The Ambivalent Image

The Ambivalent Image

*Nineteenth-Century America's
Perception of the Jew*

Louise A. Mayo

Rutherford • Madison • Teaneck
Fairleigh Dickinson University Press
London and Toronto: Associated University Presses

Associated University Presses
440 Forsgate Drive
Cranbury, NJ 08512

Associated University Presses
25 Sicilian Avenue
London WC1A 2QH, England

Associated University Presses
P.O. Box 488, Port Credit
Mississauga, Ontario
Canada L5G 4M2

The paper used in this publication meets the requirements
of the American National Standard for Permanence of Paper
for Printed Library Materials Z39.48-1984.

Library of Congress Cataloging-in-Publication Data

Mayo, Louise A., 1937–
    The ambivalent image.

    Bibliography: p.
    Includes index.
    1. Jews—United States—Public opinion—History—19th
century.   2. Public opinion—United States—History—19th
century.   3. Jews in literature.   4. American literature—
19th century—History and criticism.   5. Antisemitism—
United States—History—19th century.   6. United States—
Ethnic relations.   I. Title.
E184.J5M392   1988   973'.04924   87-45572
ISBN 0-8386-3318-8 (alk. paper)

PRINTED IN THE UNITED STATES OF AMERICA

To my husband Robert who was a constant source of support in all my endeavors: I shall ever be "thankful for the companionship that continues in a love stronger than death."

Contents

Acknowledgments

THE WORLD OF SCHOLARSHIP IS PARTICULARLY ILLUSTRATIVE OF THE truism that no human is an island. This work would not have been possible without the recommendations and assistance of many others to whom I owe a debt of gratitude.

The late Herbert Gutman not only suggested this topic to me, but also taught me, and countless other historians, to look at history in an entirely different way. The chairman of my dissertation committee, Arthur Schlesinger Jr., made many cogent suggestions. His invaluable encouragement and numerous kindnesses enabled me to complete the dissertation and pursue its publication as a book. Henry Feingold was kind enough to share his expertise in American Jewish history.

I owe special thanks to Professor Kalman Goldstein of Fairleigh Dickinson whose thoughtful and valuable comments made it possible to turn a dissertation into a book.

My late husband, Bob, not only encouraged me to continue my studies and then to write this book, but also served as unpaid proofreader. My children, Eliza and Jonathan, were unfailingly patient and supportive of my efforts.

The marvelous facilities of the New York Public Library, particularly the Rare Book Collection, the Newspaper Annex, and the Jewish Section, were of great value. The New York Society Library enabled me to carefully peruse the major periodicals of the nineteenth century. The American Jewish Committee was kind enough to allow me to look through their collection of Jewish publications. The New York Historical Library and the Newberry Library in Chicago were also of value.

I would finally like to express my appreciation to the City University of New York Graduate School for a top quality Ph.D. program that was particularly helpful to a returning adult student.

Introduction

THE ISSUE OF SOCIAL IMAGE HAS LONG CONCERNED HISTORIANS AND social commentators in such works, for example, as George Frederickson's notable *The Black Image in the White Mind* and Harold Isaacs's pioneering *Scratches on Our Mind* and *Idols of the Tribe*. Isaacs has noted the influence of the accumulation of "attitudes, images and notions held in common by large groups." These images tend to be "shaped by the way they are seen, a matter of setting, timing, angle, lighting, distance."[1] The "essential tribalism" of human beings is deeply rooted. However, in mixed societies, like the United States, wherever the "inside" may be, the "outside" is still quite nearby.[2] The images we have absorbed then become a part of ourselves, and we carry them into our relationships with others. Walter Lippmann has commented, "We pick out what our culture has already defined for us, and we tend to perceive that which we have picked out in the form stereotyped for us by our culture."[3] The way in which a group is perceived by the majority culture is bound to have a profound effect upon its behavior, adjustment, and treatment. Studies have shown as much anti-Semitism among those who have never known a Jew as among those who see Jews every day. Anti-Semitism, in short, does not seem to require the presence of Jews, only their images.

Jews came to America in very small numbers before the middle of the nineteenth century. There were only fifteen thousand in a total population of fifteen million by 1830. As the Jewish community evolved in America, it was radically transformed from the classic European model. In America the community had lost its corporate structure. It was more open, mobile, less religiously observant, and far more assimilated. Part of the reason for this was the absence both of an established church and of organized anti-Semitism. In many ways it was characteristic of postemancipation communities, but was unencumbered by the long history of anti-Jewish activities that haunted the European communities. There was an ease and frequency of association between Christians and Jews rarely found in Europe. This, in turn, led to changes in patterns of worship and a passion for innovation that made American Jews even less differentiated from the greater society.

From 1820 to 1870 a steady stream of German Jewish immigrants came to

America. By 1877 the Jewish population had grown to 250,000. These German Jews, children of the Enlightenment, generally found adaptation to American life to be an easy process, and they quickly entered the middle class. The majority found a satisfactory religious compromise in the Reform movement, which permitted them to function as both Americans and Jews. For the most part, these enterprising small businessmen were considered admirable Americans. Yet, they were often accused of cunning and avarice, and, by the 1840s, the verb "to jew" had become commonplace in American slang.

Gradually, the success of the German Jews had become more visible and began to trouble many longer established Americans. Most of the learned Jews had remained in Jewish centers in Europe. Although German Jews often played a culture-courier role in the German American community, the Jew who had migrated was generally the busy, ambitious businessman with less passion for learning. In America many appeared to have accumulated wealth at a faster rate than they did culture. More and more, the image of the Jew became that of the parvenu. Although American literature included the Shylock image, it took a milder and more impersonal form than in England. Most Jews continued to live quietly and comfortably in America.

The lives of these satisfied, settled German American Jews were violently jolted after 1880 as vast "hordes" of Eastern European Jews poured into America. By the end of open immigration in 1924, over two million had arrived. These "shtetl" Jews looked very odd to Americans and acted even more strangely, much to the discomfiture of the earlier Jewish settlers. Unlike the latter, the newcomers crowded together in slums. It seemed obvious that they would not be so readily amalgamated into American society. As Robert Wiebe has pointed out, in an era of mobility, "strange people constituted an omnipresent threat to the community." Anxieties were expressed in "visions of inundation" by floods of aliens, causing particular attention to be paid to the sifting of newcomers.[4] They would irrevocably change the image of the Jew in America.

Anti-Semitism is, perhaps, the most ancient ethnic or religious antagonism. "Anti-semitism possesses a stock of images more deep seated and protean than does any other form of inter-group hostility known to Western man, because it is the summation of self-confirming experience extending over two millennia."[5] There have been a plethora of studies about the nature of Christian perceptions of the Jews from psychological, sociological, and religious points of view. The Jew was often seen as the quintessential alien, part of a community of strangers, determinedly different, a tribal anamoly, "a particularly suitable projection screen for modern man's conflicts."[6] The qualities of the Jew were so manifold, inconsistent, and ambiguous that the observer could see whatever he wanted in the Jew. Characteristics attributed to Jews often reflected the needs and repressed desires of the hostile individual.

Religiously, a profound ambivalence prevailed. Jews were "God's chosen people, who one at the same time gave us the Messiah and rejected him."[7] Psychologically, Jews may represent the father who is feared and loved at the same time, the basis of a deep ambiguity, a mixture of hatred, fear and attachment. From the beginning of their association, Christians saw Jews as living rejections of their faith. At the same time, many Christians themselves felt a certain ambivalence about Jesus and his ideals. What better way to lessen feelings of guilt for their own rejection of the precepts of Jesus than to displace them on the "killers" of Christ. In that sense, anti-Semitism can be a form of self-hatred. Christianity demanded that Christians repress desires. The resulting resentment could be focused on the Jews who, after all, had given birth to Christianity. As Herbert Gold colorfully remarked, "The chosen people is exempt from so many sins. They are free to do all the nasty things we want to do, make money, wallow in luxury, do funny things to women."[8] It has been suggested that the Jew, originator of the Father, God, became a universal father figure himself, representing the "inhibiting depriving forces in society." At the same time, claiming a Jewish heritage, the church saw itself as the true chosen Israel. In this complex interplay of symbols, the younger brother supplanted the older in his father's affection and seized power. This was a direct and successful aggression against the father. Judaism, the elder brother, was still present, however, constantly around to scream "father," inspiring "violent and mixed feelings: hatred, fear, remorse."[9]

Concurrently, the economic role of the Jew added grounds for hostility. The cultural alien and murderer of God undertook the suspicious role of merchant and moneylender. This occurred in a medieval society where commerce was suspect and usury was condemned by church sanctions almost as strenuously as heresy. Judas, after all, had sold his God for silver. The Jew became the devil—usurer and god-killer—even developing the physical characteristics of the devil such as a long nose, red hair, unpleasant odor, and straggly beard. This created what Trachtenberg has called "mass memory."[10] In the Middle Ages the Jew was magician and sorcerer; in the modern period, international communist and international capitalist. The basic structure is the same: the Jew is both omnipotent and menacing. Both identify the Jew with humankind's current fears.

In Europe, even the "friends" of the Jews agreed that they were immoral, crude, and avaricious. The argument was whether these vices could be overcome. Liberal gentiles who pressed for emancipation "saw it as a way for Jews to shed their Jewishness . . . to shed whatever it was that caused them to be rejected."[11] The liberals believed that the oppressive environment had caused Jewish errors. Eliminating the restrictions might ultimately turn Jews into citizens like everyone else.

If one concedes the presence of widespread hostile imagery, even among "liberals," transmitted from generation to generation, to what extent was this core of Jewish-image woven into the pattern of American culture? Ben Halpern has argued, "The situation of Jews in America, however special its character, is not fundamentally different from what it has been elsewhere; and the configuration of America's attitudes towards them . . . remains confined within the traditional framework of ambivalence between anti-semitism and toleration."[12] Hannah Arendt has remarked that anti-Jewish feeling becomes politically significant only when it is a part of major political issues or when Jewish group issues come into open conflict with those of a major class in society.[13] These conditions did not exist in nineteenth-century America. In many European countries anti-Semitism was organized, had a clearly enunciated program, and had a chance to achieve political power. By contrast, American anti-Semitism was one of impulse, more casual and aimless, and lacking political effectiveness. The key, as Charles Silberman has pointed out in his popular recent book, *A Certain People,* is that American anti-Semitism has never been a part of government or church policy. Instead, "powerful forces built into the marrow of American policy confine anti-Jewish attitudes to the private domain," rather than as government policy.[14] In addition, group animosities were dispersed, finding more suitable targets in Catholics, Mormons, and blacks. "Polite anti-Semitism," manifesting itself in social discrimination against Jewish nouveaux riches by the established elite group, was the typically American outgrowth. Father Flannery has noted that the same conditions that staved off rabid and organized anti-Semitism helped to cause this American response. "A land of immense natural resources and dynamic economic growth had less need for scapegoats to heap failures upon . . . but these favorable conditions produced a species of status-seeking and social snobbery" affecting Jews.[15] There has always been a public ideological anti-Semitism and a private social variety. The latter has been far more characteristic of the United States.

Twentieth-century historians have offered widely varied explanations of American anti-Semitism in the nineteenth century. In the 1930s and 1940s observers like Carey McWilliams tended to favor an economic interpretation of anti-Semitism, tracing it to conservatism and privilege. Oscar Handlin minimized its impact in the consensus atmosphere of the 1950s. As late as the 1890s, he argued, the culture was "actually marked by a distinct philo-semitism." Although he conceded the widespread presence of the Shylock image, Handlin claimed that it implied "no hostility or negative judgment." Unflattering images might seem to be anti-Jewish but there is "evidence that they were not meant to be taken as such." A new negative image of the Jew did not emerge until the late 1890s, when it was advanced by agrarian radicals—the modern image of the Jew as evil and powerful international money broker.[16]

Somewhat later, John Higham both rejected and incorporated parts of the two earlier views, concluding that most Americans wavered "between conflicting attitudes of anti and philo-Semitism." The Jewish stereotype represented ambivalent perceptions. Religiously, the Jew was both the "glorious agent of divine purpose and the deserving victim of his vengeance." In economic terms, the Jew exemplified the virtues and vices of capitalism by his "keenness and resourcefulness in trade, yet . . . cunning avarice." As the century wore on, the Jew increasingly became the symbol of plutocracy, often to those very groups which believed in their country as a haven for the oppressed. Higham felt that, during the 1870s, an increased scramble for social prestige dislocated the American status system. Propelled by "assertive manners and aggressive personalities," German Jews advanced more rapidly than other immigrants, leading to a vastly exaggerated impression of their financial power. The image of the Jew as the "quintessential parvenu" was set by the 1880s.[17] Mass immigration from Eastern Europe "further complicated the Jewish problem." These immigrants came during a "larger, more complex upswing of anti-foreign feeling." Higham agreed that the picture of the Jew resembled other ethnic stereotypes, but he concluded that they were all unflattering. The depression added to the social and economic dislocations leading to antiforeign agitation. Hostile perceptions of the Jew were strongest when social discontent combined with nationalistic aggression.

Handlin is forced to ignore or minimize numerous expressions of nineteenth-century anti-Semitism in order to support his conclusions. Higham's understanding of the complexities and ambiguities comes closer to the realities of nineteenth-century America. It is far from a total explanation, however. No other ethnic group's image was as deeply rooted in history as that of the Jew. The impression of a sharp upswing of expressions of anti-Semitism in the 1870s and in the depression of the 1890s is not born out by a study of the press. Manifestations of anti-Jewish sentiments, which are often cited as typical of the "status anxieties" of the 1870s, existed well before then. In fact, the image of the Jew remained remarkably constant throughout the century, increasing mainly in quantity as observers became more cognizant of the presence of Jews in America. The added factor in the 1890s was a class fear of a Jewish proletariat, very different from the standard Jewish stereotype.

In a more recent book, Michael Dobkowski categorically rejects the views of Higham and Handlin. He argues that American historians have minimized the intensity of anti-Semitism here, and have emphasized transitory social and economic causes, rather than more permanent ideological and religious motives. He believes that Americans readily accepted European notions of Jews an clannish, ostentatious money-grubbers attached to an "archaic" religion that kept them from ever becoming good citizens. Dobkowski concludes that "there were few countervailing images to balance the barrage of ideological anti-Semitism that permeated American culture." All Jews, according to him, were presented as unpleasant, "Jews are not given credit for being a people like any other. . . ."[18] While this provides a necessary corrective to overly sanguine earlier viewpoints, it ignores the numerous favorable and even philo-Semitic works that appeared throughout the century. The presence of anti-Semitic ideology in America cannot be denied. However, one should also not minimize the importance of such counterideologies as America's role as a haven for the oppressed, democratic pluralism, compassion for victims of persecution, and acceptance of capitalist virtues.

The image of the Jew was undoubtedly the most complex of all the ethnic stereotypes. For one thing, it combined religious preconceptions with ethnic differences. On the one hand, there was a clear line from the ancient and deeply ingrained concept of the Jew as Judas or Shylock. On the other, there was the positive prototype of the Jew as hard working in the approved Horatio Alger way, of superior intelligence, charitable instincts, and the undaunted survivor of centuries of unjust persecution. The arrival of thousands of poor and seemingly unassimilable Eastern European Jews had a profound impact on the Jewish image in the press (although not in literature, comic magazines, or the stage). American rhetoric called for aid to the oppressed, and sympathy in response to the barbarous policies of the czar was widespread. Yet many Americans worried that years of persecution had made these immigrants "undesirable," unable to understand democracy and social restraint. Older and newer, often contradictory, perceptions of the Jew existed side by side. The image by the end of the century was a compound of class attitudes and ancient stereotypes.

The nature of America itself was an important component in this basic ambivalence. Harold Isaacs points out that America was the only country that had the goal of "building an open society, the making of one 'nation' out of many. . . ." There was bound to be a wide gap between rhetoric and reality. There undoubtedly was rejection and exclusion, just as in Europe. However, the difference was that "the dominant credo of the society was in constant contradiction with this behavior."[19] In *The Segmented Society*, Robert Wiebe argues that one of the prerequisites for real equality, a basic American ideal, was an effective sorting and ultimate assimilation of strangers. They were expected to totally divest themselves of all "alien" traits. "The essence of assimilation in the nineteenth century was invisibility."[20] Jews would be judged by the extent to which they met this standard.

In his discussion of the "biformities" so pervasive in America, Michael Kammen notes that American culture has been "particularly perplexed by ambivalence and contradictory tendencies." These inconsistencies manifested themselves in such conflicts as those between high moral standards and the ethics of the marketplace. In America to be "shrewd" was "to be admired and condemned at the same time." "Progress" itself could be viewed as a mixed blessing, leading to development or disintegration. These "biformities" arose from tensions between "inherited ideals and environmental realities;" from the diversity and strains inherent in a nation of immigrants; from heightened expectations and elevated ideals impossible to fulfill; from mobility, innovation, and change; and from conflicts between individualism and conformity, among others. This "ambivalent condition of life" in America may well be responsible for some of the ambiguities in the image of the Jew.[21]

This book attempts to examine the image of the Jew in nineteenth-century America from a variety of perspectives. It covers works of fiction and drama, Sunday-school texts and religious books, histories, polemical works, comic magazines, songs, burlesque pieces, and representative newspapers and periodicals, in an attempt to understand the perception of Jews by nineteenth-century Americans. While it is possible to examine most major magazines, newspapers have to be dealt with selectively due to their vast numbers. The major New York newspapers are covered in detail. The American Jewish press, particularly the *American Israelite,* was of assistance in quoting praise or condemnation of Jews that appeared in newspapers throughout the country. Books about Jews in various cities also provided clues about coverage of Jews in those areas. Foreign and domestic political issues with which Jews were concerned (many of which are the subjects of separate books) are discussed only in relation to the light they shed on the image of the Jews in periodicals. Their deeper implications and the actions taken are outside the scope of this study.

Nineteenth-century American views tended to verify Harold Fisch's comment that "the Jew is inevitably a figure of polarity, of radical ambiguity."[22] The ambivalence of American attitudes was reflected in complaints voiced in the 1890s by Abram Isaacs. There was a flood of works "glorifying the Jew." The Jew was treated with "superlative praise or superlative condemnation." Isaacs felt that the real Jew could be found neither in the words of his detractors nor in the praise of his admirers. "The Jew pleads for justice not glorification."[23] By understanding the sources of the ambiguous nineteenth-century image of the Jew, it may be possible to more thoroughly comprehend American attitudes toward Jews in the twentieth century.

1

The Religious Image

HISTORICALLY, THE RELIGIOUS REACTION TO THE JEW HAS BEEN THE most deeply engrained on the Christian mind. In the United States there was a profound ambivalence towards "God's chosen people who one and the same time, gave us the messiah and rejected him."[1] This basic Christian attitude goes back to the early Christian writers who taught that the dispersion of the Jews was divine retribution for the crucifixion. Judaism in Christ's time, it was assumed, had become a religion without soul, desiccated by its legalism, formalism, and ritual.

Most important, the Jews had rejected and caused the death of their one true leader, like the father who destroys his own child. In this case, the unrepentant father who had killed his child, Jesus, had also rejected his other child, Christianity. Yet Christianity did owe a debt of gratitude to Jews who had preserved the worship of one God. They were the divinely elected upholders of the law, the people from whom Christ came. Many Americans, Protestants and students of the old Testament, were acutely aware of their Hebrew roots.

A father may be loved as well as feared. The Jew was considered responsible for the crime, but it was a crime from which the Christian reaped moral and psychological benefit—redemption from sin. The Jew also represented a marvelous and incomprehensible phenomenon. Despite extreme persecution, this strange people had survived for thousands of years. Perhaps this was part of a vast divine plan in which the Jew would be restored to greatness by acknowledging Christian truth.

These religious preconceptions played a significant role in the way in which Americans perceived Jews, particularly earlier in the century. An ambivalence that had been brought over by the Calvinists, was widespread: "The Jews were forever guilty of deicide . . . but as foreordained witnesses to the divine plan of salvation in Christianity, must be tolerated and protected. . . ."[2] The view that the Jew was the Christ-killer, rejected by God and justly punished for his transgressions, was widely accepted.[3] A related popular idea was that the Jewish religion was merely a precursor of Christianity and, therefore, no longer relevant in the modern world. Proselytizers were active, although believing as they did in the central role of the Jew in bringing God's kingdom to earth, not always unsympathetic.

Although many Christian writers supported these attitudes, others, often in secular journals, placed greater emphasis on gratitude to the Jews for bringing religion to the world. They also expressed admiration for the miraculous survival of the Jewish people in spite of oppression, interest in Jewish religious customs and disdain for the futile efforts of the conversionists. They dismissed the crucifixion as either not the fault of the Jews or not related to their modern descendants. The seemingly contradictory attitudes of religious hostility and sympathy existed side by side in America, often on the pages of the same publication. At any rate, the multiplicity of conflicting attitudes was far more characteristic of the American religious reaction to the Jews than elsewhere in the Christian world.

In a discussion of the reasons for anti-Jewish prejudice, *Harper's Magazine* of July 1858 recognized the centrality of religious motivation: "Is it surprising that a civilization called from the name of Christ should hold under perpetual ban of dislike . . . the whole race which is descended from those who rejected the leader of Christendom . . . and who refuse him to this day?" The magazine felt this was a very natural and obvious prejudice and admonished Jews not to expect its rapid disappearance.[4]

Early histories of the Jewish people and Sunday-school texts for children, adults, and teachers illustrated widely held preconceptions, often balanced by expressions of sympathy. In one of the first published histories of the Jewish people (1812), Hannah Adams declared that the persecutions, antiquity, and rites of the Jews were "a standing monument to the truth of the Christian religion." Jews had been selected to preserve the knowledge of God, but after the prophetic age, Jews had corrupted and perverted their religion. When Christ was "ignominiously rejected and put to death by the Jewish nation," the result was terrible calamities and dispersion. Yet it is interesting that, despite this righteous condemnation, she expressed great sympathy for the "cruel oppression and pillages this devoted race have suffered." She admired their survival despite all their misery and hoped for the future conversion of the "descendants of those illustrious patriarchs."[5]

Sunday-school books designed for the young were often particularly severe in their judgments of the Jews. *Sabbath Lessons* by Elizabeth Peabody, for instance, spoke of the "conspiracy of the Jewish rulers against Jesus Christ" and reproofed the Jews for "indulging themselves in reviling, covetousness. . . ." Despite endorsing this view of God's rejection, an 1832 volume, *Annals of the Jewish Nation,* pointedly typified the ambiguities of the attitudes of religious fundamentalists toward the Jews. In spite of all their misdeeds, "an extraordinary providence" attended the Jewish people in fulfillment of the prophecies and in their preservation as a distinct people. They continued to be a "monument of God's displeasure" against the crucifixion. "Still they are preserved in mercy. . . . For it is clear . . . they will be restored to the privileges of the Church" from which they had been temporarily cut off by unbelief.[6]

An 1853 volume, *Stories from the History of the Jews*, presented sympathetic tales for children about the scattering of the Jewish people throughout the world where they remained strangers and were persecuted and massacred; "still we shall find them in quiet industry, making their way." The child was reminded that the Jews had "rejected and murdered the Savior" and that "the punishment, though heavy, was just." The author did, however, firmly believe that it was time for all oppression to end: "If Christians will think and act in the mild spirit of their teacher, the Jew will, in time . . . throw off their coating of pride. . . ."[7] Sunday-school texts have long been identified as sources of anti-Semitism.[8] Works such as these might reinforce the view of the Jew as abandoned by God, yet they strongly opposed modern persecution.

Religious press and books designed for adults and Sunday-school teachers were similar, even in tone and level of sophistication, to those written for children. Occasionally, their tone was far more vitriolic. In 1855 *The Churchmen*, an official Episcopal organ, reported an "outrage" to the Christian religion. A rabbi responded to a toast offered to the clergy of the state at a state legislature dinner. In a Christian city, "a disbeliever—a reviler of Christianity" dared to appropriate the finer sentiments to his own "defiant infidel system" and responded from his "evil heart of unbelief" to a Christian assembly! It was "blasphemy" and hypocritical—whoever heard of the Jews regarding gentiles as their "brethren?"[9]

Adult religious books often combined the basic image of the Jew as despised Christ killer with real, if incongruous, sympathy. In his *A Pictoral Descriptive View and History Of All Religions*, Reverend Charles A. Goodrich noted that in the dispersal of the Jews the readers of the Bible would "learn the evil and danger of despising divine admonitions." Still, Goodrich repeated the belief that God must have had a reason to preserve this people "in so extraordinary a manner," with the "same trust in the promise of their God, the same conscientious attachment to the institutions of their fathers," which he described in careful detail. In a similar vein, Hannah W. Richardson, in her 1861 book, *Judea in Her Desolations*, accepted the generally held belief that "the great mass of the Jews . . . conspired the death of this just One assuring an awful responsibility." Yet, although the national existence of the Jews was annihilated as a result, "still this sturdy stock resisted the rude blast of centuries . . . " surviving to the present as witnesses to the truth that "the savior of the world was a Jew." Therefore, she admonished her readers, Christians must never "despise these now down-trodden ones."[10]

Supposedly more sophisticated works delineated hostile images that found greater favor in the twentieth century. John Mears believed that the Jews could not accept Christ as the Messiah because they had expected a monarch-warrior since "their views and hopes were almost entirely worldly." W. D. Morrison's condemnation in *The Jews under Roman Rule* (1891) could still be heard in the modern world. The Jews were detested in the Roman world because of their practice of refusing to associate with gentiles. This was "utterly opposed to the humane sentiments of national brotherhood which were taking root in the ancient world." The Jews brought contempt upon themselves by their "separatist customs." The inference was clear that this continued to be the case.[11] This accusation has found an echo in modern complaints about "clannishness."

Religious books and publications, whether designed for children or adults, popular or scholarly, tended to reinforce the view of Jews as murderers of God's son, and the Jewish religion as a fossil destined to give way entirely to the "New Israel," Christianity. In his poem "The Star of Calvary," Nathaniel Hawthorne expressed this most basic of all Christian attitudes:

> Behold O Israel! behold,
> It is no Human One
> That ye have dared to crucify
>   What evil hath he done?
> It is your King, O Israel!
>   The God-begotten Son![12]

Yet God had continued to preserve the Jewish people. There must be some profound divine purpose for this miracle. Religious writers, therefore, frequently cautioned their readers that they must renounce persecution.

Perhaps the reason for the miraculous survival of the Jews was their ultimate conversion. Indeed, this became a basic tenet of fundamentalist ideology. In early America conversion was often the aim of even the most sympathetic Protestant leaders. For example, Ezra Stiles, president of Yale and close friend of the great merchant Aaron Lopez, often expressed the wish that his friend would see the light of truth some day. In his 1798 *Life of President Stiles,* Reverend Abiel Holmes (the father of Oliver Wendell Holmes) recommended his subject's benevolent approach in seeking the conversion of Jews. Stiles civility was certainly worthy of imitation in dealing with "this devoted people." Instead of treating them with appropriate "humanity and tenderness," Christians often persecuted and condemned them, tending to "prejudice them against our holy religion, and to establish them in infidelity."[13]

The most active and significant conversionist organization was the Society for Meliorating the Condition of the Jews. It was founded in 1820 and included among its members outstanding men such as DeWitt Clinton and

John Quincy Adams, briefly a vice-president. The Society's *Reports* clearly illustrates the conversionist mentality. They described the Jews as "that interesting and *deeply injured* people" who had shed the blood of the messiah and had its consequences visited upon themselves and their children. Despite this, the organization wished to express "the kindest sympathy and affection towards the outcasts of Israel." Even though the Jews themselves tried to prevent the dissemination of Christian knowledge, and "abuse and villify" conversionist efforts, it was still "a matter of duty to feel and exhibit the spirit of benevolence to the person of every Jew." Only the ultimate conversion of the Jews would bring about the "Millennial glory." The Bible was unequivocal in teaching that "our salvation is of the Jews."[14] Many books combined sentiments of admiration, condemnation, and missionary hopes in a similar fashion. They all commented on the "marvelous" tenacity of the "Jewish race" and the miracle of its "indestructibility," which only God could have caused. They expressed gratitude to the conveyors of the Old Testament and, while accepting the idea of Jewish guilt, unanimously warned against Christian rapacity and malignancy as the main obstacle to conversion.[15]

Isaac Mayer Wise in his *Reminiscences* recalled such activity as particularly widespread in the first half of the nineteenth century. He noted, "It was more acute here at that time than even in England or Prussia." It was humiliating for the Jews since the pietists campaign plans consisted of arousing "pity for the poor persecuted and blinded Jews." Significantly, however, Wise felt that they had to employ such tactics since the European weapons of hatred and persecution could not be employed here because of freedom and "the tolerant spirit which was prevalent." Rabbi Wise also recalled meeting a simple backwoods missionary who had been particularly anxious to meet a Jewess. The "simple trusting piety" of the man and his wife, who were not at all hostile as they prayed for the conversion of Wise and his wife, gave him "insight into American conceptions of the Jew."[16]

The ardent evangelical admonition to "weep over the unbelieving Jews and pity them and strive to reclaim them" was terribly condescending and naturally resented by Jews. However, the *actions* of those who zealously accepted such ideas could hardly have been anti-Semitic. Once, one author wrote, Jews feared to lift their heads, but now they do and "rank among the chief men of the earth" whom the Lord will take to rebuild his Holy Land. Another declared that Jews possessed "more native talent, keenness of perception and energy, joined with activity of mind," than any other group. As fellow men they were entitled to both sympathy and equal rights.[17] Unlike Europe, in the United States even the most ardent conversionist tended to favor equal rights.

The secular press showed a continuing fascination with proselytizing, reporting even the meagerest success in converting Jews. Both *Harper's*

Weekly and the *New Englander and Yale Review* were enthralled by the "Kishinev" movement of the late 1880s. Its leader, the convert Joseph Rabinowitz, declared that the "lamentable condition" of Eastern European Jews was caused by their rejection of Christ. He hoped to form an independent group of Jewish-Christians (Jews for Jesus?). Since Jews scorned those who reject their own religion, his followers would remain Jews to a certain degree, retaining circumcision and the seventh-day Sabbath. These would not be permanent, but were harmless concessions to the "weaknesses of those who cannot . . . throw off at once all Jewish feelings and prejudices."[18] The intensity of interest in this small and obviously insignificant splinter group was a vivid illustration of the continuing attraction exerted by prospect of converting the Jews.

More frequently, however, the ardent efforts of the conversionists were ridiculed by the secular press. In the early years of the century *Niles Weekly Register,* a most influential publication that was not particularly kind to the Jews, expressed its cynicism about missionary efforts among the Jews. An 1816 article, for example, commented that in the previous five years $500,000 had been spent for "the conversion, real or supposed, of *five Jews.*" The rate of $100,000 per Jew was a considerable sum to pay even to purchase the "scattered nation. . . . Whether Jews convert Christians or Christians convince Jews, what is it to us in this land of civil and religious liberty?"[19]

Most newspapers showed little patience with missionary efforts, which increased as the number of Jews in America grew. An 1871 editorial in the *Philadelphia Sunday Dispatch* commented on a report issued by the Society for the Promotion of Christianity Among the Jews. The association could claim the conversion of only a few Jews over a period of several years, a "miserable return," which the paper estimated as "a sixth of a Jew per annum." Despite funds contributed by "over-zealous Christians," the missionary L. C. Newman was forced to admit that he had not been able to convert even one of New York's one hundred thousand Jews in 1870. The lack of interest in supporting his efforts was, undoubtedly, evidence of the good sense of New York Christians. "New Yorkers know that there can be no hope in attempting to convert the Jews to Christianity as long as they feel Christianity is an untrue doctrine." Jews believed in the Messiah, the paper informed its reader, but held that He was yet to come. The missionary's salary was being increased, so "it may be expected that he will wander drearily about the country, seeking for impossible Jews whom he never expects to convert."[20]

Similar editorials appeared in the 1870s in the *New York Times* and the *Detroit Post.*[21] Not only was the success of conversion societies minimal, the *Times* noted, but the few who did convert were "of a sort whose private life and reputation does not render them very valuable acquisitions." In view of recent outbreaks in Europe, it was suggested that conversion funds might be fruitfully employed "in teaching Christians humanity." The *Detroit Post* felt that it was really impossible to convert the Jews. "The heart of a true Jew loving Israel's God with all his heart cannot be changed."

The entrance of Eastern European Jews caused renewed vigor in missionary efforts. Missionaries, who spoke to increasingly hostile mobs on the lower East Side, continued to meet with disapproval on the part of the newspapers.[22] While the *New York Tribune* in 1898 condemned the throwing of eggs at a missionary, it concluded, "The missions to the Jews are responsible in the first place. . . ." The Jew was unwaveringly loyal to his faith and "the blood of persecution was the cement with which the family union became strengthened." Here they could worship freely and "they thoroughly appreciate the blessing." If good people wished to give to improve the conditions of the Jews," let them give to those who are trying to make East Side people better Jews."

The *New York Evening Journal,* a mass circulation daily, was even more vigorous in its condemnation of conversionist activities. The *Journal* dubbed an 1899 missionary "Provoker of Riots." The paper emphasized that he had "no right to go around telling children that their parents are going to hell and trying to persuade children to give up the faith of their fathers." All the missionary succeeded in doing was keeping a law-abiding area in a state of "savage ferment."

There was more criticism of the feeble efforts of the conversionist movement in the secular press than there was approval of its goals. The ceremonies of the Jews might be mistaken, but America granted freedom to even the most peculiar ideas.

The ever present current of emotional religiosity in the nineteenth century found its way into popular poems, songs, and novels.[23] These tended to reflect the same mixture of contradictory attitudes toward the Jewish religion, the crucifixion, and the possibilities of conversion as those found in religious nonfiction. Many were impelled by similar motives as the "lo, the poor Indian" genre that was widespread at the same time.

Many early songs and poems were preoccupied with what James Russell Lowell called "thou blind unconverted Jew." These often showed great sympathy for the sufferings of the Jews and concluded that persecution would cease with conversion to the true faith. Songs, such as Mrs. Moran's 1830 "Fallen Is Thy Throne," depicted the plight of poor Jews who had been driven out of their fatherland and taken captive because they rejected the Messiah.[24] "The Jewish Maiden" lamented her lost homeland, "I n'er shall repose on thy bosom again." Reverend Eastburn's "The Hebrew Mourner" acknowledged that Jehovah had forsaken "this city of God," but held forth the prospect "He preserves for his people a city more fair. . . ." Other songs, like "The Maid of Judah," and "The Hebrew Captive," had similar themes. Though conversionist in ideology, they certainly could not be classified as malicious. Rather, their tone tended to be sympathetic.

Religious novels enjoyed great popularity throughout the nineteenth century, particularly in mid-century at the height of religious revivalism. Some were designed for the edification of children to reinforce the lessons of formal study.[25] The American Sunday School Union was particularly active in their publication. Historical novels for adults with proselytizing themes became very popular starting in the 1830s. The first really successful author in this genre was William Ware, a Unitarian minister. His best seller was *Zenobia*, written in 1837.[26] One character was a religious Jew, Isaac, who was, paradoxically, presented as admirable while Judaism itself was condemned for its aridity and lack of love. Isaac eloquently defends his fellow Jews against charges of avarice and usury. This mixture was typical of the basic ambiguity characteristic of these novels.

A similar ambivalence was apparent in the works of the most popular of the authors of biblical novels, the Episcopal priest Joseph Holt Ingraham. He enjoyed immense success with three novels romanticizing the "grandeur of Hebrew History." His books were so popular that publishers outbid each other to pay him the previously unheard of sum of $10,000 plus royalties for the second book of his series. *The Prince of the House of David* (1855) went through twenty-three editions and is said to have sold between four and five million copies. *The Pillar of Fire* (1857), the story of Moses and Joseph, was issued nine times. *The Throne of David* (1871) had twelve editions of its tale of David and Solomon.[27] The popularity of these books helped to stir up sentimental sympathy for Jews, overlaying antagonisms. Reverend Ingraham, himself, was careful to dedicate each of the books to American Jews, descendants of the biblical figures, in the expressed hope that they would finally see the light and convert. The inscription to *The Prince of the House of David*, for example, is an interesting illustration of the complex attitudes involved: "To the daughters of Israel, the country-women of Mary . . . this book is inscribed . . . they, as well as the unbelieving gentile, may be persuaded as they read that this is the very Christ."[28] The book is the story of Christ and the heroine is a Jewish convert, but the Jewish origin of Christ and his disciples is made clear. The other two books, dealing with chronologically earlier periods, are more unambiguously complimentary to the biblical Jews, also expressing the hope that modern Jews might one day "see the light."

The climax of the biblical novel was the ever-popular *Ben Hur* by Lew Wallace, which came out in 1880. This most phenomenally successful of all religious novels was typically equivocal in its attitudes toward Jews. The Jewish characters, as a whole, are presented as fine, intelligent, and noble people, the best the world had to offer up to that time. Although the crucifixion was presented in the traditional way, Wallace was careful to note that there were people of many different nationalities present, voicing hatred.[29]

The success of *Ben Hur* led to a flood of novels on biblical themes in the 1880s and 1890s. Most followed a similar pattern.[30] Florence Kingsley, who wrote four popular religious books, was most significant in promoting theological anti-Semitism.[31] The New Sabbath library published the books at five cents a copy and sold over one million, largely to young people. They presented vindictive, bigoted, and evil Jews who contrasted with virtuous Christians who turned the other cheek in the face of Jewish malice. Because of their deicide, the Jews were "a people displeasing to God and enemies to all mankind."

Although many of the biblical romances reflected similar viewpoints, there were some striking exceptions. In *The Archko Volume* (1887), William D. Mahan, a clergyman, attempted to bring humanity to his Jewish characters. He declared, "The Jews were honest in all their dealings with Christ . . . Hence much of the prejudice among Protestants against the Jews is groundless. There never was a people more honest and more devoted to their country and their God than the Jews."[32] Mrs. T. F. Black, in one of the innumerable variants of the story of Esther, presented the tale as a moral caution against modern anti-Semitism. After two thousand years in the age of Christianity, "in what condition does it find the oppressed race so kindly delivered from persecution by a *heathen* monarch! The cause of this oppressed race is now undergoing the most infamous persecution since the days of the destruction of Jerusalem."[33]

Another popular genre was conversionist fiction in which individuals, or even entire families, were brought into Christianity in vivid contrast to the paltry real results of the proselytizing efforts.[34] Some, such as *The Jewish Twins* by "Aunt Friendly" (Sarah Schoonmaker Baker), were aimed at children. The twins, Muppin and Huppin, convert but remain Jews since, after all, "the Virgin Mary and the twelve disciples were of that people to which the Blessed Savior had chosen to belong. . . ." Mrs. C. A. Ogden's *Into the Light,* written in 1867, was a popular volume in the American Girl Series. All the Jews in the book, with the exception of the villain, convert. The Christian minister-hero tells his Jewish-convert wife, "Let us remember his chosen people and plead for their speedy restoration to the land of their heritage. . . ." "Aunt Hattie" (Harriette N. W. Baker) produced two versions of this theme. In *Lost but Found* (1866) the Seixas family converts and the aloof, cold Mr. Seixas becomes "kind and affable to all." Mrs. Baker expressed the hope that *Rebecca the Jewess* would bring the light of the true religion to "some beloved child of Israel who is groping in the dark." Although Annie Fellows Johnston's *In League with Israel* (1896) indicated that only by accepting Christ could a Jew fulfill his heritage, it was kindly in its portrait of Jews. It condemned Christians for mistreating Jews. The author hoped that her book would "turn all bitterness and prejudice into the broad spirit of brotherhood."

Much of the religious literature reinforced the picture of Jews as Christ-killers and of the Jewish religion as antiquated ritual that must inevitably give way to the higher truths of Christianity. However, there were many benevolent exceptions. The rampant sentimentality of the time was easily extended to a "poor oppressed people."

The secular press tended to oppose negative religious stereotypes for the most part. A reviewer in *Scribner's Monthly* in 1876, discussing George Eliot's influential *Daniel Deronda,* commented on objections to the Jewish element in the novel. Many Christians, the critic noted, remember that Jews killed Christ. They forget "that the race also gave birth to Christ. That Christ should be killed by any people among whom he might appear was inevitable. . . . The exceptional and marvelous thing was his production. . . ." He concluded with the retort of a Jew upon whom a Christian had spat, "that half Christendom worship a Jew and the other half a Jewess." *Harper's Magazine,* in a similar vein, complained in 1879 that "men of no Christian principle whatever flout better men today because other men murdered the founder of Christianity."[35]

An article in the April 1887 issue of *Ironclad Age* presented an interesting theological counterview to the hatred of Jews as deicides. Christians, it argued, could not condemn the Jews for crucifying Christ without condemning the salvation that flowed from that act. It was all part of God's "scheme." Therefore, the magazine concluded, "let us love the Jew for killing Christ."[36]

Even folk humor reflected the view that eighteen hundred or more years was a very long time to hold a grudge against a person or group.[37] Two similar stories from different sections of the country illustrate this. In both tales a Jew (storekeeper in one case, peddler in the other) is knocked down by a cowboy or Tennessee mountaineer who has just attended a camp meeting. When the Jew demands an explanation for this unprovoked violence, the ignorant Christian replies, "You crucified our Lord." The Jew responds that the event in question had occurred more than eighteen hundred years earlier and that he had nothing to do with it. The back country bumpkin apologizes profusely, explaining that he had just heard about the event and, thus, thought that it had happened recently. The joke and its popularity point to the skepticism of the average religious American about any continuing responsibility of the Jewish people for the death of Jesus.

Many writers felt that the Christian world owed the Jews gratitude as the people of the Bible, the originators of Christian belief, and the people who gave the world Christ and his disciples. A July 1826 article in the *North*

American Review on interpretations of the New Testament pointed out the necessity of studying the Old Testament, which contains the origin of all Jewish institutions. The author reminded his readers, "Christ came not to destroy the law and the prophets, but to fulfill them." An 1867 review in the *Nation* discussed the Talmud. It acknowledged the ignorance of most Christians about that favorite bugaboo of the anti-Semite. "The morality of the New Testament is not original," the critic noted, it can be found in the Talmud. In that sense, "Christianity popularized Talmudic morality."[38]

The reminder that Christ himself was a Jew was frequently reiterated by those seeking to counter negative stereotypes. *Niles Weekly Register,* in an 1846 report of an "Israelitish Convention" to reform the Jewish religion in Germany, commented that Jews have been called a blot upon mankind, "yet the Redeemer was one of them." His descendants were worthy of respect. Whenever they had the power, "they exert it to elevate their race." They employ wealth to "spread among themselves education—a higher philosophy, a purer charity and a truer religion."[39] The same idea was expressed in 1882 in *Frank Leslie's Illustrated Newspaper,* a publication usually described as unfriendly to Jews. It reprinted a well-known poem by Joaquin Miller that enumerated the debt the world owed to the Jews and concluded:

> Who gave the patient Christ? I say,
> Who gave you Christian creed? Yea, yea,
> Who gave your very God to you?
> The Jew! The Jew! the hated Jew![40]

A few of the respondents in the *American Hebrew* discussion of the causes of anti-Semitism addressed themselves to this issue.[41] Reverend Washington Gladden conceded that prejudice had been fostered "unwittingly" by Sunday School teachings. As a solution, he urged, "We ought to keep it before our children that Jesus himself was a Jew." Oliver Wendell Holmes gave one of the most revealing responses. He noted that his own background had tended to stress the curse upon the Jews for rejecting Jesus. "The Jews are with us as a perpetual lesson to teach us modesty. . . . The religion we profess is not self-evident. It did not convince the people to whom it was sent." In his concluding poem, "At the Pantomime," Holmes described his visit to a theater filled with stereotypical "black-bearded Hebrew" men and "orient-eyed" women. They rushed in, poking him and bringing out his prejudices against the "cursed unbelieving Jew," the "spawn of the race that slew its Lord." Then he looked more closely at the Jew closest to him:

> Soft gentle loving eyes that gleam . . .

> So looked that other child of Shem,
> The Maiden's boy of Bethlehem!

—And thou couldst scorn the peerless blood
That flows unmingled from the Flood. . . .

Thy prophets caught the Spirit's flame,
From thee the Son of Mary came'
With thee the Father deigned to dwell,—
Peace be upon thee Israel!

In 1891 the *New York Tribune* summarized the attitudes of men of good will in an article on Judaism and Christianity. Benevolence, it declared, was finally eliminating "insensate emnity and antipathy born of ignorance." When our "Jewish brethren" erected a magnificent Temple on Fifth Avenue, the feeling was not that of hatred or envy, but of "generous sympathy." A Christian "cannot help respect a faith out of which his was born." The Jews maintained their ideals through centuries of oppression. Americans must admire "a faith that makes so much for a noble manhood and an exalted ideal of citizenship."[42]

A related favorable image concerned the "marvelous" and mysterious survival of the Jewish people despite centuries of persecution. This aroused a combination of guilt feelings for Christian misdeeds and pride among many Americans who saw their nation as a haven for the oppressed. In 1829 *The Constitutional Whig* ran a series of articles about Judaism by Isaac Leeser, one of the pioneers of American Judaism. The editor reproved Christians who despised Jews. If, as some believed, the Jews were being punished by God, this "ought to entitle them to the . . . compassion of the more favored Gentile." If, as most people would do, one rejected the idea that "perfect justice can punish the thousandth innocent generation . . . then we ought to admire . . . that high and unbending spirit of the Jews which have preserved their nation. . . ." Christians should feel "awe, admiration, sympathy and reverence" for the Jew who remained the same as the one who worshiped at the Second Temple two thousand years earlier. "We think it a glorious distinction to our country that here the Jews have found a substantial fulfillment of the promise of being restored to the Chosen Land. . . ."[43]

The *North American Review* expressed a similar viewpoint, as did the *Boston Journal*.[44] In an 1831 discussion of Milman's popular history of the Jews, the critic in the *Review* remarked that Jewish history since the destruction of Jerusalem was "truly wonderful." Though scattered, they were able to adapt themselves to each area with "a wonderful flexibility." The character of the modern Jew, particularly his fortitude, was the same as in ancient days. Americans should respect Jews and abandon foolish attempts to convert them. How could anyone expect them to embrace the faith of their persecutors? An 1845 review of four books about Jews in the same magazine also characterized Jewish history as a history "of wonders." They had exerted "a mighty influence over the faith and practice of mankind." Their sufferings, surpassing human endurance, and their survival was "the standing miracle of modern times." An 1837 *Journal* article, "The Jews," noted that, despite inducements to abandon the religion of their forefathers, they had remained Jews. "They have never for a moment forgotten or denied their religion, their customs or NAME. . . ."

Many well-known Americans expressed the same point of view in letters and speeches.[45] Zebulon Vance, in his widely delivered lecture, noted the contradiction of people who despised the Jew "but accept and adore the pure conception of a God which he taught us and whose real existence the history of the Jew more than all else establishes." Every Christian church was an off-shoot of its Jewish roots. If one were to eliminate all of Judaism from Christianity, "nothing but an unmeaning superstition" would remain. Jews "may safely defy the rest of mankind to show such undying adherence to accepted faith, such wholesale sacrifice for conscience sake."

Authors and speakers in the last two decades of the century, when foreign persecutions were most intense, were particularly struck by Jewish survival.[46] Sidney Lanier, the poet, in an 1881 lecture at Johns Hopkins, rhapsodized that when he saw even the poorest old clothes dealer, "I seem to feel a little wind fresh off the sea of Tiberius." Although the Jews lacked a homeland, they "made a literature which is at home in every nation." He believed that to gather the Jewish people together and restore them in their "thousand-fold consecrated home" was the noblest mission possible. Crawford Howell Toy, in an 1890 work, *Judaism and Christianity,* praised the religious instinct that had produced prophets and poets inspired by God. "It is a proof of the intense vitality of the Jewish people that they did not . . . succumb to the oppression of foreign religious domination. Their energy came from their . . . consciousness of possession of highest truth. . . ." In the same year, Charles Loring Brace, in *The Unknown God,* concluded, "we do not suffi-ciently render justice to the Jews' great services in human history . . . they deserve the lasting respect of mankind."

Harper's New Monthly Magazine of January 1894 included an interesting article titled "The Mission of the Jews." The author neatly reversed the common view of the dispersion of the Jews as a sign of God's punishment. Instead, he accepted the Reform Jewish notion that it was an indication of God's mission to serve as priests and prophets. "It was by a wondrous design of Providence that the people of Israel was dispersed over the world, in order that it might penetrate with its spirit the whole humanity." The Jews had achieved through their dispersion a remarkable steadfastness of belief. As a result, Jews had become the "chief bearers of spirituality."[47]

The most passionate defense of the Jews, summarizing many of the themes discussed above, can be found in a mid-century work, *The Progress of Religious Ideas through Successive Ages,* by Lydia Maria Child.[48] She was a well-known abolitionist and reformer, with the New England interest in the People of the

Old Testament. She was most concerned about "the relentless, universal and prolonged" persecution of the Jews. "Their constancy and fortitude equaled their unparalleled wrongs." The "darkest blot" in the history of Christians was their treatment of the Jews even though "we reverence their scriptures . . . Christ and his Mother and Apostles were Jews." Only a very few of the people were responsible for the crucifixion. Even those "acted with the blind bigotry so generally manifested by established churches toward non-conformists.:" Although so few were actually implicated, the church fathers irrationally condemned all Jews as Christ-killers, "as if each one of them had put him to death." Christians should acknowledge Jewish resisters as heroic martyrs who "at the cost of incredible sacrifice . . . still set their face steadfastly toward Jerusalem." She concluded, "We owe the Jews an immense debt of gratitude."

While Lydia Child's extreme judeophile views were, perhaps, unusual, there was extensive coverage of the Jewish religion in the press. There was a fascination with Jewish customs, practices, and rites, particularly the "exotic." Interest in movements within Judaism and celebrations of the building of synagogues were widespread. The treatment of Judaism showed the same ambivalence as the discussions of the religious history of the Jews. While many of the comments were openly admiring, some others were sternly censorious of "outdated" rituals.

The *North American Review* was particularly concerned with the movement for reform within Judaism as shown by Isaac Harby's pamphlets for the "reformed Society of Israelites."[49] The writer had assumed that "the minds of Israelites were so wedded to their religious peculiarities as to be impenetrable to the spirit of innovation." Jews had been considered to be the most reactionary religious group. Christians, who had observed the "singular rites" in synagogues, had not suspected that there were Jews who had surmounted such peculiarities as an "air of indifference," indistinct and rapid chants, and constant comings and goings. Harby merited praise. Although inwardly a firm Jew, he was willing to accommodate the forms "to the conciliatory, compensating and sacrificing spirit of the age." His opponents ideas were treated with respect due to their "solemn associations of antiquity," although the author clearly preferred the "new school." In the end, the author felt certain that the spirit of the age would convert the synagogue "with its obsolete ceremonials, its unintelligible language . . . into a more rational sanctuary." This was the viewpoint of an enlightened member of the upper class, probably a Unitarian. The condescension was obvious. It is also revealing, however, that there was not the slightest hint that the Jew should ultimately convert to Christianity. The main hope he expressed was that the new "reformed" temples would attract thousands "to be strengthened and enlightened, and their hearts to be warmed, consoled and purified."

The consecrations of synagogues were reported early and in great detail.

Evidently this was a subject of some interest to readers. *Niles Weekly Register* in 1823, for example, described the "impressive ceremony" in the Great Synagogue in London with rolls of law in "peculiar cases, most splendidly ornamental. . . ."[50]

The description of the consecration of "Roudoufe Sholum" of Philadelphia in 1843 by the *United States Gazette* was typical of mid-century press coverage. The ceremony was described in painstaking detail. The scrolls "attracted general and undivided attention." (Christians were often curious about the central importance of the Torah scrolls.) The singing was "beautifully performed" by the (as usual) lovely ladies of the choir. Most of the state justices, a large representation of the Christian clergy, the bar, and the press were present. The building was described in detail as well.[51]

An 1851 synagogue dedication in Chicago was widely and favorably reported in the local press.[52] The *Chicago Democrat* congratulated the Jews for their "enterprise, liberality and religious zeal." They had made a "glorious beginning for themselves." They had taken up a "pecuniary burden difficult to be borne," but they were happy "for there shall the parchment of the law be unrolled and read." The *Chicago Daily Journal* commented on the dedication in breathless prose:

> It was a novel, yet beautiful spectacle . . . Now rose the Hebrew chant in sweet and novel harmony; and now the sacred parchments were borne in solemn procession. . . . It was one of the most melodious things to which we have ever listened, and as it floated through the charmed and trembling air, it brought back the memories of the old glorious time historians chronicle. . . .

Other Jewish events were also reported conscientiously by Chicago papers. The *Daily Democratic Press,* for instance, described Passover in 1855, "the anniversary . . . of the great Exodus." Readers were informed that six thousand pounds of unleavened bread had been sold in the city, and that Jews were gathering in family groups "around the festival board."

James Parton, in a complimentary article in 1870 in the *Atlantic Monthly,* "Our Israelitish Brethren," noted that Jews, unlike Christians, really rested on the Sabbath. Judaism, he believed, "is a religion of one idea and that idea is God." Most of all, he was impressed that Jews seemed to know "how to associate religion with the *pleasing* recollections of Childhood." The Jewish Sabbath was "wholly joyous. . . . There is no terror in the religion of the Hebrews, no eternal perdition." he was pleased to report, "they are all Universalists."[53]

At the other extreme, the Sunday School Union book, *The Jew at Home and Abroad,* condemned many Jewish practices. Even though the Jews were "indestructible" and deserving of gratitude for the Old Testament, their rejection of Jesus had led them into delusion. They had turned to the Talmud, which contained many offensive sections, "ridiculous laws," and directions for "absurd and superstitious practices which are so numerous" in Jewish rites. The author stressed the resemblance between Judaism and "Popery." Both were beset by tradition with little judgment allowed to individuals. Still, the writer cautioned, Christians must continue to show "compassion."[54]

Most of the newspapers regularly reported Jewish festivals and events by the 1870s. The *New York Times,* not yet Jewish-owned, was a good example.[55] Like many other periodicals and newspapers, the *Times* was interested in the rising Reform movement. On 3 April 1870 it reported that "Reformed Judaism" had "excited a good deal of attention in the Christian world." This movement illustrated the "strange vitality of a downtrodden and persecuted but strong-willed race." The power of amalgamation that was creating a great people out of may diverse elements in America, "has also touched the chosen race and is bringing them more into harmony with the modes of thinking that prevail around them." There followed a continuous stream of editorials commending the "reformed school" as superior to a medieval Orthodoxy, which was oblivious to the needs of a new era. A story, "Jews in America," described the congregations of the city. The finest and costliest was Emanuel, which was the first to declare the "domination of reason over blind and bigoted faith." It stood for the triumph of the "Judaism which proclaims the spirit of religion as being of more importance than the letter."

Other articles in the *Times* in the 1870s covered Jewish religious life. An 1872 feature, "Sunday at the Synagogue," was about the "superb" Temple "Immanuel." The reporter commented on the many beautiful women, but noted that he could not tell whether they were Polish, German, or aristocratic Sephardim. Under the subtle influence of America, "the Semitic characteristics had been toned down, softened, or completely removed. The great peculiarity of the congregation was that it was difficult to recognize them as Jewish at all." In the same year the paper described a family Passover service in which "three or four generations assembled about the festive board." An 1878 review discussed the Talmud in some detail and with complete objectivity. The average reader, the writer claimed, knew very little of "the peculiar tenets and religious beliefs of his Jewish fellow-citizens and still less of the wonderful works. . . ." Popular prejudice against the Jews had, until recently, extended to their books, but "the Jews and the Talmud have outlived their persecutors."

Cities with small Jewish populations were at least as scrupulous in reporting Jewish holidays and special events. Salt Lake City papers were typical in that respect.[56] The *Salt Lake City Tribune* was particularly conscientious. An issue of 2 October 1872 described "Rosh Hasheno," followed by "the holiest of all Sabbaths, a day observed by Israelites from time immemorial. . . ." The paper noted sadly that the Western world had been contaminated by apostasy and wondered whether any of "our Jewish friends" had caught the disease. It was relieved, on the following day, to witness a large attendance at the service, "indeed we were not previously aware that so many inhabitants of this city were of Jewish extraction." On Yom Kippur the paper was again pleased to report scrupulous observance. The *Tribune* informed its readers during Passover week of 1876 that Jews celebrated the occasion by "abstaining from all food except unleavened bread as commanded by the great lawgiver." Somewhat later, when the cornerstone for a new synagogue was laid, the paper commented enthusiastically, "The building will be an ornament to the city." The dedication services were "impressive and interesting . . . a more attractive place of worship does not exist in the West."

Some observers even responded positively to mysterious Orthodox services, as demonstrated by an 1875 visit to an Orthodox synagogue by a writer for *Liberal Christian*. Although the commentator, like all visitors noted the "business-like air" and the "walking about and talking," he did not regard these as basic. The service itself was entirely in Hebrew and was "musical, plaintive, devout, triumphant." The reporter queried, "What Christian church can boast a service of such antiquity? Where is there a ritual so free from idolatry and error? Where is there a service more democratic?"[57]

The *New York Tribune* often evinced a friendly interest in the Jewish religion.[58] A September 1889 article, "A Memorial of Jewish Antiquity," noted that while many people were busy exhuming Greek and Roman relics, they showed little concern with "existing relics" that had never been lost. On that day, in their synagogues, the paper declared, Jewish fellow-citizens would celebrate their New Year "with a ceremonial containing features much older than any of the remains." A man who entered an Orthodox synagogue would soon be able to "imagine himself transported thousands of years into the past. . . . The worshippers will appear to him wrapped in Oriental prayer scarfs; the sacred scrolls will be chanted to him in an unspeakably ancient tongue." The most remarkable aspect of the ceremony was its antiquity. "It has lived along with the marvelous race that has preserved its unity without a home while persecuting empires have gone down to their graves and the monuments of their civilizations have crumbled into dust."

The *Tribune,* like many other publications, was impressed with the efforts of "Jewish Reformers." An August 1890 report on the movement to shift the Jewish Sabbath to Sunday, concluded that these Reform efforts were due to "increased enlightenment" of the people among whom the Jews dwelt. The removal of prejudicial hindrances had led the "sons of Israel" to achieve success in areas once closed to them. It had been their exclusion from contact with advanced ideas that had led them to "petty finance and to the narrow-minded teachings of their rabbinical books." This certainly appears to contradict the admiration that had been expressed for the antiquity of Jewish observances. While many commentators admired Jewish persistence, they also tended to expect a future of greater assimilation with more "modern" religious ideas.

The arrival of large numbers of Eastern Jews to New York increased the interest in Jewish ceremonial. New York newspapers described "exotic" Jewish holidays in considerable detail for the benefit of their Christian readers.[59] The *New York Tribune* was particularly careful in its descriptions. The New Year was a season of "impressive ceremonies" with "weird, tearful, wailing melodies," which the listener could never forget. Even the Feast of the Tabernacles, with its strange booths, was fully covered. Most of the services took place in "the humble synagogues of the poor." The strongest impulse in the ghetto was the maintenance of religion in these tiny synagogues where one found not a single trace of New York, "not a word of English." The *Evening Post* reported that each little town of the Pale of Jewish settlement was represented by a synagogue in New York. Chanukah was a "merry season of domestic fun making." The *Post* advised people who thought of Jews as "a sullen folk in dismal homes" to witness this celebration. They would find "many prospering lords of large families dispensing 'mehr fun als a circus.'" The *Times* contrasted the Reform and Orthodox services of the rich and poor. On the East Side, the "weeping and wailing of the supplicants could be heard for blocks." In the fashionable temples attended by richly attired men and women, while the services "were also fraught with deep emotion," the worshippers displayed no such open feelings. The rituals of the Eastern Jews were "oriental" and strange. The services of the Reform Jews were certainly more comprehensible and "American" to newspaper observers and, therefore, far more thoroughly reported.

Issues of church and state were extremely important to postemancipation Jewry. Jewish periodicals were often disturbed by what they perceived to be efforts to impose Christianity as the official religion of the nation. The Christian and secular press, on the other hand, tended to assume that Jews should be so grateful for their welcome to America in contrast to persecution elsewhere, that they should never question the Christian basis of American society. One typical example of this prevalent attitude was the controversy over an 1844 Thanksgiving Proclamation by Governor Hammond of South Carolina, which exhorted citizens to offer thanks to "Jesus Christ, the Redeemer." Charleston Jews protested the sectarian nature of the document. The governor revealingly responded, "I have always thought it a settled matter that I lived in a Christian land. . . . I know that the civilization of the age is derived from Christianity." Jews who still scorned the Christ they had crucified had no grounds for demanding inclusion in public Christian worship.[60] Other such issues included Sabbath observance and Christian teachings in public schools. However, the nation's press tended to take the

Christian foundations of the country for granted. Periodicals were unaware of any dichotomy in attitudes when they welcomed Jews, expressed admiration for the Jewish religion, and assumed that all would fit in with Christian practices in public policy. In fact, they rarely even discussed church-state issues of concern to Jews.

In America the religious image of the Jew was filled with ambiguities. There is no question about the continuing power of the old view of the Jews as crucifiers of the Son of God, a people who had been punished for eternity for that heinous crime. Indeed, that idea of the religious place of the Jew has continued to be potent in the minds of some Americans to the present day. A related view with widespread circulation was that the Jewish religion had existed only as a precursor to Christianity, and had long since outlived its viability in the modern world. Not only did religious and Sunday-school texts propagate this perception of the Jew, but religious novels, some of which were among the most phenomenally successful books of the century, also often reinforced such ideas.

It is also true, on the other hand, that some of the very religious writers were also the most aware of the Jews as the people of the Bible and the originators of Christianity. Even the most ardent conversionists were not always unkind in their estimates of Jews. Believing, as they did, that the Second Coming was dependent upon the restoration of the "chosen people" and their acceptance of the true Messiah, many expressed a benevolent interest in the Jews. Although patronizing or even scornful about Jewish religious rites, most preached that respect and tolerance was the best approach.

In addition, there was a strong countercurrent in America, especially apparent in the secular press. This was the image of the Jews as the ancient people of the Bible who had preserved the worship of one God, who had courageously overcome the most terrible persecution the world had known, and to whom Christians should be grateful for their basic ideas and for Christ himself. It was a great source of pride that these ancient people could worship with complete freedom only in America. This confirmed America's superiority to the bigoted Old World and should not be tampered with. For that reason, the secular press was largely opposed to missionary activities. There was a genuine interest in the religious customs of the Jews, and while this interest was sometimes condescending, it was rarely unkind. The building of synagogues were universally welcomed, and the consecrations were characteristically attended by the leading citizens of the community. While most Christian observers seemed to prefer Reform Judaism as more "American," this was a reflection of the desire to assimilate Jews into the American mainstream, rather than an unfriendly wish to eliminate the Jewish religion. At any rate, by the latter years of the century, hostile religious images of the Jews diminished considerably, a reflection of a more secularized society. By that time, other, nonreligious images—both positive and negative—had become more significant.

2
Literary Images

In his excellent study, *From Shylock to Svengali*, Edgar Rosenberg examines the picture of Jews in British literature.[1] British writers appeared to be obsessed by Jews. To a great extent, nineteenth-century American literature was derivative from the English in its accepted conventions.

One of the most important archetypes was the Jew as supervillain, the Shylock character. This usurer was a secretive coward, clannish, servile to Christians whom he detested, and always an opportunist about money. Physically, he was stooped, and he had an outlandish nose, an unpleasant odor and, frequently, a speech impediment. This ancient stereotype can be traced back to St. Paul's description of Judas, making a direct line from religious to literary stereotypes. Like Judas, this character always demanded his thirty pieces of silver. In that sense, some of the powerful attraction of this figure can be related to the crucifixion. It surfaced in accusations of ritual murder of Christian children, repeated in Chaucer's *Canterbury Tales*. Shakespeare gave flesh to this repulsive person in *The Merchant of Venice*. The type reached its depths in Dickens's Fagin, compared to whom even Shylock was civilized. This horrible child's view of the devil was always "less sinned against than sinning." Trollope, in *The Way We Live Now*, created a modern secular Shylock who no longer extorted money because he hated Christians, but was part of a decadent society that encouraged such opportunists.

The miserly old usurer often had a beautiful daughter. His love was characteristically divided between her and his gold. This young woman was the second basic stereotype, "la belle juive," the beautiful Jewess. This lovely girl was the object of lust and seduction attempts by the Christian hero. The original was Shylock's Jessica, but she reached her apogee in Scott's Rebecca, an absolute paragon in word and deed. This character was often permitted flaming speeches in affirmation of her Jewishness and in denunciation of the persecution of her people, even though similar language only added to the distaste for the aging villain. Her fate was either to run away with the gentile

40

hero or, more often, to suffer an "inevitable doom," resulting from her love for a Christian.[2] Above all, however, she was mysteriously beautiful, with a special kind of dark allure.

Finally, there was the institutionalized countermyth to Shylock, the benevolent Jew. During the Enlightenment, some writers sought to justify Jews to gentiles. The finest such work in Western literature was Lessing's *Nathan the Wise*. In English literature, the archetypal good Jew was Sheva in Richard Cumberland's 1794 play, *The Jew*. Sheva was a professional do-gooder. This Jew, although misunderstood and maligned, was selfless and self-sacrificing, beyond all belief. This "bloodless abstraction" was almost as popular as the villain. He displayed most prominently the New Testament virtue of turning the other cheek. In George Eliot's *Daniel Deronda* (also influential because of its early espousal of Zionism), the virtues turned into saintliness. The didactic purpose of this characterization could be seen in Eliot's comment that she wrote the book, "on purpose to enoble Judaism." Whether good or bad, the Jewish male in English literature was generally judged by the single yardstick of money. His chief virtue was his usefulness to Christians, generally shown by financial aid to worthy Christians.

Other mythic Jews who appeared in English literature included the Wandering Jew and the sorcerer. The Wandering Jew could be a mysterious and fearsome figure or, as in Shelley, an admirable martyr and rebel. The figure of Svengali was the ultimate Jew with supernatural power, a strange combination of God's mouthpiece and sordidness. In any case, the Jew was always the alien, a man apart whether he was an object of contempt or awe. Rosenberg concludes that "the image of the Jew in English literature is depressingly uniform and static." In fact, the Jew did not receive any real consideration as a human being until the ghetto studies of Israel Zangwell in the 1890s. As late as 1914, Zangwell complained, "It seems curious that the cad and the money-lender still practically monopolize the boards."[3] The same basic stereotypes and attitudes could be found in much of the literature of Europe.[4]

In many ways American literature followed English literary conventions and disregarded American realities. Generally, there was little relationship between the picture of the Jews in American fiction and the Jews actually living in America in the nineteenth century. The image of the Jew in American literature through the century showed as little tendency to change as the British. Imaginative writing was far less reflective of the upheavals in the American Jewish community than the press. One could have read American fiction of this period without realizing that a fairly sizable group of German Jews had entered the country and achieved success, or that a far larger group of Eastern Jews had poured in, altering the character of the Jewish community.

Although the British stereotypes of the Jew were part of American literature, it is important to note that American writers were simply not as obsessed by Jews as their British counterparts. In Britain major writers focused upon Jewish villains and heroes. Dickens and Trollope created memorable Jewish arch-villains. Scott romanticized the quintessential beautiful Jewess. Dickens, in a mood of repentance, and George Eliot sought to counter with "good" Jews. On the other hand, few American writers of consequence mentioned Jews at all. James Fennimore Cooper, in *Oak Openings,* whimsically characterized the Indians as a lost tribe of Israel, but he only had one Jewish money-lender as a lesser character in a minor work. Hawthorne had one beautiful Jewess and one incidental peddler. Mark Twain, despite a charming little Judeophile article and a clear awareness of the Jewish presence in the West, never created a Jewish peddler as a character in his novels.[5] Henry James dealt tentatively with one beautiful Jewess and dabbled in occasional aristocratic condescension toward Jewish art dealers. Despite his claims of realism and his encouragement of Abraham Cahan, William Dean Howells did not include one significant Jewish character in the pages of his numerous works. Even Lindau, the socialist in *Hazard of New Fortunes,* is referred to as a German, although he was patterned upon a German Jew Howells knew. Only Melville, among the major American authors considered Judaism and the Jewish people in one of his books. For the most part, when one considers the image of the Jew in American literature, one must discuss less significant authors. Many of these authors shifted the locale of their stories out of the United States. Clearly, American writers did not feel the same danger from the Jew as European authors.

Shylock: The Villain in America

The Jew as Shylock or Fagin has haunted the imagination of the English-speaking world. The Shylock archetype of a merciless, murderous usurer is, as Leslie Fiedler has observed, something more profound than the standard villain. He is "a representative of the tribal fury of Jewry that will not admit its maltreatment is merited. He loves only one thing more than gold: the sweet savor of vengeance."[6] The treachery of Judas, paid for in silver, was paralleled by the usurer's terrible passion for wealth and revenge. The mythic weapon of this creature was a knife, the classic instrument of castration. Guilt feelings about treatment of Jews intermingled with fears of inevitable retribution. This villain satisfied the need to prove that negative attitudes towards Jews were caused by Jewish misbehavior. There may also be some element of the angry father, in Freudian Oedipal terms, in this character. The father, after all, holds and withholds the purse strings. Judaism fathered Christianity and then rejected both its tenets and its holy child. Sometimes, the hero was a Christ-like figure who was as beset by Jews as Jesus was by Judas. All of these villains tended to suffer a downfall and humiliation similar to the prototype, Shylock.

As one might expect, Americans, having a much better record in treatment of Jews and encountering far fewer than Europe, felt a less urgent need to focus on the Jewish villain in their literature. Although British literary tradition remained potent in determining the representation of Jewish characters, male Jews played a more peripheral role in American fiction. The stereotype of this classic miscreant was somewhat softened, stitched in less acid lines than his English cousin. There was also a tendency to switch the scene of his misdeeds out of the United States. Serious anti-Semitism was relatively uncommon.

The earliest American portraits of the hawk-nosed, gold-hording, heavily accented usurer occurred in books and plays dealing with adventures among the Barbary pirates. At the time of American conflicts with the Barbary states, two powerful Jewish banking families were partners of the ruling Dey. They helped to supervise the piracy, served as diplomatic channels, and lent money to Western consuls for expenses and ransoms, often at extortionate rates. Their presence lent credence to the accepted stereotype.[7] The standard was set by Susanna Rowson's popular play of 1794, *Slaves in Algiers*.[8] It featured Ben Hassan, moneylender and forger, who plans to betray the American captives after taking their money, and admits to "having cheated the Gentiles as Moses commanded." He speaks with an accent and lisps, which was, for some unaccountable reason, considered a Jewish trait. In the manner of Shylock, he has a beautiful (and unaccented) daughter who, like Jessica, wishes "some dear Christian man would fall in love with me and carry me off." Overhearing her, the American hero declares, "I'm your man." However, in a marked deviation from the old tale, when her father suffers his inevitable ruination, the daughter bids her lover good-bye, proclaiming, "When my father was rich . . . I did not think much about my duty; but now he is poor and forsaken, I know too well to leave him alone in his affliction." The author's approval of this daughterly reaction was indicative of a more ambivalent attitude and less deep-seated hatred of the villain.

Other versions of this popular story followed Mrs. Rowson's success.[9] Royall Tyler in *The Algerine Captive* (1797), one of the first American novels, utilized the same theme with more typically American ambivalence. On the one hand, he characterized Jews as "this cunning race" who follow a messiah of gold, "content to be apparently wretched and despised, that they may wallow in secret wealth." On the other, however, he described the blood libel as "this horrid tale which should have been despised for its absurdity and inhumanity." The enlightenment hero, a Yankee doctor enslaved in Algiers, saves the life of a wealthy Jew's son. The Jew's house is outwardly desolate to avoid provoking envy, but is furnished in Oriental splendor. This picture of secret wealth was prevalent in later books about Jews, in part out of a need to explain the apparent poverty of so many of the supposed money-grubbers, and in part as wish-fulfillment. The "benevolent Hebrew old man" befriends the hero and promises to ransom him. But, when he dies suddenly, the "wily" son robs the hero and sells him into slavery. Both good and bad Jew are thus presented, but the function of both revolves around money.

Quaker City, written in 1844 by George Lippard, was a vastly popular blend of sex, violence, and socialism. Gabriel Von Gelt is a minor character, a Jewish gangster in a gallery of grotesques. "Jew was written on his face as though he had fallen asleep for 3000 years at the building of the Temple." His demands for repayment of a loan cause his death at the hands of the villain. Probably most readers of this fantastic novel did not single out the lone Jew from the huge army of criminals. Yet, as Leslie Fiedler has noted, "It is not unimportant that in the nightmare phantasmagoria of the populist imagination run wild . . . the figure of the hawk-nosed conniving Jew takes his due place." He was the true ancestor of the twentieth-century fictional Jewish gangster such as Wolfshein in *The Great Gatsby.*[10]

As the century wore on and the Sephardic merchant princes were replaced by German peddlers as the prototypical American Jews, the image of the usurious villain remained relatively constant. In Peter Hamilton Myers *The Misers' Heir* (1854), Hakes, a Chatham Street old clothes man "whose features and occupation proclaim him a Jew," is also a money-lender who sits "spider-like in the back part of his den, watching for prey." When the innocent young hero enters, the sharper gives his rates, "Ten per shent . . . I gif him one tousand now—he pay me ten tousand when he ish a man." This "Jewish ten percent" was a subject of constant comment in other books as well.[11]

In *The Clipper Yacht* by Joseph Ingraham (of biblical novels' fame), the description of Moloch the moneylender is more flattering than usual. When Captain Dowling asks for money to cover his forgeries, Moloch responds with great relish, "so you haf come vor more monish? . . . Te Christian pleads humbly to the Jew when he would haf money; and curses him when he no longer needs him." When Moloch converses in the "Hebrew tongue," however, he speaks with "dignity of accent." (Most of the authors knew so little about Jews in the first half of the century that they believed that the latter spoke biblical Hebrew in conversations among themselves.) Moloch turns out not to be so evil after all. He has been plotting to marry his niece to Captain Dowling to revenge himself on the Duke, Dowling's father, who had struck the moneylender many years earlier. Rather than the usual humiliation, all of Moloch's plans come to fruition and everyone lives happily ever after—a uniquely American version of the old story![12]

John Beauchamp Jones was one of the few novelists to present Jews as nonexotic storekeepers in the West.[13] Although their occupations were more mundane, however, their characters were very similar to the standard usurers. One of the heroes remarks that Jews "cheat Christians with their own wares." A Jewish merchant destroys his own store by fire, one of the earliest examples of a charge that would later become commonplace. Even these more realistic Jews were given the traits of Shylock.

Henry James occasionally wrote about Jews as art connoisseurs with Shylock's ability to make a quick profit. In an 1883 story, "Impressions of a Cousin," Mr. Caliph, "a Jew of the artistic, not of the commercial type," is the executor of the estate of an heiress. Although he claims to be trustworthy, the narrator asks, "Who ever heard of a naif Jew?" Caliph does indeed mismanage the estate, which is only saved by his virtuous non-Jewish half-brother who loves the heiress. However, since James was incapable of writing mere clichés, the heiress forgives Caliph for his dishonesty and probably marries him in the end.[14]

F. Marion Crawford was one of the most popular novelists of the last decades of the nineteenth century. He thought of fiction as a "marketable commodity," and, in his own time, was more famous than Howells or James. In many of his numerous works Jews appeared as exotic peripheral figures. In *Witch of Prague,* however, Crawford combined negative and positive images. The hero is a young Jew who "in form and feature . . . represented the noblest type of the Jewish race . . . a young eagle." Yet the description of the Jewish quarter is chilling, a stronghold "in which Israel sits, as a great spider in the midst of a dark web, dominating the whole capital with his eagle's glance . . . " As a means of revenge, the "witch" brings the Jewish hero back two hundred years to the time of a martyr convert who was murdered by his fellow Jews. The earlier Jewish quarter was pictured vividly in Crawford's lush prose:

> Throngs of gowned men, crooked, bearded, filthy, vulture-eyed . . . grasping fat purses in lean fingers, shaking greasy curls . . . pointing long fingers and crooked nails . . . intoxicated by the smell of gold, mad for its possession . . . poisoned to the core by the sweet sting of money, terrible in intelligence, vile in heart, contemptible in body, irresistible in the unity of their greed.

In short, an entire community of Shylocks! In Crawford's book the Shylock image was again juxtaposed with religious hostility. Nevertheless, there is a more complex view here since the hero is also a Jew.[15]

As people encountered more real-life Jews, the character of the usurer-criminal-villain began to lose most of his exotic traits, but remained as a staple. In the 1898 *New York, a Novel,* Lysko, a Polish Jew who "can smell a dollar ten times further than I can see one," offers the hero money to commit arson, which was by that time widely accepted as a typical "Jewish" crime. *An Exile from London* (1896) described a villainous Rothschild-like family who were involved with an equally disreputable American Jewish lawyer. Russian Jews were briefly considered by Richard Savage, a successful and prolific writer of the 1890s. In *The White Lady of Khaminavatka* (1898), a town of

Orthodox Jews was described as the home of "the trading vultures who fatten on the Russian peasant." They were "parasites," feeding on a decaying country by trafficking "in usury." Here was an entire nation of Shylocks![16]

At the time when Eastern European Jews were pouring into American slums and sweatshops, one important novelist, Frank Norris, included a Polish Jewish character in his popular 1899 "naturalistic" novel, *McTeague*.[17] Zerkow was the classic Shylock, with "the thin, eager cat-like lips of the covetous . . . and claw-like prehensile fingers—the fingers of a man who accumulates, but never disburses." The glint of gold "was in his eyes." He keeps begging the servant girl, Maria, to tell him the story of one hundred solid gold dishes her family had supposedly once owned. Eventually, he marries her just to hear the preposterous tale. When she develops "brain fever" and forgets the story, his avarice drives him into a terrible rage and he murders her. He is discovered later, floating in the bay, clutching a sack of one hundred rusty old pots and pans. While this might be dramatically effective, it is significant that a "naturalist" novelist in 1899 could include this kind of portrait of a Jew in the face of real life among the garment workers in the ghetto.

The Shylock-Fagin figure, the Jewish usurer-criminal, also remained an important character until the twentieth century when, altered slightly, he turned into Jewish gangsters in the works of Fitzgerald, Hemingway, and T. S. Eliot. It should be remembered, however, that, whatever psychological need he fulfilled, he did not occupy nearly as important a role in nineteenth-century American fiction as in British. Serious American writers were simply not as obsessed by the evil Jew as their English counterparts. The wicked Jew was placed far more frequently in foreign, exotic environments than in America and he was often counterbalanced by "good" Jews in the same novel.

The Wandering Jew

A few American authors were peripherally interested in the Wandering Jew, a symbol of the dispersion of the Jewish people after their rejection of Christ and the subject of much European fiction. Nathaniel Hawthorne was the most significant American writer to present this character first in an 1842 short story, "A Virtuoso's Collection." In this tale, a museum guard who has shown an astonishing familiarity with the past turns out to be none other than the Wandering Jew. He offers the narrator eternal life, but the latter refuses. To the Wandering Jew "earthly life is the only good," and he is uninterested in spiritual matters.[18]

Hawthorne's fine short story "Ethan Brand" contained the one realistic portrait of a nineteenth-century peddler, "an old German Jew traveling with a diorama on his back." There was an aura of truth about the picture of the "old Dutchman," who passes through the village "in the hopes of eking out the profits of the day." Far from living in secret splendor on the ill-gotten gains of usury, he makes a pitiful living by exhibiting "Pictures worn out, tattered, full of cracks and wrinkles and in pitiable condition." One cannot doubt that Hawthorne must have encountered just such a struggling show-man. In this case, however, he is also the mythic Wandering Jew. There is a typically Hawthorne-like aura of evil in his mysterious relationship with the haunted Ethan Brand. He turns the "dark and strong outline of his visage" to Ethan, urging him to look into the box. Although others can see only an empty canvas, Ethan sees and understands. "I remember you now," Brand mutters. "Ah Captain," the Jew replies with a dark smile, "I find it a heavy matter in my showbox—this Unpardonable Sin. By my faith Captain it has wearied my shoulders this long day to carry it over the mountain." The old man then packs up his wares and disappears from the story.[19] In this way Hawthorne managed to suggest mysterious evil and the Wandering Jew in an unstereotyped tale.

The immense success of Eugene Sue's *The Wandering Jew,* which became a runaway best-seller in its English translation in 1845, led less talented au-thors to tackle the same theme.[20] F. Marion Crawford, a popular purveyor of romance, altered the myth when his villain was revealed to be an insane Christian who merely believed himself to be the Wandering Jew. This character was far less interesting to American authors than the Shylock figure. Perhaps the lack of American fascination with the Wandering Jew was the result of a feeling that the Jew could cease his journey in free America.

The Rebecca Image—La Belle Juive

The exotic figure of that magnificently beautiful woman with the liquid dark eyes, the lovely young Jewess, was as popular a character in American literature as the villainous old usurer. In fact, she often appeared as the daughter of that evil and deformed old man, just like Shylock's Jessica or Isaac's Rebecca. In some cases, it was the role of the hero to carry her off to a better, assimilated life. Leslie Fiedler feels that this legend is part of a "dream of rescuing the desirable elements in the Judaic tradition (maternal tender-ness . . . the figure of Mary) from the unsympathetic (patriarchal rigor and harsh legalism: the figure of the high priest . . . ."[21] This identification of the Jewish woman with Mary can be seen in *The Clipper Yacht* when the Duke scorns anyone who would stoop so low as to marry a Jewess. He is admon-ished by Moloch, "The mother of thy Christ" was a Jewess."[22] For the most part, however, it is difficult to see most fictional American Jewish women as representations of Mary. In general, Americans were far less involved than Latin peoples with the figure of the Virgin Mother.

The Jewish woman was almost never presented as a typically maternal figure, but rather as a female with mysterious sexual allure. If she was the mother Mary, she fulfilled the desire for a seductive mother. She was often contrasted, as she had been in *Ivanhoe,* to the pale listless, pure, and asexual Anglo-Saxon maiden. She was the erotic dream figure, the "dark Lady," who was permitted to assert her sexuality. To some extent, she was also a manifestation of the romantic ideal. Although it was occasionally true, as Fiedler asserts, that she did not survive the books' endings, "being death-ridden as well as death-bearing," more often she did far better than that. Frequently, she was permitted to voice sentiments that would never be allowed to the male Jewish characters. She was, with rare exception, sympathetic and considerably more "liberated" than her Christian counterpart. The authors often used these women to give expression to otherwise repressed sexual feelings.

One of the earliest and most interesting Jewish women to appear in American fiction was Mrs. Achsa Fielding in Charles Brockden Brown's *Arthur Mervyn,* which appeared in 1800.[23] She departed considerably from the cliché of the Jewish woman, lacking both the villainous father and the striking physical beauty that were the hallmarks of the conventional exotic Jewish heroine. A figure of grace and intelligence, she was the ideal mate for the Enlightenment man, created in the image of the woman Brown hoped to marry. In the novel, Arthur Mervyn, a young rustic, comes to Philadelphia where he learns all about corruption and intrigue. In the second volume of his adventures, he meets Mrs. Fielding, a woman of "dignity and independence, a generous and enlightened spirit," well versed in music and literature. Although she is "too low" in stature, "all personal defects are outweighed by her heart and intellect. . . ." She had been brought up by doting parents indifferent to the distinctions of religion. She married an English nobleman at sixteen and entered the Church of England. She is apologetic about her conversion, ascribing it to youthful "thoughtlessness" and a reaction to the "scorn to which the Jewish nation are everywhere condemned." After a series of personal tragedies, Mrs. Fielding eloquently opposes "vain distinctions of property and nation. . . . Her nation has suffered too much by the inhuman antipathies of religions and political faction." Her Jewishness is not even an issue to Mervyn. He proposes to her at the urging of a friend who concludes, "A brilliant skin is not hers, nor elegant proportions . . . yet no creature has more power to bewitch. . . ." The book ends happily with their marriage. Mrs. Fielding, with the exception of her "Jewish eyes," was the only totally nonstereotyped Jewish woman in nineteenth century American fiction. Her Jewishness is reflected mainly in her greater experiences in the world's tribulation and her resulting wisdom. She is also one of the few examples of a truly liberated woman in that fiction. The beautiful Jewess was preferred by most authors. Shelley, for example, could not understand why Mervyn did not prefer to marry the pretty, insipid, childlike Eliza, who was the typical Christian heroine.

Most nineteenth-century works presented the standard Rebecca image. Seductive Jewish eyes were the salient feature of every female Jewish character in American fiction at this time. Veronika, in Henry Harland's *As It Was Written*, is typical. She is a pure "white soul" with bottomless eyes, "far, far in their liquid depths the spirit shone. . . ." A Jewish woman, unlike a Christian, could be mother and child at the same time. Veronika is an innocent, "but she was a Jewess and all the experience of the Jewish race, all the martyrdom of the scattered hosts were hers by inheritance."[24]

Almost invariably, she was the daughter of a Shylock and the lover of a Christian man. The father of Daria Leon in E. S. March's *A Stumbler in Wide Shoes*, is the standard usurer whose "strong yellow teeth unpleasantly suggested a missing link in the direction of carnivorous animals." She, as usual defying heredity, has "blue black hair . . . melting eyes" and "the beauty of Spain on her face." Though she claims that she will only marry a Jew, she has a fatal weakness for Christians. The problem is "they cannot turn Jew for her; she will not turn Christian for them." In spite of this, however, she decides to "stoop in taking a Christian."[25] Although this proclivity for Christians sometimes led to a tragic death from a broken heart, more often, in American fiction, the Jewess married the Christian hero. Rachel, in *The Clipper Yacht*, for example, was permitted to marry the dissolute hero, reform him completely, and become a prize ornament of the English royal court!

As in European fiction, the beautiful Jewess was often described as a desirable "sex object." At any rate, she was permitted to project an open sexuality denied to Christian heroines. Sartre has commented on the sexual significance of "la belle juive." He noted that the words carried a different impact from "beautiful American," for example. There was "an aura of rape and massacre . . . she whom the Cossacks . . . dragged by her hair through the streets of her burning village."[26] It was rare for that aspect to appear in American fiction. Here her sexuality was far more robust. Thus, Rachel, who ultimately became such a great lady, had "an air of the most finished coquetry." She wore tight fitting scarlet satin to show off "her finely developed bust . . . and affording a striking relief to her jet black hair and nut brown complexion."[27] Generally, like Rachel, despite her sex appeal, she was a most virtuous individual.

Occasionally, the beautiful Jewess was not so pure. George Lippard, in *The Nazarene*, combined the sensual Jewess and all the sexual implications of that image with the Wandering Jewess in his usual sensationalist fashion.[28] One of the survivors of a shipwreck is a once magnificent actress who, even amid famine and death, retains traces "of that gorgeous loveliness peculiar to the daughters of Palestine from immemorial time." She has "voluptuous warmth," with hair in heavy masses falling to her waist and "neck and shoulders as beautiful as alabaster." She reminds one of "the warm and glowing Bathsheba or the wild and beautiful Herodia. . . ." She reveals that she is indeed the Wandering Jewess who was once the voluptuous Herodia. Then she undulated to and fro, clasping a human head in "incestuous embrace" to the "warm bloom of her bosom," as she danced with delight, the blood falling on her robe. For this act she was condemned never to grow old or feel emotion, "to be loved—worshipped—and not to feel love again." She specializes in tempting men to their deaths.

The very persecution that embittered and helped to explain the villainy of the Shylock figure merely served to add to the allure of the Jewish heroine. European fiction tended to treat the beautiful Jewess as a "desirable suffering sex object" who did not protest or struggle against the current, but allowed herself to drown.[29] In America, in contrast, she could show "the proud hatred a beautiful Jewish woman can only express when she speaks of the persecution of her race." She might even reject the advances of a Russian nobleman to care for her people, informing him that her heart was "pierced by the murder of my kindred . . . my soul made sorrowful by the sight of the wrongs inflicted on them by you and your caste."[30]

Serious writers were also attracted to the romantic Rebecca figure. Nathaniel Hawthorne's Miriam in *The Marble Faun* was an interesting variant.[31] Miriam is only partly Jewish, but it is clear that the Jewish blood is responsible for her "warmth and passionateness." As an artist she paints a portrait of a magnificent looking woman with "a Jewish aspect . . . dark eyes into which you might look as deeply as your glance would go . . . black abundant hair . . . this was Jewish hair and a dark glory such as crowns no Christian maiden's head . . . what Rachel might have been when Jacob deemed her worth the wooing seven years and seven more." The portrait is of Miriam herself. Unfortunately, the spirit of evil hovers about her, although she herself is not at all wicked. She precipitates the loss of innocence and death of Donatello, the "faun," who adores her. The destiny that is connected with love for Miriam may represent the punishment that flows from the yearning for vibrant, full-blooded sexuality, a result typical of Hawthorne's works.

Henry James described another half-Jewish Miriam in *The Tragic Muse* (1890).[32] Miriam Rooth is the daughter of a "Jew broker," who, like many of James's Jewish men, also deals in art. Although upper class, she is an ambitious actress who aspires to be "the English Rachel." She cares little about being Jewish, but wants always to be "interesting." Miriam has inherited her talent and artistic sensibilities from her father. "The Hebraic Mr. Rooth, with his love of old pots and Christian altar cloths, had supplied in the girl's composition an aesthetic element, the sense of color and form." Far from pining away, as Jewish maidens were sometimes wont to do, Miriam gives up her stuffy upper-class Christian lover to pursue her career. In the end, she is a successful, accomplished actress and woman of the world.

The Jewish women presented by Hawthorne and James were strong figures, capable of accomplishing much good or evil. On the other hand, Ruth, the heroine of Herman Melville's *Clarel,* the beautiful young Jewess who awakens the hero from his passivity, represented the kind of vestal love usually associated with Christian women.[33] She wears a snowy robe and veils. She is Eden before the Fall, all innocence and hope for release from life's complexities. "She looked a legate to insure that Paradise is possible . . . an Eve-like face. And Nereid eyes with virgin spell . . . Hebrew the profile every line. . . ." Such a love, however, cannot be, and Ruth, the innocent, must die, not because of her Jewishness but because of her otherworldliness. Elsewhere in the book a character remarks jestingly, "there is no tress can thrall one like a Jewess's." In his light-hearted version of history, all the great beauties and coquettes are Jewish. Melville, thus, presented two aspects of the beautiful Jewess character.

The lovely dark young Jewess remained a staple of American fiction through the century. This idealized picture of Jewish feminine beauty was so widely accepted that it could be routinely found in news articles as well. As poor wan immigrants began to flock in from Eastern Europe, the character began to lose her allure. The presentation of the Jewish woman in modern American fiction appears to bear little resemblance to that of her ancestor.[34] In many respects, the "Jewish princess" in her selfishness and contemptible familiarity is the complete opposite of the exotic, noble, beautiful Jewess. Perhaps, however, she is more a product of Jewish self-hatred than of Christian hostility.

Sheva: The Benevolent Jew

Among the literary conventions imported from Britain was the positive stereotype of the counter-Shylock. He may well be traceable to the realization that Christ himself was a Jew. This incredibly benevolent soul looked just like Shylock and lived the same kind of life as the moneylender, but he utilized his money to help out worthy but needy Christians. The function and purpose of the "good" Jew revolved around money as completely as did that of the evil Jew. Most of these exceedingly popular characters derived from Sheva, the hero of Cumberland's *The Jew,* who had been conceived in expiation for the author's numerous Jewish villains. Within a year of its 1794 performance in London, *The Jew* had been performed twice in Boston and in New York, Providence, Hartford, Charleston, and Philadelphia. Within another year it had been republished five times and was considered a smash hit. The purpose of the character was clearly understood at the time to be an answer to Shylock. A 1795 reviewer in *New York Weekly Magazine* declared, "the idea of vindicating the Jews and bringing forth on the stage a kind of white [!] Shylock is certainly a very happy one." An 1801 reviewer, commenting on another play with a Sheva-like character, praised it for "its evident tendency to obviate those unjust and illiberal prejudices which have too long been entertained in every country against this unfortunate race of men."[35] Clearly, this character existed largely to expunge guilt feelings, rather like efforts to upgrade the black image on modern television.

Sheva-like characters appeared very early in American fiction. In George Walker's *Theodore Cyphon or the Benevolent Jew* (1803), a central character is Shechem, a Jewish moneylender who uses the proceeds of his huge rates of interest to pay for his "charities and benevolence." Even after the execution of the heroic Theodore, Shechem continues to "extort from the spendthrift, to accumulate bond to bond, and in defiance of every Christian example to bestow charity without applause and benefit mankind in secret."[36]

The well-known Southern writer William Gilmore Simms gave Jews a pivotal role in his uncharacteristic historical novel *Pelayo* (1838). The plot concerns the establishment of the Spanish nation by Pelayo, who is aided by a Jewish army. The wealthy patriarch Melchior lives in the usual opulent apartment, hidden by a modest exterior, and has the standard beautiful motherless daughter who falls in love with the Christian hero. However, unlike the Shylock figure, Melchior would gladly give up all of his great wealth to obtain freedom for his people. He agrees to support Pelayo only when he sees that the hero is free from anti-Jewish prejudice. Melchior is a stereotyped figure, but he is based less upon Sheva than upon Nathan the Wise. He is given to expressions of Enlightenment sentiments such as a belief that it was narrow of the Jewish people to seek Christ's death since "he strove for the rescue of Israel from the tyrannic sway of the Romans. . . . He was a good man, and his deeds and designs were holy; but I cannot think, my child, that he was a god as the Christians regard him."[37]

Otto Rupius's *The Peddler* was written in German in 1859 and later translated into English. Realistic descriptions indicate that the author was familiar with the life of the peddler, but the story itself is pure Sheva. A young, innocent German intellectual, who has just come to America, aids a little Jewish peddler boy whose wares have been scattered by a runaway horse. He encounters the boy's elderly uncle who offers to be of service when the hero is robbed. The hero notices "real sympathy and honest interest through the naturally crafty expression of his eyes. . . ."[38] The peddler obtains a job for the hero and proves the young man's innocence when the villain tries to frame him. In a sequel, *The Peddler's Legacy*, the old Jew makes the hero executor of a large estate and guardian of his nephew, all out of gratitude for picking up a few items from the street!

An interesting variant of the benevolent moneylender brought to America was the Jewish pawnbroker hero, Solomon Isaakski, in J. Richter Jones's historical novel, *The Quaker Soldier*. Based upon the Revolutionary War financier, Haym Solomon, this Solomon is presented as a wealthy Polish Jew drawn to America by his sympathy for the rebelling colonies for whom his

precious money "was lavished unsparingly." His shop is a cover for revolutionary activities although, "possibly with his noble qualities he mingled
some of the hereditary habits of his race." Like other fictional moneylenders,
his private quarters reflect Oriental tastes, including arches, Persian carpets
and an exquisite young wife, "the fairest of Circassians." (Here the contrast
to the real Haym Solomon is particularly vivid.) Solomon explains his
devotion to the cause of Revolution in a broken English that belies his
supposed brilliance: "Every vare ve Hebrews are treated as brute-beasts, not
as mens, ve hab no rights . . . If dis cause succeed, ve vill be mens and citizens
. . . Me vill fight in dis cause till de death." An enthusiastic Puritan chaplain
tells him, "You ought to have lived in the days of your great fore-fathers, you
are worthy of the best of Beni Israel."[39] Perhaps the free air of America could
transform Shylock into Sheva.

The appearance of George Eliot's *Daniel Deronda* had some impact in
adding to the picture of the noble Jew. It was widely and favorably reviewed
in American periodicals. Edwin Whipple's comments in the *North American
Review* in 1877 were representative. Mordecai was an heroic ideal whom
George Eliot "endows with the Hebraic fervor of imagination, while she
emancipates him from the Hebraic narrowness of view. . . ."[40] In spite of its
enthusiastic reception, however, *Daniel Deronda* did not lead to any significant number of American books containing a more multifaceted picture of
the Jew. American novels tended to remain wedded to Sheva, rather than
Deronda.[41]

Caroline Willard did present a most unusual Jewish hero in *A Son of Israel*
(1898). David Rheba is a silversmith who has "warm hazel" eyes and a
"delicate and clear cut" nose. A Christ-like image is clearly suggested in his
appearance and saintliness. "The face was of the highest Christian type with
all its fire and mysticism." The villain is a virulently anti-Semitic Russian
official. The depiction of ordinary poor Russian Jews "crushed down, bru-
talized . . . they haven't one farthing to rub against the other," is another
unusual aspect of this book.[42] Although David departs from the stereotype
considerably, he is Sheva-like in his willingness to do good deeds for those
who have harmed him. It is significant that authors tended to endow "good"
Jewish characters with the Christian ideal of turning the other cheek. Perhaps
this was the only alternative they could see to Shylock's terrifying need for
revenge.

Many of the books written late in the century emulated the original Sheva
story and utilized both the stereotype of timidity and the Shylock image
reversed, to make the Jew a hero. A "little Hebrew" peddler named Saul
Shemuel, for example, is a "greasy spectacle" who always whines. Yet, although always frightened, he is totally unselfish in his devotion to the
patriot-hero of *Cardigan*. When it appears that he has been murdered, the
hero offers a dubious obituary for the "little peddler" who, "for all his squalid

weakness of limb . . . his physical cowardice," had remained in the service of his country. "Nothing save the innate love of liberty in his grotesque and dirty body had lured this errant child of Israel to risk his life. . . ." Despite the fact that he was last seen being brained by British soldiers, he survives in stereotypical fashion: "Under my hat I haff a capful of shillings." To the end, in the midst of spirited combat, when the hero thinks he has "cut away to make up time in trade," Shemuel continues to perform noble deeds for hero and heroine.[43]

The more sophisticated works of Harold Frederic exhibited considerable ambiguity. In an early story, "The Jew's Christmas," Aaron Ashermeyer, an unusual combination of pawnbroker and Talmudic scholar, buys Christmas presents and agrees to adopt an overworked little orphan girl. He explains, "Upon such common holy ground as charity we both stand, you the Christian, I the Jew." Frederic produced an outstanding series of articles for the *New York Times* on the persecution of Russian Jews in 1891, well balanced and sensitive in their understanding of the situation. His 1898 novel, *Gloria Mundi*, was pro-Jewish in an ambivalent way, coupled with uneasy suggestions of Jewish power. The hero's great uncle Julius has married a great Jewish heiress "so noble and clever and wise and strong that I couldn't help becoming a decent fellow in spite of myself." A utopian society, which is the core of this book, is attempted by their son, Emmanuel. He is a magnificent and benevolent person "with one extraordinary limitation . . . a Jewish limitation—for I have seen it pointed out that they do not invent things," but simply expand on the ideas of others. He sets up his perfect paternalistic village which, however, lacks enough originality to survive. "What you see in him is a triumph of the Semitic passion for working a problem out to its ultimate conclusion." The failure of his conservative attempt at utopia is traced to this "Jewish" weakness. Still, Frederic liked Jews of "the right sort" and condemned anti-Semitism in his 1899 novel, *The Market Place*.[44]

In general, however, the benevolent Jewish man, a character as popular in America as the evil usurer, was similar, both in life-style and preoccupation with money, to the villain. The differences were his extravagant and unintelligible benevolence and his tendency to do his good works in America. He was a product of the wishful feeling that the Jew would respond to persecution in a Christ-like way, blessing those who mistreated him, and that the freedom of America could turn Shylock into Sheva. While the character lacked depth, his benignity was certainly a positive characteristic. As Ellen Schiff has remarked, "apparently the Jew had to show he could be nice before he was entitled to substance and versatility."[45]

Jews on the Mind of New England: Judeophile and Anti-Semite

On 31 July 1818 the venerable former president, John Adams, wrote a letter to the Mill Street synagogue in New York on the consecration and dedication of its sanctuary. He declared:

I have had occasion to be acquainted with several gentlemen of your nation
. . . whom I found to be men of as liberal minds, as much honor, probity,
generosity and good breeding as I have known in any sect . . . I wish your
nation may be admitted to all the privileges of citizens in every country of
the world. This country has done much, I wish it may do more . . . It has
pleased the Providence of the first cause . . . that Abraham should give
religion, not only to the Hebrews, but to . . . the greatest part of the
modern civilized world. . . .[46]

This attitude was typical of a large segment of educated New Englanders.
Probably no portion of the English-speaking world felt as distinctive a
closeness to Jews and the Old Testament tradition as the New Englanders,
the founders of a "New Israel."

Edmund Wilson has pointed out that many Puritans regarded their faith as
a kind of Judaism "transposed into Anglo-Saxon terms." Through the nineteenth century their conviction persisted that Jews were a special people,
chosen by God for a unique role. They felt that they too were a chosen
people. Thus, Harriet Beecher Stowe described one character as a "Hebrew
of Hebrews," and declared that New England bred "better Jews than Moses
could." In *Old Town Folks,* she characterized the devotion of her grandfather
to the Hebrew tradition: "No New Englander could really estimate how
much of himself had actually been formed by the constant face-to face
intimacy with Hebrew literature . . . (He) spoke of Zion and Jerusalem, of
the God of Israel, the God of Jacob, as much as if my grandfather had been a
veritable Jew."[47] Her husband, Calvin Stowe, was a bearded, long-haired
scholar of Hebrew and Talmud who even wore a skull cap. (This, however,
did not prevent her from including a Jewish slave trader in *Uncle Tom's
Cabin.*)

Wilson feels that the Protestant of the Puritan tradition finds in Judaism,
"the spiritual austerity he already knows, but not bedeviled . . . by the fear of
a despotic deity who seems to favor or condemn by whim." Many of these
New Englanders tended to glorify the Jewish past. Ralph Waldo Emerson,
for example, said, "The Hebrew nation compensated for the insignificance of
its members and territory by its religious genius, its tenacious belief; its
poems and histories cling to the soil of this globe like the primitive
rocks. . . ."[48] As philo-Semites, they revived forgotten legends of ancient
Judaism, but they showed little interest in the realities of contemporary
American Jewish life.

Henry Wadsworth Longfellow was typical in this respect. Several of his
works have Jewish themes. *Sandolphin* was based on a Talmudic story about
the Angel of Prayer. *Judas Maccabeus* was a five-act tragedy about that
towering figure. In *Tales of a Wayside Inn,* several of the tales are narrated by a
Spanish Jew. Longfellow, stressing the mysterious aura of the Jew, transformed a staid Boston merchant of his acquaintance into a Spanish vender of
rare silk to suit the romantic purposes of his poem:

> Like an old Patriarch he appeared . . .
> With lustrous eyes and olive skin,
> And wildly tossed from cheeks and chin
> The tumbling cataract of his beard.

In his famous poem "The Jewish Cemetery at Newport" (1852), Longfellow considered the centuries of persecution the Jews had suffered:

> They lived in narrow streets and lanes obscure
> Ghetto and Judenstrass in mirk and mire;
> Taught in the school of patience to endure
> The life of anguish and the death of fire.
>
> Pride and humiliation hand in hand
> walked with them through the world where 'ere they went;
> Trampled and beaten were they as the sand
> And yet unshaken as the continent.

In the free atmosphere of America, however, Longfellow believed that the uniqueness of the Jew would disappear. Their fading saddened him, but he felt that their fate was sealed—they would inevitably dissolve into the enveloping American society:

> But ah! what once has been shall be no more!
> The groaning earth in travail and in pain
> Brings forth its races, but does not restore,
> And the dead nations never rise again.[49]

Whittier also used biblical and Talmudic themes in several of his poems, such as "The Two Rabbins" and "Rabbi Ishmael." In the latter he utilized an interesting passage in the Talmud based upon the uniquely Hebraic concept of man blessing God. As a Christian, he was unable to accept, or perhaps even comprehend, this idea, so he altered the whole point of the story.[50]

Sometimes the New England stress on the mysterious Jew could lead to a genteel anti-Semitism. Oliver Wendell Holmes described the struggle within himself to combat latent feelings of bigotry. He ascribed the problem to the Puritans' exclusivity, which led them to emphasize the curse upon the Jews for refusing the Gospel. "The old Calvinist spirit was almost savagely exclusive." In *Over the Teacups* Holmes commented that on occasion the Jews one met "in our ill-favored and ill-flavored streets were apt to be unpleasant specimens of the race." However, the Jews had begun to achieve remarkably and "forced the world to recognize and accept them." Christians "have insulted, calumniated, oppressed, abased and outraged" them and continued to do so because of the Jewish refusal to accept Jesus. Holmes reported that years before, he had come to terms with those underlying feelings and had emerged with a truly brotherly feeling. In later books he directed withering fire at anti-Jewish legends.[51]

Some authors worried that the world was in danger of imminent Jewish takeover. James Russell Lowell exhibited the most extreme example of this mania.[52] He admired the "universal ability of the Hebrew," but that ability appeared so formidable to him that Jews became a menace toward whom he directed morbid suspicions. The dichotomy in his attitude was revealed early in an 1847 review of Disraeli's *Tancred* in which he noted "that the descendants of those who . . . would kneel before the golden calf, should be the money changers of Europe has in it something of syllogistic completeness." Yet the article went on to defend the Jews against absurd prejudices. Humans seemed to require someone to keep down. In America it was the Africans. "In Europe the Jews have long monopolized the responsible privilege of supplying an object for this particular craving of the supreme Caucasian nature." Disraeli believed that the Jewish mind still governed the world. Lowell agreed, but in a more negative sense: "Instead of absolute truth, it accepts corrupt Hebrew gloss. . . . The Gospels are still too often read backward, after the Hebrew fashion."

As he aged, Lowell's obsession with the Jews increased. He wrote to Henry James, "All roads lead to Jerusalem at last." In 1878 he remarked of Gambetta that the strength of his Jewish ancestors has been, "that they could always supply you with an accommodation at heavy interest. Where would a Jew be among a primitive society without pockets. . . ." Yet, in the same year, he remarked about Disraeli, "I think a good deal of the prejudice against Beaconsfield is medieval!" In his well known 1884 essay, "Democracy," he defended the Jews in somewhat ambivalent fashion. Emancipation had been denied to them for centuries even though Jews were "a race in which ability seems as natural and hereditary as the curve of their noses, and whose blood, furtively mingling with the bluest bloods of Europe, had quickened them. . . ." They were driven, but they had their revenge, as the mistreated often do. "They made their corner the counter and banking-house of the world, and thence they rule it with the ignoble scepter of finance."

Lowell was fond of asserting that the genius of the Lowells came from remote Jewish ancestors. In 1892 Leslie Stephen commented on "his astonishing faculty for the detection of Jews . . . his ingenuity in discovering that everyone was in some way descended from the Jews. . . ." Stephen concluded, "this was the only subject upon which I could conceive Lowell approaching within measurable distance of boring." A reporter in the *Atlantic Monthly* commented that the subject of Jews was "almost a monomania" with Lowell, who believed that they had penetrated "the human family more universally than any other influence except original sin." This was not entirely a bad thing since they had "talent and versatility." When the writer asked Lowell what the Jews would do when they had control of finance, the military, the press the government, "and the earth's surface," Lowell responded, "That is the question which will eventually drive me mad."

Other genteel anti-Semites were far less ambivalent. Henry Cabot Lodge was willing to grant the economic capacity of Jews but believed that they lacked "the nobler abilities which enable a people to rule and administer and to display that social efficiency in war, peace and government without which all else is vain."[53] Professor C. H. Toy of Harvard commented that Jews had personal and social habits that had grown unpleasant as the result of centuries of isolation. "Most Jews are socially untrained and their bodily habits are not good."[54]

Henry Adams and his brother Brooks were the best known of the upper-class anti-Semites. Henry was obsessed by the Jewish menace. It became an integral part of his personality and was related to his difficulty in adjusting to modern society, his sense of alienation from an industrial capitalist America. The Jew, for him, symbolized the "economic man" who had succeeded despite all the obstacles in his path, while Adams, despite all his advantages, had failed. The Jew was bringing about the social and economic changes that endangered the privileged orders. "With a communism I could exist . . . but in a society of Jews and brokers, a world made up of maniacs wild for gold, I have no place." The Jew controlled politics, finance, and even journalism. Adams's anti-Semitism was a part of his dismay at the disintegration of his world. In *The Education of Henry Adams* he ruefully commented about himself: "His world was dead. Not a Polish Jew fresh from Warsaw or Cracow—a furtive Yacoob or Ysaac still reeking of the ghetto, snarling a weird Yiddish to the officers of the customs—but had a keener instinct, an intenser energy and a freer hand than he—American of Americans."[55] Such feelings were not frequently expressed in his published works, however. In fact, in *Democracy,* the Schneidekoupons who are "descended from all the Kings of Israel," though given an unkind name, are close friends of the heroine and are not particularly unpleasant. In his private letters to friends, though, he felt free to give open expression to his loathing for the Jew who "makes me creep." His more tolerant friend John Hay joked that when Adams "saw Vesuvius reddening . . . [he] searched for a Jew stoking the fire." Hays remarked, "I was amazed to see so sensible a man so wild."[56]

One of the most interesting examples of the love-hate relationship many New Englanders felt for Jews was that of John Jay Chapman. Few people expressed a more passionate regard for Jews. "There is a depth of human feeling in the Jew that no other race ever possessed. . . . What monstrous perversion that we should worship their god and despise themselves!" He felt that the history of the Jews was the most remarkable of all the peoples in the world "and I feel this same power in the Jews I know. They are the most humane and the strongest people morally, mentally and physically. . . ." Despite such expressed sentiments, Chapman gradually shifted from friendship to fear of a Jewish conspiracy. This change in attitude was precipitated by encountering a large, loud group of German Jews vacationing in Atlantic City. It evidently was a traumatic experience for him to discover Jews who did not measure up to their biblical ancestors. Edmund Wilson feels that perhaps the Jews succeeded too well in convincing the descendants of New England Puritans of their privileged relation to God. New England visionaries assumed that there was something supernatural about the Jewish people. It would upset them to discover that Jews were merely human beings. For the apocalyptic mind this simple explanation for the faults of real Jews would be difficult to accept.[57] For some this would lead to the anti-Semitism of a disappointed lover.

As the poverty-stricken Jews of Eastern Europe came in ever increasing masses, New England gentility was offended. There were some like Charles Eliot Norton, Edward Everett Hale, and Thomas Higginson who were more sympathetic and opposed the immigration restriction movement, which was directed, to a large extent, against Eastern Jews. Alice James, sister of Henry and William, was disgusted by the attitudes of her friends who favored restriction: "What a spectacle! . . . the Anglo-Saxon races addressing remonstrances to the Czar against expelling Jews from Russia, at the very moment when their governments are making laws to forbid their immigration." Her brother William agreed and expressed the hope that "the Anglo-Saxon race would drop its sniveling cant."[58]

The attitude of their brother, the great novelist Henry James, was more typical of the distaste felt by aristocratic New Englanders for the new Jewish immigrants. Even upper-class Jews were treated with condescension. In an 1896 story, "Glasses," Jews were described vacationing at a fashionable resort: "There were thousands of little chairs and almost as many little Jews; and there was music in open rotunda, over which Jews wagged their big noses." Around the turn of the century, James was taken for a tour of the Jewish section of New York, which he described in *The American Scene*. James praised the intellectual vigor of the Jewish people and their ability to survive "without loss of race quality." Nevertheless, one can detect more than a faint trace of queasiness in the description of the crowded streets of New York: "There is no swarming like that of Israel . . . here was multiplication with a vengeance. . . ." There was certainly a sense of fear in the discussion of "the extent of the Hebrew conquest" of New York and of the "New Jerusalem."[59]

New Englanders conceived of themselves as having a unique relationship with the Jewish people. But the Jews they imagined were Old Testament figures. They knew almost nothing of real Jews in America. It disturbed them deeply that these should be merely ordinary people. Sometimes this gap between expectations and reality led them into anti-Semitism. At times the Jew appeared, not as an Old Testament prophet, but as a representative of the forces of decay in the deferential society they loved and expected. This led to the change from the "honor, probity, generosity and good breeding," in the description of the Jews by John Adams to the "rotten unsexed, swindling, lying Jews" of his great-grandson, Brooks. If the German-Jewish businessman disturbed them, the Eastern Jewish worker living in overcrowded slums would evoke fastidious distaste. Few were able to sense the excitement and intellectual vigor that impressed Hutchins Hapgood in his 1902 classic, *The Spirit of the Ghetto*. Few would understand the ferment in Yiddish poetry, journalism, and theater, or care in any way.

Sympathetic Observers: Melville, Sidney Luska, Cahan, and Others

Herman Melville was the only major American writer in the nineteenth century to include a serious consideration of Jews and Judaism in one of his works. For the most part his descriptions and discussions were singularly unprejudiced and unstereotyped, although not particularly knowledgeable about contemporary American Jewish life. In 1857 Melville went on a pilgrimage to Palestine. He used many of the sights he saw and the people he met in *Clarel*, written years later.[60]

Clarel is a difficult book, in verse, about the search of a young divinity student for truth in the Holy Land.[61] While there, he falls in love with Ruth, an American Jewess. Her father is an early-day Zionist who has settled in Palestine and is eventually killed by hostile Arab raiders. Ruth dies of fever and grief, depriving Clarel of the fulfilment he had hoped to find with her. He must seek it within himself, with only her memory to comfort him.

Ruth, the heroine, is a conventional beautiful Jewess, more suggestive of Mary's virginal saintliness than of the usual sexual allure. The other Jewish characters, however, are far less conventional. Ruth's father, Nathan, is an American Zionist who is a study of American doubt and the struggle to believe. He converted to Judaism out of love for his wife Agar, but turned to passionate Zionism. Nathan holds to his dream fanatically despite attacks by the Arabs, the death of one of his children, and the pleas of his wife to return to America.

Ruth's mother, Agar, is a representative of the good domestic woman, subordinate to her husband's wishes. She is an ideal Victorian woman and Jewish mother. She remains loyal and, when her husband is killed, she too dies from grief. She is a unique character in nineteenth-century American fiction—a Jewish mother (old men and their beautiful daughter had been the norm) who stands for what Melville considered to be the maternal and wifely virtues.

There are also several minor Jewish characters who add to the richness of the book. Abdon, the host at the inn in Jerusalem, is a "Black Jew" from Cochin where "his kin, never from true allegiance torn, kept Moses' law." He represents experience through age and the virtues of ancient orthodoxy. Abdon is the only old Jew in the book, and he is most certainly not a villain or comic miser, or even a Sheva stereotype. Clarel also shares a room for a night with a gay young French Jewish salesman who has come to Bethlehem to have fun with the pretty girls. He represents extravagance, carefree youth, and a light-hearted, strangely innocent sensuality that is a temptation to Clarel in both homosexual and heterosexual aspects. The only unpleasant Jewish character is criticized, not because he is a Jew, but as an apostate, cynic, and unbeliever.

Melville was particularly effective in describing Jewish customs, ritual, and quality of life. These are not presented as exotic or romantic. Thus, the unextinguished lamp burns, for it may not be quenched on Saturday, "the unaltered Sabbath of the Jew." Agar's family had kept its Jewish heritage as "a treasured store/Like plate inherited . . . ," which graced "That family feeling of the Jew" which "Makes home a temple—sheds delight. . . ." What a contrast this presents to pictures of miserly money-lenders living in secret Oriental splendor! In spite of all the changes in the world, Rolfe (who represents Melville himself) strongly believes:

> Nor less the Jew keep fealty
> To ancient rites, Aaron's gemmed vest
> Will long outlive Genevan cloth—
> Nothing in time's old camphor chest
> So little subject to the moth.

In many ways *Clarel* was remarkable for its time. Judaism, Jewish customs, and characters were intertwined with Clarel's search for faith. The characters were generally not Jewish stereotypes. Despite an apparent absence of Jewish friends or real interest in Jews as they then lived in America, there is a tolerance and understanding that goes beyond any other American book of this period. It was a reflection, perhaps, of a great and wide ranging mind, but it was scarcely typical and did not lead to any upsurge of interest in American Jewish life.

In some ways it is fair to say that "Sidney Luska" created the Jewish American novel and novelist. He was hailed by spokesmen of Jewish culture and by William Dean Howells as an authentic interpreter of Jewish life in America. But, in fact, Sidney Luska was really Henry Harland, a discontented, "alienated" Protestant. As Leslie Fiedler remarks, "There is a certain irony in the fact that the first Jewish American novelist was not a Jew at all, or that, more precisely, he was the creation of his own fiction, an imaginary Jew."[62] In New York Harland had become acquainted with Felix Adler, the founder of the Ethical Culture Society. He entered German Jewish society and saturated himself with everything Jewish. His books featured Jewish themes, and included carefully documented Jewish customs and rituals.

Harland's biographer quotes Van Wyck Brooks, "In this exile world of old country merchants, artisans, teachers, rabbis and beggars, whatever one had known at home was turned upside down . . . The contrasts, the mysteries and surprises one encountered . . . might have furnished Henry Harland with a thousand tales."[63] At the height of his fame, Sidney Luska shaved his beard, became Henry Harland again, and fled America. He ended his life as a Catholic in France, denying he had ever heard of Sidney Luska.

As It Was Written (1885) was his first novel. It was a success, selling 50,000 copies. Ernest Neumann, a Jewish musician, is engaged to Veronika, a typical fictional Jewess, who is murdered. He is first accused, then acquitted of the crime. He drifts around in sorrow for years until he meets a kindly gentile who congratulates him on being a Jew: "I should be proud of my lineage if I were a Jew . . . I believe the whole future of America depends upon the Jews." This was always the heart of Harland's message. The Jewish element had to be amalgamated to leaven the whole and color the mixture in America. It would add "a dose of rich strong wine. It will give fire and flavor." The Jewish element would cause America to produce great music, art, and poetry.[64] There was an underlying threat in all this extravagant praise. What if the Jew refused this necessary assimilation? From the beginning, a current of hostility lurked beneath the extreme Judeophile surface of Harland's works. Ernest Neumann, the supposed "new man" praised by his gentile friend, turns out to be capable only of destruction. He discovers that he actually did kill Veronika while possessed by the vengeful spirit of his father who hated her as the descendent of an enemy. (The lust for revenge was considered a particularly Jewish failing.) The *New York Times* reviewer, unlike most observers, realized immediately that the author was not a Jew. "It is an eminently Christian whim . . . to attribute to the Jews various magnificent characteristics over which the latter smile."[65]

Mrs. Peixada (1886) tackled the theme of intermarriage more directly. Arthur Ripley, a young Christian lawyer, takes a case to locate Mrs. Peixada who has been acquitted of murdering her husband. She is a stereotypical beautiful Jewess with those ever-present "deep" eyes. He informs her that Jews are "the kindest-hearted and clearest-minded people one meets," but he is glad that "there is a tendency among the better educated Jews to cut loose from their Judaism. I want to see them intermarried with Christians . . . and help to form the American people of the future. That of course is their destiny." Mrs. Peixada would prefer "to retain the name of Jew until it has grown to be a term of honor," but she agrees that destiny lies in the direction of amalgamation. After he marries her, Ripley discovers that she had killed her husband in self-defense. She had been "bought" to satisfy her father's debt by a pawnbroker who was the personification of every evil ever attributed by Christian writers to Jews. He had "a hawk's beak for a nose . . . yellow fangs . . . fit features of a bird of prey. . . ."[66] This monstrous person was, implausibly, a leading figure in synagogue and community. He was also responsible for a Fagin-like organization of criminals. Thus, the author, who claimed to write about "real" Jews, included the most devastating stereotype in his work. The novel does provide a fleeting glance at the hearty German-Jewish bourgeoisie. Strangely, Mrs. Peixada's new husband turns out to be a weakling who faints in the midst of her tribulation with the law. The book ends with her nursing him back to health, in an unconsciously ironic comment on this "ideal" intermarriage.

Harland's best and most famous book was *The Yoke of the Thorah* (1887). In it he gave the fullest expression to his views on intermarriage. A young Jewish artist, Elias, falls in love with a golden-haired Christian beauty. His upbringing by his uncle, an Orthodox rabbi, made him "intensely a Jew." Racial antipathy toward gentiles had been "reinforced by the terrors of a supernatural religion." His uncle assures him that God will prevent the match, and, when he suffers an epileptic seizure at the wedding ceremony, he believes it is a sign to leave her. The uncle says the girl "is a Christian . . . despised and abominated of the Lord . . . Now she must bear her punishment."[67] Elias marries the pretty but crude daughter of German-Jewish merchants. Although she is kind and good, he cannot love her. Having rejected that union with the gentile world which would have been his redemption, Elias dies hoping to catch a glimpse of his former love. The novel stirred great bitterness among many New York Jews. They felt that their former champion, a man who had lived among them and written for their papers, had attacked their deepest beliefs. Harland was astonished at their reaction. He was obviously unaware of the latent anti-Semitism under the surface of his philo-Semitic stories. He reiterated his basic viewpoint: "If Jews care to see an end to the prejudice . . . they have it in their power to do so. Let them cease to be exclusive; let them associate freely with their gentile neighbors. . . ."[68]

There was a real value in *The Yoke of the Thorah,* however. It included German Jewish merchant families who were not projections of Anglo-Saxon hatred or guilt feelings, but were real people. They talk too loud and "their grammar isn't of the choicest." They love good food and matchmaking. They are coarse and vulgar, sentimental and platitudinous, but they are also "thoroughly good and wholesome . . . the core is sound and sweet." They are not artists, writers or musicians whose amalgamation will save America, but they are human. Their presence is so lively and vigorous that Elias, who represents the author's hopes for the future, almost completely disappears in their presence. This was probably the only genuine genre study of German-Jewish life in nineteenth-century America. Interestingly, the Jewish press objected to the portrayal of uncouth Jewish merchants almost as strenuously as it did to the picture of the bigoted rabbi.

The Yoke of the Thorah was widely, and generally favorably, reviewed.[69] The

New York Times critic remarked that the author has a "predilection for Jewish subjects," but found this book far superior to his earlier ones. Luska was "very good natured to the Jews. If he does smile at them, he does it in a kindly way." The *Tribune* was more enthusiastic. Luska was "a gifted young writer" who analyzed the emotions of "race and religion" and "the fierce prohibition of that unwritten code of law called the Thorah with which Orthodox Judaism has supplanted the Law of Moses [!]" Intermarriage is particularly threatened "with terrific curses. . . . It is contamination of the race for whose preservation in purity God created and maintained the world." There was delightful humor in the study of middle-class Jews who experience the "pains of learning grammar and other refinements of an artificial society." With kindly eyes, "Luska" did "full justice to their domestic virtues, their generosity, their charity, and their open hearts." Unlike the Jewish critics, this reviewer felt that the bondage to the "Thorah" was treated as "an exceptional survival of obsolete beliefs. For the Jews as a body he evidently has a liking. . . ."

Harland wrote one more complete book about German Jews, without any editorials in support of his assimilationist views. It was *Uncle Florimond* (1888), a boy's tale. A young French orphan runaway meets a kindly Jewish "trummer . . . a voolen salesman" and his father-in-law, "one of the pleasantest looking old gentlemen I had ever seen in my life."[70] This delightful version of the benevolent Jew stereotype gives the boy a job and sends him to City College. When the idolized Uncle Florimond comes to visit from France, he turns out to be threadbare and poverty-stricken and also moves in with the old Jew. The boy marries a nice Jewish girl and everyone lives happily ever after. This was an obvious effort to placate the Jewish community. The *American Hebrew* was pleased. Both Jewish characters, it felt, were "large-hearted and generous to a fault." However, "the dialect of the younger man is hardly as permissible as in the case of the elder."[71]

In May 1888, *Lippincott's Monthly Magazine* published Harland's "Mr. Sonnenschein's Inheritance," one of the first American genre stories about poor Jews. The hero is a poor German Jew, but the story included some ominous stereotypes of the newest "Polish" Jews. Mr. Sonnenschein is an old, white-haired, bent man who "ain't naifer mait no money . . . I was a rekular schlemiel." He lives in a tenement with his crippled daughter whose hideous needle work he peddles. When a rich brother in Germany dies and leaves him "terventy-nine tousand, seven hoonert tollars," he puts the money in his friend Levinson's "burglar proof safe" in a second-hand store. The store burns and the money is supposedly destroyed. The gentile hero asks the fire marshal if there was anything suspicious about the fire. The marshal replies, "Whenever a fire occurs in a premise occupied by a gentleman of Mr. Levinson's race, class and profession, I may say it is suspicious. These low-class Polish Jews think no more of setting a fire than they do of lying." The "unspeakable" Levinson is uncovered and goes to jail. The money is recovered and the hero's father invests it for Mr. Sonnenschein, providing him with a nice annual income. Sonnenschein takes care of Levinson's wife and children. "Though a Jew by birth and faith, he is as good a Christian as most of the professing ones."[72] Both the Sheva and Shylock stereotype appear in this story. The unusual aspect was that Sheva was poor and an incompetent business man. Few other fiction authors recognized the existence of such Jews.

Grandison Mather (1889) was Harland's last book to include German Jews. The hero, Thomas Gardner, is a writer who clearly represents Harland himself. When he and his wife lose their money, they find inexpensive lodgings with a German Jewish family, the Grickels. Tom comments, "it doesn't correspond very well with the popular idea of the Jewish character, the way she lowered her price to suit our manes." His wife replies, "very likely the popular ideas of Jews are absurd." The father, Raphael Grickel, is obviously based upon Felix Adler, the man through whom Harland had become interested in the German Jewish community. He believes in the teachings of Christ as "the greatest of prophets," and has founded the "Society for Humane Culture," obviously the Ethical Culture Society. "The Christians despise him as worse than a Jew, and the Jews rate him as an apostate," but Tom and his wife become followers. The book even included a passing reference to Harland's favorite theme of intermarriage.[73]

This was the last reference to New York's German-Jewish community in Harland's works. He left for England and continued writing under his real name. Later he moved to France where he gained some fame as a distinguished Catholic author with a best-seller, *The Cardinal's Hat*. He became friendly with the European aristocracy. His later books contained passing unflattering comments about Jews in the manner of the upper classes. He never acknowledged his former identity as "Sidney Luska."

If Harland presented the only realistic picture of German Jews in America, Edward King's *Joseph Zalmonah* (1894) included the sole attempt by a non-Jew to describe the real life of the Eastern European Jewish immigrant. King was an American-born journalist and novelist. The book was based upon the life of the labor leader Joseph Barondess. It is a melodramatic tale of the hero's struggle to improve garment-industry working conditions and avoid socialist extremism. Joseph is forced to fight a trumped up criminal charge (as was the real Joseph Barondess) and to resist the wiles of an anarchist femme fatale. The story is unconvincing and poorly constructed, but it does present a realistic portrayal of the daily existence of Russian Jews in New York. Their customs are accurately described and the problems they faced in America are sympathetically presented. One of the characters, for example, is a good natured peddler whose life consists of "seventeen hours of unremitting daily toil." Joseph is distressed that his newly arrived wife "must be told that the misery into which they had fallen in New York was almost as deep as that they had left behind them."[74] Despite its weaknesses, heroes and villains in this book are all Jews, and none is a conventional stereotype.

These few books exhaust the realistic portrayal of Jews by non-Jews in the nineteenth century. There was a need for Jewish writers to identify and employ materials from the lives of real American Jews. We are so accustomed to a literature in which American Jewish writers play a major role, that it is astonishing to discover the paucity of nineteenth-century American Jewish writers who were willing to write about Jewish experiences. These earlier Jewish immigrants achieved their successes largely in commerce and small business, and produced little in the way of literary activity. With the exception of Emma Lazarus, their few works were almost never read by non-Jews and, therefore, had no impact on the image of the Jew in America. The advent of the Eastern European Jew provided the intellectual ferment to produce a flourishing Yiddish literature and, in the twentieth century, American Jewish literature in English as well.

Abraham Cahan, who had immense significance as a journalist within the Jewish community, became the foremost interpreter of the Russian Jew to the gentile world. He wrote many articles about Eastern European Jews for American periodicals and was the real originator of American Jewish fiction. His first novel, *Yekl* (1896), was the first significant American Jewish novel, a small realistic gem. (Many years later it was made into a movie, *Hester Street.*) The hero, Jake, is a cloak maker who left his wife and child in Russia three years earlier. Now, "the thought of ever having been a Yekl would bring to Jake's lips a smile of patronizing commiseration for his former self." The book is filled with marvelous descriptions of the ghetto, "a seething human sea fed by streams, streamlets and rills of immigration." Here one could find "specimens of all the whimsical metamorphoses wrought upon the children of Israel of the great modern exodus." When Jake's wife, Gitl, arrives in New York, his heart sinks at this "wigged, dowdyish little greenhorn" whom he begins to regard as an obstacle. He turns to Mamie, his Americanized dancing partner. Finally, Gitl agrees to a divorce in view of Jake's growing hatred. After a few months Gitl herself develops that "peculiar air of self-confidence with which a few months of life in America is sure to stamp the looks and bearing of every immigrant." Although Jake appears to be victorious, his wife is able to find another man who appreciates good cooking and Jake is entrapped again in a marriage to Mamie.[75] Despite its slightness and unwillingness to tackle the real misery of the ghetto, this book did evoke its flavor. It showed the impact of America on the life of the ordinary immigrant Jew. *Yekl* defied the tradition that had arisen of the romantic tenement tale. It did not show the nobility of poverty. In fact there was a clear indication that poverty had a negative effect on character. In his later stories Cahan dropped the caricaturized dialect that marred *Yekl* but continued to pursue its underlying theme of the gains and losses of Americaniza-tion.

Yekl was not successful financially, but it did launch Cahan on the Amer-ican literary scene. A review by Nancy Banks in the *Bookman* remarked that the book had been "unreservedly praised" by many outstanding critics. She wondered if Cahan really wanted the reader to believe that "the types represented in this book are truly representative of his race? That it is as sordid, as selfish, as mean, as cruel, as degraded as he has shown it to be?" She missed the kind of sympathetic portrayal one would find in the works of Zangwell, "that dignity of faith which compels respect from Christians; that helpfulness of each other which shames the selfishness of Gentiles." Instead, she complained, this was a frank revelation of "racial weaknesses." William Dean Howells, however, was far more favorable in the 26 July 1896 Sunday edition of the *New York World*. The headline proclaimed, "The Great Novelist Hails Abraham Cahan, the Author of 'Yekl' as a New Star of Realism. . . ." The glowing review was reproduced on posters throughout the city. Howells declared that Cahan's "sense of character is as broad as his sense of humor is subtle and deep." He added, "He sees things with American eyes, and he brings in aid of his vision the far and rich perceptions of his Hebraic race."[76] This made Cahan a celebrity. Articles about him began to appear in the nation's press, including a long biographical piece in the *Boston Sunday Press* in September 1896.

Possibly as the result of this publicity, Cahan had several stories published in prestigious magazines. "A Ghetto Wedding," in the February 1898 issue of *Atlantic Monthly*, dramatized the meaning of poverty in the ghetto. This was an O'Henry-like tale in which the hero and heroine, a peddler and a knee-breech worker, decide to spend all of their meager and dwindling savings on a grand wedding, to get fine presents for their apartment. However, "the Ghetto was groaning under a long season of enforced idleness and distress." Only 20 of the 150 invited guests show up. Most were kept away "by lack of employment; some having their presentable clothes in the pawnshop; others avoiding the expense of a wedding present. . . ." The couple ends up with no money, no furniture, and no guests. Dressed in their wedding outfits, they return to their empty rooms. As they pass a saloon, hooligans throw vegeta-bles and yell, "look at dem . . . A sheeny feller and his bride." But they proceed hand in hand through the "somber impoverished street . . . a stream of happiness uniting them . . . a blissful sense of oneness."[77]

This story appeared with several other tales by Cahan in an 1898 book, *The Imported Bridegroom and Other Stories of the New York Ghetto*. These included "A Providential Match" and "A Sweatshop Romance," both of which had been published in *Short Stories* in 1895, and "Circumstance," featured in *Cosmopolitan* in 1897. The latter was a vivid exposition of the difficulties faced by the immigrant intellectual, in this case a young lawyer, who is forced to eke out a skimpy living in a button factory when he comes to America. "The Imported Bridegroom," the longest story in the book, concerns a wealthy immigrant who returns to his old shtetl to "buy" its leading young Talmud scholar as a husband for his Americanized daughter, Flora. She rejects her father's choice, insisting that she must marry a doctor. The young man, Shaya, comes to live in their household and is rapidly seduced by secular learning. He agrees to become a doctor and marry Flora, much to the joy of father and daughter. The father's pleasure turns to sorrow when he discovers that his son-in-law has become a total nonbeliever. The final irony comes when Flora realizes that she is shut out from her husband's intellectual life with its incomprehensible discussion groups in Comtian philosophy.[78] The discontents of Americanization came to life vividly in these stories.

Cahan continued to publish short stories in a variety of magazines, presenting a truthful and occasionally harsh picture of immigrant Jews. *The Century* (1899) featured "The Apostate of Chego-Chegg," about a convert, "yearning for her father's house and her Jewish past." "The Jew who deserts his faith for that of his oppressors," Cahan noted, was met with a "loathing which the Gentile brain could not conceive." With his usual honesty, which annoyed many Jews, Cahan described how she is chased and pelted in the Jewish settlement, yet her pursuers and "the whole Jewish town" are "dearer to her heart than ever." Although she is a "living stigma," she tries to keep kosher and light the sabbath candles. She is miserable: "The God of Israel is not in the habit of refunding one's money . . . Once a Jew, forever a Jew." The town finally raises money for her to leave her husband and return to Judaism, but, at the last moment, she decides to stay with him and suffer.[79] The December 1899 issue of *Scribner's* included "Rabbi Eliazer's Christmas," a bittersweet tale of a lonely old craftsman in fine lettering, an anachronism in industrial America. The description of the kindly social worker, who comes upon the old man in her search for needy cases, was particularly biting. When she speaks with him, she is "tingling with compassion and with something like the sensation of an entomologist come upon a rare insect."[80]

Cahan's stories were often attacked by the Jewish press, edited by "uptown" Jews who objected to the portrayal of Jews of the "lower depths," a "vile class." Nevertheless, he was the first American Jewish author to be widely read by non-Jews. His stories boldly challenged many basic assumptions about Jews and Americanization. His works, culminating in his great 1917 novel, *The Rise of David Levinsky,* ushered in a new era in which Jews launched literary explorations of their own experiences. Through Abraham Cahan, "the Yiddish *knaytch* (style, tone, twist) enters American literature."[81] In the early twentieth century there was a whole series of immigrant novels and short stories by Jewish authors, some of which were realistic in tone. Their theme, like Cahan's, was the "inner conflict between the old world ties and new world enticements," setting the groundwork for much of the twentieth-century American Jewish fiction.[82] The search for American Jewish identity, which has played so important a role in American fiction, had begun.

The Jew in nineteenth-century American fiction was generally an exaggerated figure, usually larger than life. Whether villain or hero, he was most often in a mysterious and romantic mist, inconceivably evil or unbearably noble, but almost always an exotic. American authors appeared to have real difficulties in their attempts to come to terms with the real Jews in America. Jonathan Sarna has noted this puzzling dissonance between the "mythical Jew" and the "Jew next door."[83] In American literature ancient stereotypes vied with Enlightenment attitudes of tolerance.

In the earlier years of the century few Americans had any contact with real Jews. There was a tendency to believe that, while Jews might be villainous in exotic settings in Europe and North Africa, they would turn out fine in the free air of America. The image of the knife-wielding usurer, the rejecting father, was deep in the Christian unconscious, and he appeared in American works with some regularity. However, it is important to remember that he rarely appeared in books taking place in the United States. He did his dirty work in England and Algiers, but almost never in New York. The beautiful Jewess turned up in both exotic settings and, possibly as a result of wishful thinking, right here in America. The benevolent Jew, on the other hand, often carried out his good works in the United States. Frequently, as in Ruppius's *The Peddler* and Jones's version of Haym Solomon's heroics, it was stressed that the good deeds took place as the result of gratitude for the unusual freedom of the New World. If the Jew did possess unpleasant characteristics, America's environment might successfully alter them.

As German Jews entered the country in increasing numbers, the picture of the Jew as moneylender remained in the new guise of pawnbroker. This was supplemented by the old-clothes dealer and peddler. Generally, one would have looked in vain for a respectable merchant, lawyer, doctor, or artisan. (The works of Henry Harland are the major exception.) The Shylock image remained in the face of changes in Jewish life in America. The picture, however, was considerably less pervasive and central in American fiction than in European. There is also little question that the image had less bitterness to it than the European version. This may well have been due to the greater assimilation of Jews in America and to freer interactions.

The tremendous increase in Jewish immigration from Eastern Europe at the end of the century had only a minimal impact upon fiction. Although literature is often presumed to reflect reality, novels tended to ignore the newcomers and employ accepted stereotypes. Fagin was present in a "realistic" novel by Frank Norris, just as readily as he had earlier found a place in the romantic sensationalism of George Lippard. The presence of these very "different," bearded, Orthodox, strangely garbed individuals, packed together in dirty tenements, did help to stoke the fires of anti-Semitism among some presumably respectable people, however.

Nineteenth-century American literature did begin to come to grips with the problem of what would ultimately happen to the Jews in a free society. Through centuries of persecution, many Marranos had maintained their Judaism in secret. Within a few generations after emigration to America, they had all but disappeared through intermarriage. Would the lack of institutionalized anti-Semitism mean that the Jews, no longer required to stay together for self-protection, would assimilate and disappear? Longfellow believed, with some sadness, that the Jews would vanish. Harland preached that the Jews should fade away in the ethnic amalgam of America, adding a valuable element to American society. On the other hand, Cahan tried to find a true Jewish-American identity which would enable Jews to survive the perils of freedom. As we have seen, Melville also believed that Jewish survival was inevitable.

Nineteenth-century American literature contained the seeds of many of the issues considered by twentieth-century works. One could find the anti-Semitic image of the Jew with his overwhelming concern for wealth. The good and worthy, if often incomprehensible, Jewish citizen was also present. Serious concern about assimilation and survival was expressed by several authors. Only the beautiful Jewess seems to have disappeared into the mists of time, too exotic a figure to survive realism. The attitudes of Americans, as revealed by literature, were ambivalent in the nineteenth century—and they continued to be so in the twentieth.

3

Popular Images

THE JEW WAS FOUND IN ALL OF THE FORMS OF MASS ENTERTAINMENT IN much the same guise as he appeared in more sophisticated works. Shylock, Rebecca, and Sheva made their appearances in even more exaggerated forms. In fact, Jews could be discovered more frequently in popular entertainment than in more serious literature.

The Dime Novel

By the middle of the century technological improvements in printing had produced an expanding working-class readership and a mass popular literature. Produced on cheap paper in small print with paper covers, these sensational works flowed from the presses of what has been described as the "culture industry."[1] These "novels" could be purchased by the average worker. The fantastic popularity in the 1840s of George Lippard, the "D. W. Griffith of cheap stories," whose books pioneered in this method of production, gave impetus to the movement. The dime novels of the next generation were, however, of much lower literary quality.

Beadle, one of the main entrepreneurs in this field, combined acute business shrewdness with extreme feelings of patriotism.[2] The house of Beadle and Adams and later competitors poured out thousands of formula novels from the 1860s to the 1890s. This pulp literature, much of it nationalistic in spirit, had an enormous influence on the way Americans perceived others. As might be expected, these books presented the standard stereotypes of the Jew, with a similar ambivalence. The prolific authors did not hesitate to present a Jewish villain in one book and a hero or heroine in another. Often, just as in more serious writing, the Jew was not what he appeared to be. The face he presented to the world was frequently a mere facade—his real character was shrouded in mystery. Occasionally, the image was surprisingly positive, more so than in "serious" fiction.

Sylvanus Cobb and Edward Judson, two of the earliest writers in this genre, were also leaders in the Know-Nothing movement. Their lack of any real malice toward the Jewish characters indicates how little the nativist movement of the mid-century was involved with anti-Semitism.[3] Cobb's *The Marmeluke* (1852) was an early example of the standard romantic tale. Mordecai Kerenzac is an old banker, "bowed by the weight of tyranny." Inside of his dreadful looking house is the usual magnificently appointed apartment. He has the inevitably beautiful daughter, Judith, who is rescued from a harem and sent to Paris for a musical career. (Beautiful Jewesses could usually sing.) Fortuitously, her father dies, and she is free to marry the Christian hero and go to live and perform in America.

Judson, in *Morgan Or the Knight of the Black Flag* (1860), included the popular duo of the Jewish money-lender and his beautiful daughter. When Morgan first sees the dwelling where old Solomon lives, he remarks contemptuously, "A Jew may live in such a den, but a Christian would not." Outside, the dwelling is "squalid and filthy in the extreme," but once doors within doors are unbolted, there is revealed "magnificent splendor and Oriental luxury." As might be expected, Solomon's daughter has "that rare and striking beauty so peculiar to women of the Jewish race." Despite her sad songs of Judah's plight, she defiantly declares, "Give us hate . . . pity us not, for we yet are proud amid all our suffering. . . ." She has all the family virtue authors often ascribed to Jews, "While I live, I owe all my love and devotion to my father." Her father saves her from disgrace at the hands of King Charles, declaring, "I, like my child, begin to value gold less than once I did."

In Judson's *Rose Seymour: Or the Ballet Girl's Revenge* (1865), Miriam represents the sexual implications of the beautiful Jewess character. She lives in a dirty shop with her disgusting pawnbroker father. When Rose, the heroine, faints, she awakens to see watching over her "a beautiful fair Jewess . . . her face bore the signs of pain and suffering." She tells Rose, "They would force a hateful life upon me and I resisted, see." She lifts her blouse to reveal long red cuts produced by a heavy whip. The hag who possesses influence over her father ties her to the wall naked to the waist and, in a scene of explicit sexual violence, flogs her with savage ferocity. This is one of the few occasions in which this character was the European style "la belle juive," with its aura of "rape and massacre."

Albert Aiken was one of the most prolific of dime novelists. A number of his books included Jewish characters, frequently in the most unfavorable light.[4] *The Genteel Spotter* (1884), for instance, included two Jewish villains. One, Moses Cohenstein, is an old pawnbroker and fence, withered and "fox-like," with a sneaky manner: "A man who never by any chance looked anybody in the eye, and who always cringed and crouched as though he was afraid someone was going to strike him." He is called, "Slippery Moses." He has eyes like a hawk, but wears "a pair of old fashioned spectacles to conceal the expression of his eyes." This is another Jew who hides his true character—

he can "control every muscle in his face with the skill of a practiced actor." Another stereotyped miserly "typical Hebrew" can be found in *Lone Hand in Texas* (1888). Oppenheim "cringed and rubbed his hands together whenever he talked to anyone." A more interesting Jewish character in this book is Jacob Plunkett, the landlord, an English Jew, "although beyond his promi-nent nose—with the true Hebrew hook" one could not tell his "race." Although the landlord is scornful of old Oppenheim's stinginess, both turn out to be in the employ of the villain. In *Dick Talbot, the Ranch King* (1892), containing another "greasy" Jewish villain, Aiken was somewhat apologetic about his constant use of the negative Jewish stereotype in his Westerns. He blamed the locale, "Although in my time I have met with a great many Jews who were every bit as good as any Gentiles . . . as a rule these gentle Jews don't flourish in a climate like this."

Aiken was not always so unremittingly hostile. He often used the popular device of having the Jew turn out to be on the side of good in spite of being a money-lender or pawnbroker.[5] In *California Detective* (1878) Isaac Abrams, a diamond broker, despite the usual hooked nose and keen eyes, is "a jolly contented looking gentleman . . . one evidently used to good living and at peace with himself and the world." He is instrumental in helping the hero to expose the villain. In *Phantom Hand* (1877), the hero, fallen into bad times, is helped by an old Jewish pawnbroker who offers him a bed at a nominal rate, "you pays me when you gets ready." The hero is touched, "Abal your heart's all right old boy." The Jew responds proudly, "s'help me I am an honest man."

Aiken attempted one beautiful Jewess, as usual the daughter of a moneylender and pawnbroker, in *Lone Hand the Shadow* (1889). When outlaws break in, she has fire in her flashing black eyes, "which told she was made of sterner stuff than her affrighted parent." Although her father swears, at first, "I hafe so little monish," when the outlaw puts a knife to his daughter's throat, he forgets his own terror and cupidity "in contemplation of the danger which menaced Rebecca." Rebecca "had the warlike spirit of old Israel strong within her." The Lone Hand quickly realizes that "this girl was one who would be quite free of the weaknesses of her sex." He agrees to help find the outlaws even though many are prejudiced against the Jew who is a "tough cuss at a bargain." In spite of his weaknesses, the old Jew works with the Lone Hand to capture the villains.

Gilbert Jerome, another "master" of the dime novel, was openly hostile in his two books containing Jewish characters.[6] In *Dominick Squeek, the Bow Street Runner* (1884) Aaron Lackstein is a Polish Jewish fence, a frequent occupation for Jews in dime novels. His face is "repulsive" with "eyes twinkling with avarice." His wife, an unusual Jewish female character, is a "tall woman of masculine appearance" who saves the hero and kills the major villain and herself, in anguish over her son's death. Lackstein is happy that his wife is dead so he can return to his house and resume his dishonorable business. (It is interesting that the villainous Jews often escaped punishment in popular crime stories.)

Jess Cowdrick's *The Detective's Apprentice* (1885) was another standard "half-dime" selection.[7] The story takes place on Baxter Street, "the stronghold of the Jews. . . . Here if your general makeup proclaims you to be from the country, not a dozen steps will advance ere you will be caught by the sleeve and almost pulled out of you boots by some enterprising dealer in ol' clos, who seems determined to force a sale upon you at almost any sacrifice." Ikey, a "good looking little cuss, smart as lightening," is the son of a hardened Jewish criminal. He is trained by the chief villain to take the hero's place as the son stolen in infancy from a millionaire. Ikey is ultimately discovered, but Hal, the hero, says, "take care of him . . . and let him have a chance to grow up honest." At the end, Hal and Ikey are both at school together, preparing for college. This appeared to suggest that the American environment and good training could turn the Jew into a useful citizen.

Edward Wheeler, another well-known dime novelist, portrayed several Jewish characters of varying types.[8] Moses Monk in *Apollo Bill, the Trail Tornado* (1882) speaks a broken Jewish dialect, but is really a Yankee who pretends to be a Jew because, "the average American admires the shrewd business tact of the Jew, if not the Jew himself, and therefore patronizes him." On the other hand, Dr. Albert Alberts, the villain in *Boss Bob, King of the Bootblacks* (1886) is a "modern merchant of Venice," who prefers being a pawnbroker to practicing medicine. His keen grey eyes are "the mirror of an evil soul." Pearl, the heroine, has been pledged to him as collateral for a loan by her millionaire father. (Dime novelists seemed to feel that this was a common practice among the upper classes.) He desires Pearl because she has admission to the highest circles of society: "She would loosen my purse-strings and make me so popular that the world would forget that I am a Jew." Naturally, his villainous designs are balked in the end.

Wheeler also wrote about "good" Jews. The hero in *Jim Bludsoe, the Boy Phenix* (1878) was another fat pawnbroker, Isaac Isaacs, "an exceptionally fine fellow for a pawnbroker." He is "keen as a razor," and despite his 365-pound bulk, an extraordinary dancer. He strikes the villain down and walks away "with the utmost *sang froid*." The hero acknowledges his invaluable assistance by calling him a "right good friend, and Jew though you are, you have indeed proven yourself an honest man." The tendency to mix stereotypes, and to qualify praise of a Jewish character in this manner, was not unusual.

Wheeler presented a far more unconventional Jewish hero in *The Ventriloquist Detective* (1887). When a drunken Irishman (another popular dime novel stereotype) tries to force his attention on a young lady, a "foppishly attired young Jew with red hair and a hooked nose," intervenes and knocks the miscreant out to the cheers of bystanders. He is a most unusual Jewish character—young, brave, energetic, and, in spite of admitting, "I haff some of dose anxiety to get rich vunce in a vile," not overly involved with accumulating money. He saves the heroine, collects a reward, and sets up a detective agency with his pretty wife, Rebecca.

Prentiss Ingraham, the son of Joseph Ingraham of religious novels fame, is reputed to have written six hundred dime novels. Several contained Jewish characters, some standard stereotypes, and others who were far more unusual.[9] The Jew in *Gold Plume, the Boy Bandit* (1881) is a comical figure, the familiar coward who has come West to cheat the miners. He is rescued from an irate lynch mob but is forced to treat the crowd to drinks to save his skin, a fate almost as bad as death. Ingraham's Jewish heroes, in contrast, were extraordinary. *The Jew Detective* (1891) is vividly introduced as a handsome, obviously Jewish man, with the dark magnetic eyes usually attributed to Jewish women. Wrongly accused of murder, he exclaims, "Oh, God of Abraham! that I should have come to this . . . it must not, it shall not be, for those of my race never die at the hands of a hangman." At his trial, Cora, the heroine, admits that she did the killing in self-defense. The Jew detective defies numerous stereotypes—he is a charming conversationalist, has courtly manners, is a lawyer, and is poor. He runs around rescuing the heroine and bailing out her horrible anti-Semitic brother. He also saves an old Jew who speaks with the usual accent in English, but perfect mellifluous Hebrew. The old man is a stock character—his daughter is one of the ever-present beautiful Jewesses and he is a pawnbroker, interestingly characterized as a "much abused but necessary class of businessmen." The poor young detective becomes rich as a result of his good deeds for the old Jew. He rejects the beautiful Jewess in favor of the much abused Cora. "Though I am not a Jewess, my Christian friends deserted me," she declares in a marvelous ending. "You have been my truest friend . . . and to you I now turn for happiness in life, for your people shall be my people, your creed my creed, and your God my God." One can only wonder what the faithful dime novel readers made of this story, a total reversal of conventions, in which the handsome young hero is a Jew and the beautiful heroine a Christian who converts to Judaism! The accepted intermarriage had always been between the gallant Christian hero and the beautiful Jewess, and any assimilation had been her decision to accept her lover's Christian faith. The presence of a young Jewish male character was, in itself, a rarity. It is all the more remarkable that this reversal was in a piece of mass fiction, rather than in a more "serious" work.

Evidently, Ingraham found this unconventional formula successful, for he returned to it in "Jule the Jewess" (1896–97) which included a Jewish hero, heroine, and villain. Adolph, the Jewish hero, is a "young man of gentlemanly bearing and dress, darkly bronzed, handsome features and the unmistakable stamp of the Israelite resting upon them." Jule, one of the heroines, is perfect in every way, "The seal of her race had been but lightly stamped on her exquisite face." When the millionaire father of Isobel, another heroine, pledges her, as usual, to a miser (non-Jewish) to save his wealth, Adolph swears he will save her "by the God of Abraham." He retorts to taunts about his Jewishness, "I am a Jew, and I am as proud of the title as you are of that of Christian and have far better right to it." Jule responds to a Christian marriage proposal that she cannot "forget the creed of my people and turn my back upon the God of Israel to love one of a race who had persecuted us. . . . There is a wall between the Christian and Jew ever so high, and only a renegade to our creed can scale it." Later, however, she does fall in love with Merton Wilbur, a Christian lawyer. Jule informs a Christian bully, "Your people are often traitors to your religion but seldom it is that one of my race is." In an echo of *The Jew Detective,* Isabel declares her love for Adolph and gratitude to Jule, "I tell you that their home shall be my home, their God my God." She adds that the only objection to Adolph had been that he wasn't a Christian "and there are some who said that he lived a purer, better life than those who are." Jule and Merton, Isabel and Adolph marry in a double ceremony, performed in surprisingly modern fashion by a rabbi and a minister. Shades of Henry Harland!

There were many Jewish characters in dime novels. Many of these were one-dimensional Shylocks, usually engaged in illegal activities of a nonviolent nature such as extortionate moneylending, fencing, or representing the interests of an even bigger villain. The image was basically the same as in more substantial literature, distilled downward. Interestingly, however, the Jew was rarely the major monstrous evildoer. Generally, his misdeeds were of a nonviolent nature. The beautiful, noble, and, often, fiery Jewess was also a frequent character. The pawnbroker or moneylender who seemed villainous at first glance but, Sheva-like, was in reality a cohort of the hero in his struggle against evil, was about as common as the Jewish villain. The young Jewish heroes and heroines of Prentiss Ingraham and Edward Wheeler were unusual in representing standard heroic virtues of honesty, courage, and self-sacrifice. However, it is interesting and significant that the reader of dime fiction was evidently willing to accept what, by convention, were very unlikely heroes. Such characters could not be found in more "serious" works.

The Theater

The popular perception of the Jew was undoubtedly affected by his portrayal in the theater. Here the image, affected perhaps by the need for more-clear-cut dramatic divisions between good and evil, was stereotypical for the most part. Ellen Schiff concludes that the first century of theater in America was "routinely anti-Semitic." She believes, however, that this was more a product of habit, routine acceptance of long-established stereotypes, and insensitivity rather than of deliberate hatred of Jews.[10]

The Jewish image in America's theater was bedeviled by the powerful character of Shylock. *The Merchant of Venice* was one of the most popular plays performed on the American stage. It may well have been the first play produced in America, in Williamsburg in 1752. T. Allston Brown's standard *History of the New York Stage* (1903) lists 130 productions on the New York stage alone, beginning with one at the John Street Theatre in 1768.[11] The *Merchant* was the first play performed in America by a regular company. Edmund Kean toured with it in 1820–21 in a performance characterized by Fanny Kemble as "divested of all poetry or elevation" but invested with "ferocity that made one's blood curdle."[12]

Edwin Booth was the best known American Shylock. His father, Junius Booth, had played the part with a Yiddish accent and hand gestures. He was reported to have attended synagogue and studied Talmud to enable him to get into the part. Thomas Gould, in Edwin Booth's edition of *Merchant* in 1867, pointed out that Junius Booth's Shylock included outward greed and revenge, but also patriarchal dignity, "the type of race as old as the world . . . marked by pride of intellect; by intense pride of race . . . as if there centered in him the might of a people whom neither time, nor scorn, nor political oppression could subdue. . . ."[13]

Edwin Booth, however, presented a very different characterization. William Winter, in *Life and Art of Edwin Booth* (1893), described Booth's Shylock as fierce and vindictive, "inspiring neither veneration nor pity . . . a fiend-like man."[14] The *New York Times* in 1867 criticized a Booth performance as "rage without purpose, noise without meaning. . . ." It was impossible to reconcile Booth's interpretation with an understanding of "how completely the Israelite was hedged in by prejudice; how narrow and slippery was the path he trod. . . ."[15] William Cullen Bryant saw Booth's performance at the Winter Garden. Booth's Shylock, he felt, was "not a Jew, but a fiend. . . . Revenge is not a characteristic of the Jew." Booth stressed Shakespeare's execration of "that unquenchable lust for lucre which marks the race, although he does not show that this passion was but the effect of persecution." (This was often given as an excuse for the Jew's supposed misconduct.) Other parts of Booth's picture also did not fit. A Jew would prefer the money to the flesh and would avoid physical contests, preferring "to triumph by intellect." The daughter's contempt for her father was also unrealistic since Jews "are universally admired for the affections which adorn their domestic life." The performance fails "to do justice to the grandeurs of the Jewish race . . . to exhibit that superiority of intellect which has survived all persecution . . . ," Bryant concluded with a paean of praise for all the great and progressive events of the age that "may be traced to the wonderful working of the soul of the Hebrew . . . which gave mankind its noblest religion, its noblest laws and some of its noblest poesy and music."[16] Bryant thus revealed a countervailing attitude among at least some of the American audience watching Booth.

The ranting, raving Shylock, patterned on Edwin Booth's interpretation, influenced hundreds of less talented actors. *The Merchant of Venice* played all over the United States. Noah Ludlow even took it by wagon and flatboat to towns like Milledgeville, Georgia[17] Thousands, who had never seen a real Jew in person, saw Shylock in his most extreme form. "Sam Slick" reported in 1858:

> I once seen a theater play . . . and there was an old Jew in it, and there was a fellow run away with his daughter and his money puss and if ever there was a critter ravin, tarrin mad, it was old mister Shylock. . . . I never see such work as he made on it, a runnin up and down the floor, and a pulling at his wig and frothin at the mouth like a "hoss with the blind staggers."[18]

American audiences may well have seen a different interpretation of Shylock when the great British actor Henry Irving toured the country in 1883 and frequently thereafter, playing Shylock with dignity and sympathy, bringing understanding where there had been only scorn. The *New York Herald* stressed the taste and tact of Irving's Shylock, "invested with a dignity that is truly ideal." The *Philadelphia Evening Bulletin* reported that Irving presented the Jew as "more than the mere incarnation of avarice," but as a character worthy of sympathy. The *Chicago Tribune* declared it a "nineteenth century Shylock. It is a creation only possible in our age, which has pronounced its verdict against medieval cruelty and medieval blindness." Irving, at this time, saw Shylock as a representative of a mistreated race whose wrongs made him fiendish in his goals. He was what man might become in an oppressive environment. Played in this manner, the sympathy tended to shift to Shylock.[19]

Irving's role in countering the Shylock image was not always so clear-cut, however. There is some evidence that over the years, Irving's Shylock grew less human and more loathsome. The *New York Mirror* in 1888 complained that Irving's performance was exaggerated and grotesque, resembling "the futile rage of an epileptic peddler." William Archer criticized Irving Shylock as neither just nor accurate. "He fails . . . to give the man that touch of dignity which raises him above the mean and malicious usurer." Somewhat later, Norman Hapgood, an observer sympathetic to Jews, witnessed a performance that stressed the justice of Shylock's cause and "grandeur to his revenge . . . Hebrew nobility and suffering." Obviously, Irving presented Shylock both ways at various times in his career. The drama critic, Henry Clapp, recalled several of Irving's American tours as Shylock, "Sometimes as a fierce money-catching old clothes dealer. . . . Sometimes as a majestic

Hebrew financier and law giver. . . ."[20] This underlying dichotomy in Irving's interpretations reflected, perhaps, the ambivalence of his audiences.

Many "modernized" versions of the *Merchant,* some intended to be humorous, played throughout the century with varying degrees of popularity.[21] John Brougham's 1858 version was more sympathetic than Shakespeare's. Shylock became "a shamefully ill-used and persecuted old Hebrew gentleman . . . whose character was darkened by his Christian contemporaries simply to conceal their own nefarious transactions." The ending turns "happy" as Lorenzo reveals, "twixt me and you, I'll tell you a secret—I've turned Jew." George M. Baker's *The Peddler of Very Nice* (1866) was intended to be a humorous version of the play. Shylock is a pawnbroker in it, and Antonio is a peddler. Shylock, sharpening a huge set of shears in a takeoff of the stage business, constantly employed by "serious" Shylocks, threatens to remove the buttons from Antonio's coat. In the end, Shylock marries Portia and promises, "I will reform, no longer villain be. . . ." The comic version performed by the Griffin and Christy Minstrels was particularly popular. Here, one can clearly see the progression from Shylock to the burlesque Jew. Shylock becomes an old clothes dealer who always asks, "how's pishness?" In the end Shylock wails, "I've lost my flesh, my monish and my daughter . . . ," and the entire chorus tosses him in a blanket. In these comic versions the Shylock character was stripped of any pretense of dignity, but was considerably less malignant.

The Jewish criminal was a popular character in the theater as well as in the dime novels.[22] In John Brougham's 1867 play, *The Lottery of Life,* Mordie Solomons, who speaks with a "strong Jewish accent," is an old clothes man, counterfeiter, crook, and possible murderer. Dion Boucicault's *Flying Scud* was one of the most popular plays of the nineteenth century. Although it opened in London first, it was produced in New York in 1867 and constantly revived thereafter. One of the major characters is a comic Jewish confidence man who receives his just reward when he is shot in the rear by one of his accomplices. Solomon Isaacs in *Jail Bird* was a more vicious criminal, "a brutal vulgar, cowardly Jew." In all these cases someone else does the dirty work.

Another species of Jewish characters in the theater was based upon Cumberland's *The Jew,* written in 1794. On 25 February 1795 it opened in the John Street Theatre in New York for its first American production. It was "a piece which remained popular for forty years."[23] It led to a vogue for sentimental plays with long-suffering, whining, saintly Jewish characters who were vindicated at the end. This popularity persisted for most of the century. Often the same theater would offer first the Shylock, then the Sheva view of the Jewish moneylender.

Thomas Dibdin's *The Jew and the Doctor* (1807) was a typical play of this type.[24] Abnego, a dealer in "pargans," finds a little girl and raises her, sending her to Christian schools. When another character calls him, "you old—old Jew, You," he responds, "Can you trow noting in my face but my religion? I wish wid all ma heart I could return the compliment." He is not normally brave, but "ven Miss Emily is in danger, I feel all de vorld so I vas a lion." At the end, when the girl's real father offers to pay him for what he has done, he replies with characteristic nobility, "I'll tell you how to pay me. If ever you see a helpless creature vat needs your assistance, give it for ma sake—And if de object should not be a Christian . . . you can never make your own religion look so well as when you show mercy to de religion of others."

This type continued to be presented even in the later part of the century. Sidney Grundy's *An Old Jew*, first produced in London, was brought to America in 1894. In his introduction the author defended his conception of the hero as "typical of his race . . . millionaire, very generous . . self-sacrificing . . . superlatively chaste and of . . . strong domestic affections . . . pride of race . . . a stern strength." One unique quality of this hero is the absence of an accent. He is permitted a ringing defense of his people: "I am proud to be one of that great family which has established itself throughout the length and breadth of the earth—citizens not of one country, but of all; and wheresoever it has gone, furnished its foster mother with her greatest sons. . . ."[25]

There were occasional productions of *Nathan the Wise*, with its far loftier concept of the "good" Jew. Norman Hapgood saw an 1899 production in which the actor presented "a wise old Jew of . . . laintly spirit . . . picturesque appearance . . . dignity . . . the picture of a large, charitable nature."[26] Shylock and Sheva, however, were far more popular characters than Nathan.

At times the benevolent Jew was also turned into a comic character. *Sam'l of Posen* (1880) by George Jessop was popular for many years and made a star of M. B. Curtis, a Jewish actor who specialized in this part.[27] Samuel enters the stage executing some sharp dealing with an upper-class snob and a lazy Irish clean-up man (another popular stereotype.) However, Samuel's Sheva-like benevolence is shown when Mrs. Mulcahy enters the shop with a pathetic shawl that she hopes to pawn to get bread for her family and medicine for a sick child. Sam advances the money remarking, "A true Hebrew never goes back on the widows and orphans." Then he returns her shawl and fills her basket with food, suggesting, "Give your children a Jewish picnic." He proceeds to foil all the machinations of the villain and to exonerate the honest though unintelligent hero. In one real reversal of stereotype, Samuel wins the hand of a beautiful Jewess who, unaccountably, does not show an interest in handsome Christian men.

Sam'l met with mixed reviews, which seemed to depend on the broadness of Curtis's performance.[28] An 1881 *New York Daily Graphic* review described the play as "vile." Curtis was conceded to have made "a wonderfully realistic appearance and characterization of a miserable type of Jewish humanity . . . painful to the refined sense." The American Jewish establishment was also not amused. The *American Hebrew,* for example, caustically referred to the "Fagins and Sam'l Posens that have served to calumniate and caricature our people." The criticisms evidently led Curtis to mute the excesses of his performance. In 1890 the *Philadelphia Sunday Mirror* commented that Sam'l was "harmless . . . easy-going." The stage Jew "had been raised a trifle from the standards . . . in bygone days . . . He had advanced. . . ." An 1894 revival garnered generally favorable reviews. Nobody "could find offence in this amiable, ingenious and kind hearted young Israelite," one critic commented. A Detroit reviewer called it the "cleverest and cleanest characterization of the Hebrew ever presented on stage."

Milton Nobles presented a far less satisfactory "good" comical Jew in a revitalization of an old play, *The Phoenix.*[29] Nobles appeared in the popular play 1,500 times in the last twenty-five years of the century. In the preface to a 1900 edition, he noted, "I was the first to place on the stage the modern American Jew, a jolly up-to-date man about town, not a villain." The character, Moses Solomon, however, was a former moneylender turned gambler.

The popular 1890 comedy of manners *Man and Woman,* by Henry De-Mille and David Belasco, was a more successful attempt to present the "modern American Jew."[30] Israel Cohen, an honest bank president, is shown as an educated, unaccented, virtuous individual. Even though the heroine rejects him for an embezzling bank cashier, he exhibits great mercy for his rival. The Jewish press was quite pleased with this play. The *Jewish Exponent* felt that the stage had at last "shaken off the prejudice of the centuries and given us a Jew unsullied, untrammeled, uncaricatured . . . a living, breathing man."[31]

Edward Tullidge's turgid *Ben Israel* (1875) was the most professedly philo-Semitic play of the century.[32] Tullidge's aims were made quite clear in an introduction dedicated to the Jews of America: "Your theme and race my Hebrew brethren constitute the grandest epic of the world . . . the nations owe to your people the crown of civilization. . . . As an author I am ashamed to say our class has been but little better than the bigot and the priest. . . ." Tullidge's play takes place in the court of Charles II, where Rachel, a beautiful Jewess, tries to stave off the King's lust. The villain frequently declaims, "Curse the Jews!" The saintly hero, David Ben Israel, responds, "Christian scoffer! Our race were princes when thy ancestors were robbers and barbarians." He advances funds to the King to protect the Hebrew maid. Only when the Christian hero risks his life for Jewish rights is Rachel permitted to marry him. Ben Israel looks forward to the time when, "every land shall bless, not curse the Jew. . . ."

Beautiful Jewesses were also obvious frequent characters in the theater. In

1836 a popular spectacular drama, *The Jewess,* was presented at the Lion Theater in Boston. It enjoyed long years of popularity—a performance was reported in 1866 at the New Bowery Theater and in 1871 at the Bowery Theater.[33] Several different versions of *Judith,* the story of the biblical heroine, were also performed. Augustin Daly's *Leah the Forsaken* (1862) was the most successful play on this theme and a favorite for more than forty years. Kate Bateman became famous for her portrayal of Leah, and, in 1892, the great Sara Bernhardt made an American appearance in the part. The heroine is a Jewish maiden in Austria who suffers great tribulations for her faith, but ultimately reunites with her Christian lover. The villain of the piece is a renegade Jew who had deserted a dying father to become a Christian. He hates his own Jewishness and goes so far as to try to frame the innocent Leah. The girl who fiercely defends her Jewishness is the heroine; the convert is the villain, in an interesting reversal of the usual Christian attitudes on this issue. The play was greeted with great popular and critical approval. One critic felt it made a powerful case against all prejudice, drawing a parallel between Jews in Europe and Negroes in America.[34]

The character of the money-hungry Jew, the petty Shylock, found its way into the popular comedy theater and burlesques, where it was added to a growing collection of comic ethnic stereotypes. Precursors appeared in the honky-tonks of the West. "Pretty Sally Solomons," sung "with appropriate gestures," described the love of a peddler for the daughter of an old clothes man. "America's Royal Ball" combined stereotypes of Chinese, Irish, and Jews in one ditty. In early burlesque, in Robey's "Knickerbockers," Charley Burke made a tremendous hit doing a "Jew character" who sang of his love for Rachel Goldstein for whom he would "build a fire . . . fail in business."[35]

The immigrant Jew himself began to appear in the parade of ethnic stereotypes. In a subtle shift, he induced the audience to laugh with him as well as at him, by poking fun at his own foibles.[36] The team of Bert and Leon are generally described as the first Jewish comedians. They appeared in the 1870s, singing such numbers as "The Widow Rosenbaum," the saga of a rich and unattainable widow whose father kept "a hock shop . . . where the sheeny politicians can be found." Frank Bush made the character of the East Side pawnbroker into a common burlesque figure. The Jewish comedian became "the ranking comic" for burlesque companies, a stock figure "with a beard, unkept clothes and sometimes a limp." Bush himself sang "My name is Solomon Moses I'm a bully Sheeny man." His career continued through the 1890s, helping to make that kind of comedy "a staple of our variety theaters." Joe Welch, a Jew himself, was another delineator of this favorite stock figure. His characteristic pose was rubbing his hands together, bowing or cringing and demanding his "monish." When a young Willie Howard wanted to appear onstage smooth faced, the manager asked, "Where's your beard?" Howard replied that he hadn't planned to wear one. The manager ordered,

"Go back and put it on. If you don't wear a beard, the audience won't know you're a Jewish comedian." Jewish comedians gave their largely non-Jewish audiences expected characterizations, just like blacks who appeared in minstrel shows in the required blackface. Some of the early "Jewish" comics were not Jews, but this changed by the end of the century. This self-deprecatory caricature led to the development of modern Jewish comedy styles, which often play with and against the stereotype (Woody Allen, for example).

The stage Jew also appeared in many comic plays, starting with *The Mulligan Guard Ball* in 1879.[37] In *A Ready-Made Suit* (1885) almost every ethnic stereotype is introduced in the parts of the husbands of a female bigamist who is on trial. Two of them are Jews from a firm of "eminent Hebrew jobbers in second-hand clothes." They explain that they both married the same woman because "ve dinks if ve can get von vife between us, dot vill be less expensive." David Warfield, a well-known Jewish actor, starred in several plays that combined a plot line with the burlesque image. He achieved great popularity as Melter Moss, the rascally Jew in *Ticket of Leave Man*. In 1899 Warfield played Sigmund Cohenski, a Jewish millionaire. To a sneering comment, "I suppose you think the pen is mightier than the sword," he responds, "You bet my life. Could you sign checks with a sword?"

The stage, "serious" and frivolous, reflected many of the same perceptions of the Jew that one could find in literature. Contradictory images abounded: Shylocks and Shevas, Sam'ls and Leahs competed for public attention. In burlesque the comic Jew, like the lazy drunken Irishman, was merely one of innumerable unflattering ethnic caricatures. Here the Shylock image lost its menacing malevolence and became an object of merriment. Just as, in a later era, Stepin Fetchit portrayed the stereotypical black, Jewish comedians presented the miserly Jew. Not only were Jews the lead comics of burlesque companies, but the impresarios and theatrical syndicates were predominantly Jewish. As Ellen Schiff has pointed out, the droll Jew, who teases himself and everything else, is largely an American Jewish creation. Villainous Jews in "serious" plays in America tended to be far less dangerous and menacing than their European counterparts. The comic Jew joined an unending parade of ethnic stereotypes. It is instructive that the British were unable to comprehend *Sam'l of Posen*, which required them to laugh with the Jewish "Hero," rather than sneering at him.[38] This, perhaps, is the nub of the difference in the image of the stage Jew in America compared to Europe.

Jews in Popular Humor

The image of the Jew in American popular humor was similar to that in other forms of popular amusement. However, as humor tends to reduce every object to its most absurd form, the Jewish image became more one-dimensional. The Jew was basically presented as someone concerned solely with the accumulation of money, willing to use any means in his pursuit of wealth, including fraudulent failures and arson. For the most part, there was no real alarm or fear connected with this image, and it joined a long list of other unflattering ethnic stereotypes that were enormously popular in nineteenth-century America.

The stereotyped humorous image of the Jew could be found in early publications well before the advent of the comic magazine. As early as 1799 a "comic" song might express the sentiment that it was money, "vat make Jew Christian, Christian Jew."[39] A tale of the old South concerned a political meeting in which a speaker was attacking know-nothingism. Noticing a "little German-Jew" clothing peddler, he asks rhetorically, "Furriner, didn't you come to this country to escape from tyrannical, downtrodden and oppressed Europe . . . to live in a land of freedom?" The peddler responds, much to the amusement of the crowd, "No sur; I comes to dis countrie to sell sheap ready-made clothes."

Thomas Haliburton's *Letterbag of the Great Western* (1840) demonstrates the early presence of the fully developed stereotype.[40] Moses Levi, in a "humorous" letter to Levi Moses, is somewhat skeptical about opportunities in the United States: "I mosht afeart America is no conetry for te Jewish . . . Te Yankee all knowish too mush for us ant too mush awake ant shoo sharp as a needle at making von pargain, vich give no chansh at all to a poor Jew to liff." The frequently reiterated idea that the Jew and that model American, the Yankee, were equally sharp in business dealings, removed much of the sting from the stereotype.

Of the early periodicals, *Spirit of the Times* was most likely to include anti-Semitic estimates of Jewish character and comic stories of Jewish foibles.[41] In 1844 the magazine included a description of Chatham Street, the "old clothes" center, where country folk would be constantly harassed and "every now and then falling into the hands of one of those fierce whiskered Jews, carried into a gloomy cavern, and presently sent forth again in a garment. . . ."

The Jew as the quintessential parvenu was an image many held well before the often-written-about status pressures of the 1870s.[42] An 1845 poem in *The Spectator,* for instance, described the way in which a wealthy German Jew was able to gain entry into New York Dutch society by means of his vulgar use of wealth, including displaying his wife and horses "in spangling fustian and brocade." In an 1857 poem in *The Knickerbocker,* the Jew and the poet were seen as the exact opposites among men. The Jew wishes that "yonder stars . . . real shining dollars were . . . " and that he could grab them. The poet sees the stars as his longings in flight. Then, each looks at the other, "full of scorn beyond expression."

In the last quarter of the nineteenth century, humor magazines reached heights of popularity, presenting far from subtle stereotypes of Jewish parvenus, misers, and cheats among their sometimes brutal collections of ethnic caricatures.[43] *Puck* was founded in 1877 by Joseph Keppler, an Austrian immigrant. It advocated total assimilation and ridiculed many creeds and groups without any real malice. While its crude oversimplifications might appear anti-Semitic today, it did not regard itself, nor was it thought of in its time, as such. In fact, it frequently attacked anti-Semitism. Irish Catholics were treated far worse than Jews in the pages of *Puck*. *Judge,* started in 1881, early ran into financial difficulties and, for a time, turned to anti-Semitic slanders in an effort to boost circulation. In 1883 new management promised to avoid such vulgarity and bad taste. The magazine was eventually taken over by prominent Republican businessmen and achieved a circulation of over 50,000. It occasionally continued to include offensive features. *Life,* started by *Harvard Lampoon* graduates in 1883, was the most consistently "Judeophobic," particularly in featuring a drama critic who saw America and its theater threatened by an Irish Catholic plot and by Jewish conspiracy. *M'lle New York,* which lasted only briefly and was the least significant, showed a perverse fascination for physically repulsive Jewish men and seductive Jewish women, both of whom it supposed to be skilled in sexual depravity.

The Jewish stereotype joined the whole range of clichéd ethnic images in the humor magazines. Generally, the comic version lacked viciousness, but the Jew, willing to do anything for money, was sharper than the other groups, who tended to be portrayed as dim witted. An 1883 *Life* tale, "The Juice," is a good example of the contrasting stereotype of the Jew and the Irishman.[44] An Irish policeman complains about those "bloodthy pagans that made the Holy Vargin an orfin. . . ." He describes how one old-clothes dealer was arrested for keeping his store open on Sunday. The Jew explains that "he kep' Sathurday for Sunday." The next week the policeman finds the store open on Saturday. "But I've changed me religion, sez he." On Sunday, when the store is again full, the Jews says that his mother has died and the people are attending a wake. "Sure enough there was the hook-nose corpse in a chape coffin an' sivinty-sivin hook-nose mourners." The following day, the cop sends a detective who finds a wax mask of a corpse. "Phwat can yez do wid dem Juice, annyhow," he concludes in disgust.

Money was considered to be the measure of all things to the Jew. In *Puck*'s "Instructive Exercise," Mr. Goldheimer, in an athletic club, sends his children to do their exercises on a pole in the shape of a dollar sign. When the child informs his father that the book he is studying says that money does not bring happiness, the father replies, "No mein sohn, its der interest vot you gets on der moneysh vot makes you happy." Even patriotism had to take a back seat to moneymaking. Told that Ikey Levy has been with Dewey in Manila Bay making history, Burnstein responds, "Voudln't it been better if he had stayed in Baxter Bay making moneysh?"[45]

Sickness, danger, and even death could not interfere with the Jewish proclivity for moneymaking. Even on the most sentimental occasions, money was the true yardstick. When the rescuer saves Mrs. Cohen, her spouse rewards him with five dollars. It was not that he was fond of his wife, but "she had her diamonds on." When Mrs. CoHenn is going down for the third time, her nonswimming husband shouts, "As you loaf me, Leah, t'row dem erringks ashore! Dey gan't be madched in der cidys." A Jew might even be willing to die if the monetary situation so dictated. The cause of the sudden death of Solomon Isaacs was that "some one told him that his life insurance would expire the next day." Naturally, the Jewish child would quickly learn what was expected of him. When the boy is asked whether he believes in quick sales and small profits, he answers, "I belive in quvick sales undt all kinds of brofits."[46]

The clothing trade, whether in new or second-hand clothes, came to symbolize the Jew. Along with pawnbrokering, manipulation of customers in clothing stores was the "Jewish" activity most frequently described by the humor magazines. The sale was the lifeblood of the Jewish merchant. When Aaron Levy was sleeping on a disabled ship, he was awakened by the cry, "A sail! A sail!" Forgetting his whereabouts, he displays his "ruling passion" by shouting, "A sale! A sale! Where?" Most of all, the Jew could be depended upon to try to make anything fit the "rube" who has the temerity to enter his store. A long-nosed Jew tells his customer-victim who has a pair of pants almost up to his neck, "Dose bants fit you jusd beautiful, mine frent, now ain'd it?" "Y-y-yes," is the reply, "But don't you think they are a trifle tight under the arms? (This evolved into a standard vaudeville routine.)[47]

This obsession with profits might lead the Jew into dishonest practices. The use of illegal bankruptcy as a means of making profit was often attributed to Jewish merchants. When Rosenbaum informs Cohen that there have been eighty-seven failures in New York, a worried Cohen responds, "Mein Gott! Such competition as dot will kill buziness endirely." When the boy asks if it is a disgrace to fail in business, Mr. Isaacs advises him "It vos better to have failed undt lost den neffer to have failed at all." The Jewish business ethic could be summed up by a neat reversal of an old adage, "If at first you don't succeed, fail, fail again."[48]

Arson was the most common crime attributed to Jews in their quest for wealth. Although arrest reports of actual arsonists did not reveal any particular ethnic correlation, the comic culprits were invariably Burnhiemer, Burnstein, or even such fanciful names as Smokenstein, Blazanheimer, and Burnupsky (the Russian Jew). It is ridiculous when the tax man asks, "if you had any losses by fire vich vas not covered mit insurance," for, as Burnupski readily admits, the cause of the fire was "der insurance." It is also absurd to inquire how Cohenstein would get out of his apartment above his store in case of fire. Obviously "in case of fire I wouldn't be in." Even Satan does not faze the irrepressible firebug. Mr. "B. Elzebub, Esq." asks the new denizen of his kingdom what he thinks of the fire. "Grandt! Grandt!" the Jew replies, "I subbose, of course, you haf efert'ing covert mit insurance!"[49]

If the Jew had pretensions of being anything more than the humble (though wealthy) old-clothes dealer or pawnbroker, he was caricatured as the quintessential parvenu. A large *Life* carton entitled "Where oh Where are the Hebrew Children?" depicts obviously Jewish nouveaux-riches awkwardly attempting such evidently Anglo-Saxon pastimes as polo, golf, and tennis. A social upstart can only look foolish bedecked in pawned diamonds and suits. To the woman who wants a guarantee that the painting she is purchasing was really painted by Holbein, Ikenstein is reassuring, "Madam, I saw him paint it meinself, ven I vos a boy, in Chermany." Even in social climbing, monetary value is central. When the impeccably attired young man informs his grandfather that he made $50 trotting his horse, the old man responds, "Goot for you Chakey! Dot vos der vay to enchoy horseback riding."[50]

In spite of these jibes, there was some anxiety about the continued increase in Jewish wealth and the supposed Jewish control of important segments of the national economy. An indicative simile was "vunce he vas as poor as a church mouse undt now he is as rich as a—as a—" "As a synagogue mouse." *Puck* was rather genial in contemplating imminent Jewish dominance. Levy believes that Jews are rapidly monopolizing the business of the country. This prospect does not please Isaacs, who sadly remarks, "Soon dere vill pe nobody left dot ve can shtick." *Judge* was far more perturbed by this prospect. A two-page cartoon depicted the "Ceremony of taking down the last sign of the Christians in New Jerusalem (Formerly New York)." The sign, "John Smith and Co." is replaced by "Moses Eichstein Son, a Levy," as a joyful Jewish crowd, including the "Pawnbrokers Union," looks on. The Jew will replace the flag with a "symbolic three balls," and the word, "monish." Washington will become "Jewville." Working girls will be "sold to the highest bidder." *Life* was equally alarmed. Not only was the Jew advancing in business, but he was becoming all too prominent in the press as well, as exemplified by Joseph Pulitzer. Another cartoon of New York City of the future depicts the metropolis as entirely Jewish. Businesses have such headings as "Cafe P. J. O'Cohenstein," "The Garrickheimer Theater," and "Cohen by the Sea."[51]

Similar attempts at humor, featuring broad ethnic stereotypes, could be found in other popular books and periodicals. Almanacs issued by Ayers and Hostetter, patent medicine purveyors, showed the Jewish peddler attempting to sell all kinds of items to credulous rural customers. Supposedly more "serious" periodicals like *Harper's* reported similar tales to their readers. Getting the best of the shrewd calculating Jew was a popular theme in Western humor. Thus, a Jewish tailor in early Milwaukee who was "noted for his sharpness in trade" stood at his door "watching for a chance to beat somebody with a shoddy coat." A brawny lumberman teaches him a lesson by putting on an offered pair of pants, picking up Samuel, carrying him into the gutter, and rolling over with him "until they both resembled a third ward porker just out of a mud-bath."[52]

There is no question that humorous publications were the most consistent disseminators of Jewish stereotypes. Yet even here, there was considerably more ambiguity than is usually conceded. An early example poked fun at Christian efforts to convert the Jews. At a meeting of the American Society for Ameliorating the Condition of the Jews, "John Donkey," suggests "ameliorating the conditions of the Five Points" and other people "whose condition both morally and physically demanded more attention than the Jews." The Society advertises a "real live reformed Jew" who will eat "a pound of pork sausages and a real ham."[53]

Even in pieces containing some negative comments, positive images of Jews might be presented as more significant. *California Mailbag* ran a poem about a widow who attended the "'Ebrew Benevolent Ball." The first part of the verse poked fun at the parvenu tendencies of some wealthy Jews. However, the widow concludes:

> But this I vill say, that the 'Ebrews is kind
> to the poor and friendless and let Christians bear in mind
> Ven they gets into debt and their rent hoverdoo
> The only vun with money to 'elp is the Jew,
> And but for circumcision and sleepin' in the boosum
> Of Abraham before 'alf the Christians I'd choose 'em.[54]

Puck was the most striking of the humor magazines in its ambivalence toward the Jews.[55] *Puck*'s explanation was, "We have never made fun of the Jews as a race or of their religion. We have made fun of the follies and absurdities of Jews, just as we have made fun of the follies of Christians and atheists." *Puck* consistently followed a liberal policy on the issue of exclusion of Jews by hotels and resorts. When Hilton announced his prohibition against Jews in Saratoga, "A Jews of a Row," a series of satirical interviews, exposed the absurdity of his policy. Mrs. Wilkins declares, "I only wish that besides excluding Jews, he'd kept out professional actors . . . I never could bear to be cheek to jowl with the common classes." Dr. Mary Walker did not like the fit of the Jews' clothes, but "between the Jews and Judge Hilton, I think I would much rather have the Jews." A cartoon depicted "The Christian (?) Sentiment Rampant." An obviously drunken member of the "Hog Family" complains, "Say ish them Jewsh shtoppin in thish hotel?" The clerk replies apologetically, "Yes, but they're very wealthy and highly respectable. . . ." Indignantly, the drunk announces, "Make out my bill! I can't live alongsider Jewsh. Ash a Chrisn'n gen'lm'n, I can't shtand 'em."

When Corbin announced a similar policy of exclusion on Coney Island,

Puck produced an interview with Moses in heaven. Moses reminds the reader, "Der fact is, I vas a Shoo myself . . . see dem hook in dot nose. . . ." Moses remarks that the Jew goes with his family and "don' droubbles nobodies." A large cartoon showed Bismarck, Hilton, and Corbin all prosecuting the Jew who stands in the middle with "sobriety, industry, music, sciences." The triumphant Jew announces, "I have thriven on this sort of thing for eighteen centuries. Go on gentlemen. Persecution helps de Pizness." In a humorous inversion, a Jewish hotel keeper declares that "he did not like Irishmen on principle. They came down to his hotel . . . with shillelaghs in their hands, broke one another's heads, spilt the blood over the place, much to the disgust of Mr. Cohen's German and Jewish guests." An 1881 editorial, with the usual mixture of sympathy and stereotype, noted that Mr. Moses Isaacs of Chatham Street might be a "sheeny," but "he vos a shaindelman un don' you forket it." *Puck* advised, "The sea, at least, is free to the downtrodden Hebrew."

Even *Life,* more consistently hostile, ran a cartoon poking fun at anti-Jewish snobbery. It shows a long-nosed bearded Jew in Heaven, carrying a key and sporting a large halo. As he passes by, he is observed by a group of Greek goddesses. Minerva comments, "Extraawdn'ry isn't it, my dear Juno, how the Jews get in everywhere."[56]

A long poem, which appeared in *Puck* in 1891, illustrated the typical dichotomy of viewpoints in popular journals. Here the Jew is clothing dealer, parvenu, and accumulator of the money he loves. Yet, he is also charitable, a good family man, and a kind human being:

> Child of torture, son of shame
> Robbed of even a father's name—
> In this year of Christian grace,
> What's your state and what's your place?
> Why you're rich and strong and gay—
> Chakey Einstein ouff Broadway . . .
>
> Fat and rich you are and loud;
> Fond of being in a crowd . . .
> Fond of life and fond of fun.
> (Once your "beezness" wholly done.)
> Open-handed, generous, free
> Full of Christian charity:
> Far more full than him who pokes
> At your avarice his jokes.
> Fond of friends and ever kind
> to the sick and lame and blind;
> (And though loud you else may be
> Silent in your charity;)
> Fond of Mrs. Einstein and
> Her too numerous infant band.

Ever willing they should share
Your enjoyment everywhere . . .

Though you're spurned in some hotels,
You have kin among the swells—
Great musicians, poets true
Painters, singers not a few
Owe their cousinship to you . . .

Well good friend we look at you
And behold the conquering Jew . . .

The ultimate fate *Puck* predicted for "trade's uncrowned king" was, however, in keeping with its basic philosophy, thoroughly assimilationist. Solomon, the first-born son of "Chakey Einstein ouff Broadway," will eventually wed a Christian blue blood, trading his money for her name, "as sure as day is day." A cartoon in the same issue was entitled, "They are the People, the Downtrodden Ones—'They have always Persecuted Us; But we Get There All the Same.'" Various rulers, down to Russia's current Czar, are portrayed passing laws aimed against Jews. In the middle, in triumph, stands a rich Broadway Jew.[57] In spite of all the stereotypes, there was a widespread admiration, even in the humor magazines, for the ability of the Jew to overcome terrible obstacles and succeed in the world.

There can be little doubt that humorous periodicals tended to reinforce existing stereotypes of the Jew as a human being to whom the measure of all things was money, a man who would often use discreditable means in his unremitting pursuit of wealth. On the other hand, these caricatures did not demonstrate any real rancor or fear. The overstatements joined a myriad of stereotypes directed at other foreign and alien groups. As John Appel has pointed out, many of these images were just as contradictory in nature. Thus, one could find diabolically clever, wise, and tractable Chinese and "good-natured darkies who became lustful beasts."[58] A contemporary writer noted, "From the commingling of heterogeneous customs and languages we shall have a medley full of fun, loud, large uproarious and rollicking in exaggerations."[59] The contrast with European humor is particularly striking. The Jew was the incarnation of the devil, the source of much of the evils of modern society, in European caricature. The Jew was "mocked, reviled and cursed, never really laughed off."[60] In American humor the Jew was more laughable than dangerous, for the most part. (After all, what great damage can be done by an ill-fitting suit?) Unlike the devil image, he was a rational human being who, unfortunately, may have used his reason to promote his acquisitiveness. This kind of calculated grasping might well be essential in capitalist America. To some extent, the criticism of the materialism of the Jew was also a critique of American society, which seemed to accept many of his values. The fre-

quent comparison of the Jew to the Yankee, an original American, under-
lined this point. The pursuit of wealth was, after all, endemic to the America
of the Gilded Age. The image of the Jew was more of a challenge to the
presumed values of the humorist than that of the other ethnic stereotypes.
One can hardly come away with the impression that many of the cartoonists
or humorists feared the evil satanic Jew who, however, obsessed Europe.

Popular image makers from whom the average American received his
picture of the Jew often reiterated preexisting stereotypes of the Jew as
money hungry. Yet the Jews were not the first or only group to be subject to
prejudice or caricature. The Mexicans, for example, were lazy, scoundrels
who would "steal anything that was not nailed down." The Irish were
irrational, dim-witted drunkards. The "deadly violence" of the Italians was a
commonplace of popular fiction and magazines, with its "specter of the
stiletto, imported terrorism and blood-lust." The Chinese were a serious
threat to the melting pot, "filthy and loathsome" with perverted sexual
proclivities and an innate craftiness and cruelty, a "dwarfish race of inferior
beings."[61] The Jew was only one part of this ethnic stereotype network. The
other groups were often treated far more brutally in print. More positive
countervailing images of the Jew were presented. Indeed, it could be argued
that the rational, calculating Jew would be of definite value in an expanding
capitalist society. The lack of heat in most of the popular sources was also in
striking contrast to Europe. Nevertheless, the main image of the Jew was that
of an economic creature, an image that has proven to be remarkably per-
sistent.

4

The Press and Periodicals

OF ALL IMAGE MAKERS, THE DAILY PRESS AND MORE SERIOUS MAGAZINES were, perhaps, the most schizophrenic in their treatment of Jews. Positive and negative pictures could often be found in one journal, sometimes in the same issue. This profound dichotomy could be discerned in the treatment of issues concerning Jews, in attitudes toward famous Jews, and in "human interest" coverage. The overall picture was at once somewhat hostile and warmly favorable.

Issues concerning American Jews arose only occasionally. The infrequency of such issues was indicative of the lack of any really deep tensions. The ways in which the press handled such issues were further manifestations of the attitudes toward Jews in America.

The Jew as Firebug

A brief but sensational incident in 1867 concerned the refusal of several insurance companies to write fire insurance policies for Jewish-owned firms. The *Banking and Insurance Chronicle,* a Chicago-based trade publication, reported that the general agent of New York insurance companies, in a circular to local agents, detailed heavy losses in the South and West on Jewish properties and indicated that the companies would be compelled to "decline all such risks."[1] A protest meeting was held. The publication felt that the agent should receive a "scathing rebuke." As a class, Jews are "intelligent, fair dealing and at the same time, a law-abiding and thrifty people. That they have rascals among them is no more the fact—nor more damaging—than we find the same kind of men among the different religious denominations." One could find "representatives of the Hebrew race" among the leading men of business in the principal cities. They sustained no more or larger losses, but, "being careful men, they are always insured." Other nationalities were simply more reckless. This did not imply fraud or collusion.

A few weeks later the *Chronicle* reported an indignation meeting in Richmond, Virginia. Mayor Mays, an insurance man himself, noted that most of his dealings were with Jews. He gave "testimony to the uprightness and honesty of their conduct." In the same issue, however, an insurance underwriter discussed the "Jew risk." The truth was that "Jews as a class have blustered and swindled the insurance companies." He quoted the city fire marshal of Hartford, who had warned, "it is better to decline risks for the 'lost tribe' unless for an individual or firm whose good character and honesty have been established. . . ." In response, the *Chronicle* urged Jews not to be discouraged "because a few black sheep have been discovered in their fold. The world at large will not condemn them." The *Insurance Monitor,* a New York publication, was far less sympathetic, decrying protests by respectable Jews acting as "champions of men with whom as individuals they would have no dealing whatever." It was foolish to call realistic actions an affront to any religion.

Newspapers were divided on the issue.[2] The *New York Tribune* was sympathetic to the Jews. The *New York Herald,* on the other hand, insisted that no insurance company had "refused to insure any respectable merchant." There was a class of swindlers who took out large insurance policies and then were "conveniently burnt out." It seemed that "an unusual proportion of this class are men of the Jewish race . . . this perhaps is the development that roguery has taken in that financiering race." Jewish leaders should expose the criminals. The *Evening Post* ran many letters from protesting Jews and a response from the president of the Metropolitan Insurance Company. He claimed that German Jewish small businessmen "of no known social standing or pecuniary responsibility" were making fraudulent claims, backed up by "witnesses of like faith." The class distinctions between scrambling small "Jew businessmen" and respectable upper-class "Hebrew merchants" was an interesting subsidiary aspect of the dispute, as was the frequent assertion that Jews would lie for each other.

The *Philadelphia Sunday Dispatch* published one of the strongest editorials opposing insurance company actions and vigorously defending the Jews. The companies were guilty of "persecution . . . utterly unworthy of the present age and country." While Jews might "have a proverbial reputation for close dealing," Christian merchants were "fully as ready to drive a hard bargain." Jews stuck to the bargains they made. "We can bear testimony to their integrity as merchants . . . and to their general refinement and intelligence. . . ." Jews were rarely accused of crimes, never required society to support their paupers and "have among them some of the most learned men of the day. . . ." Unfortunately, "the peculiarities of the Hebrew religion" tended to separate the Jews somewhat from other citizens. Many people, knowing little about them, might take the actions of the insurance companies as indicative of Jewish untrustworthiness, a charge "without foundation."

The immediate dispute over insurance quickly died down, but the image of the Jew as arsonist persisted. The *American Israelite* was troubled in 1873 by a story in the Pennsylvania *Lawrenceburg Press* in which an innocent Jew was suspected of an attempt to burn the town down. The New York *Police Gazette* reported that German Jews were receivers of stolen goods and found it difficult to get insurance "because of the frequency with which fires occur in their stores and the suspicious circumstances attending them." In 1890 the *Boston Herald* took note of the fire marshal's report that 76 percent of the city's arsonists were Polish or Russian Jews. (Note the change in the fatherland of the accused Jews.) Insurance provided an incentive for illegal gains "in the minds of people whose standard of morality is low, blunted no doubt by long years of persecution in their native land." The problem was not the ordinary Hebrew, but "the lower class of Polish and Russian Jews, many of whom were criminals before they came to this country." (Again, the class distinction.) One insurance man remarked, "There seems to be something in their religion that teaches them there is nothing dishonorable in cheating Christians."[3] By the 1890s this image had become so deeply ingrained that it was a major source of material in the humor magazines. The image of the Jewish businessman setting fire to his own investment to make a quick profit has persisted to the present time.

Hilton, Corbin, and the Jewish Parvenu

The issue that excited the most comment from the press was the "Sensation at Saratoga." In June 1877 Joseph Seligman, a leading banker of German Jewish background, was refused admittance at his usual summer watering hole, the Grand Hotel in Saratoga. The order came from the executor of the Stewart estate and soon-to-be hotel magnate, Judge Hilton. Seligman was informed that the guests would stop coming if the Grand Hotel was frequented by "colonies of the Jewish people" who made themselves "obnoxious to the majority of guests." The hotel manager explained that upper-class Jews brought guests from low boarding houses who monopolized the best chairs for shows. "Old customers stood while a shoemaker or tailor from Chatham Street occupied prime seats. They also intruded on conversations where they were not welcome and wore large and vulgar jewelry. . . ." An interview with Judge Hilton revealed a great deal of animosity toward Seligman, who had been a political opponent. He characterized Seligman as a man who "owes some of his most vaunted offices to the practice of the veriest Shylockian meanness." The Seligman Jew could be distinguished from the Hebrew. "He is to the Hebrew what the Shyster is to the law profession—he is the 'Sheeny.'" Both his origins and instincts are low even though he advertises his wealth. "He is as audacious as he is vulgar." He prepares himself for the next day of gluttony "by ridding himself of his tortured load all over the furniture with groans at its loss that disturb every decent person."

Such Jews cause contempt for the Hebrew race. Other hotel keepers in the area disagreed, commenting that they had among their guests "a large number of excellent Hebrew people." One noted that "we take all the Jews we can get," since no Jew ever left an unpaid bill.[4]

The incident monopolized headlines for a week. The practice, now brought to the public's attention, was not new, however. In this 1868 New York guide book, Matthew Hale Smith described a new hotel, built by leading families on the express condition that Jews were not allowed. "Every means has been resorted to by the people of Israel to get rooms in this hotel and fabulous prices offered," but none was admitted. "A half dozen would drive away all who were not of Israel."[5] A year before the Seligman incident the *New York Tribune* had run an advertisement by a resort proprietor warning, "Jews not admitted." When a Jew wrote to complain, the paper replied editorially, "It is hardly wise for Hebrews to be so extremely sensitive. They certainly do not wish to go to a hotel which does not desire their presence, or, if they do, they have odd notions of self-respect." The *American Israelite* decried the commotion over the Seligman incident since "the same thing has been done, said and published dozens of times." Houses for rent routinely said, "Jews can't have it." The only difference was that in this case "money-bags collide." Jews should stay away from these watering places, which were "pools of corruption," the *Israelite* advised. These prejudices against foreign Jews was directed against the "moneyed aristocracy" in Eastern cities.[6] Although it seemed that this form of social discrimination was not uncommon, the Seligman incident obviously brought it to the public's attention.

Discussions of the incident occupied the editorial pages of many newspapers.[7] Most of the comment was in condemnation of Hilton's actions. The *New York Herald* paid particular attention to the event. Its first editorial was headed, "Have Israelites Any Rights which Hotel Keepers are Bound to Respect?" An action like Hilton's might have been tolerated when Jews were "a proscribed class," but it is not acceptable in "this liberal and enlightened period." Jews had made advances in every walk of life, "finance especially," and in "the munificent foundation of great public charities." Any attempt to revive old prejudices was "a revolting anachronism," an affront to the freedom of America and a violation of the Civil Rights Act. A second editorial stressed that Jews were very successful in America "since the battle is free and it is quality and capacity that win." The *Herald* also feared that the issue involved not merely whether hotel keepers could refuse Jews, "but the framework of society itself."

Other New York publications expressed similar, although somewhat less vehement, opinions. The *Evening Post* felt that the "proscriptive spirit" of the order would not be tolerated. Hotel keepers could not reject guests out of pure whim. The nation had fought a war against mistreatment of a race "who

was honestly believed by a large number of citizens to be an inferior race."
Could people tolerate the barring of "a race whose equality with the foremost
races in the intellectual and moral activities of civilization is nowhere dis-
puted?" The very upper-class *Commercial Advertiser* demanded to know
whether the "colored population" had rights that whites lacked. It was true
that, "among a certain class of Christians," there was prejudice against Jews
which showed itself "like hydrophobia during the dog days." Most Americans, however, opposed "any attempt to draw the line of distinction between
Christians and Jews. The day of caste and prejudice has passed." The *New
York Sun* noted that Jews had become an important element in the population. At a time when England, with all her prejudices, had a man of Jewish
birth for prime minister (Disraeli), "this eccentric action of Mr. Hilton in
excluding Jews where Negroes must be admitted," was certainly illogical.
Later the *Sun* commented, "Nearly the entire community has shown its
readiness to stand up for the rights of our Jewish fellow citizens." It was
evident that if Hilton did not stand alone, "his party must be very small
indeed."

The *Daily Graphic* editorialized that Jews in America had been free from
the "unjust discrimination, oppressive laws and social ostracism" common in
Europe. As a result of hard work and "keen business instinct," they had
prospered. Except for "a cast of features which nothing but centuries of
intermarriage" would change, the average American Jew could hardly be
recognized in company. The *Graphic* did make some concessions to the views
of the more prejudiced, with the usual explanation of why Jews had traits that
were disagreeable to most Americans and were excessively sharp in business
dealings. This offensiveness was the natural result of persecution, "the Jew
has been on the stone until his brain is as keen as a knife blade. Driven out of
society, he lacks the fine manners and gentle ways which come from centuries
of good breeding." Still the Jews had made great contributions to science,
art, literature, and religion, so "we must be just to such a people with such a
history."

The *New York Tribune* displayed even more ambiguity in its condemnation
of Hilton's actions. The paper responded sarcastically to Hilton's complaints
about the "vulgar ostentation" of the Jews. "As these vices are quite unknown
to Christian society, we may now congratulate ourselves that at least one
hotel . . . will be a little paradise of refined simplicity and an academy of good
breeding." However, since a gentleman never went where he was not
wanted, Jews should not become oversensitive. A later editorial reflected
upon the decline of fashionable places due to the influx of the class of people
Hilton had described. Seligman did not belong to that class, but it did exist.
Hilton's error was in stigmatizing the Jews since, "both the old faith and the
new provide their full contingent of underbred and overdressed men and
women who make life hideous at watering places." As the incident dragged

on, the *Tribune* lost patience with the Jewish viewpoint. The incident was not related to religious persecution, which was impossible in this country, the paper argued. It was the result of the lack of social affinity between Hebrew and Anglo-Saxon. "Nature is to blame . . . the peculiarities of different civilizations . . . have increased this dislike between the two races." In addition, Jews were "naturally of a clannish disposition," congregating in the same hotels, affecting business. Many hotels had to choose between excluding them or catering to Jews alone.

Most of the newspapers and periodicals throughout the country also expressed indignation. *Harper's Weekly* felt that Hilton's actions was "monstrous," illegal, and morally and socially wrong. At least the responses showed "how sincere and universal is the protest against the indulgence of a race prejudice against white skins." The *Philadelphia Bulletin* and the *Cleveland Leader* agreed that intolerance was condoned only by "vulgar beggars of yesterday mounted on horseback by shoddy or petroleum." Other papers were confident that the persecution of Jews would fail in our democracy where it ran counter to the principles "upon which our institutions are based." It was a return to medieval attitudes. Several editors praised the Jews as "in many respects the most remarkable people on the face of the earth." The *Albany Journal,* for example, felt that any group that could boast of Mendelsohn, Meyerbeer, Rothschild, Disraeli, and Rubinstein "can smile superior at the vulgar slight of a hotel keeper." A few papers agreed with the *Elmira Gazette* that it was time Congress looked beyond the "poor negro" to see if there was need of legislation to "insure the rights of a white man." The *Providence Journal* concluded that any hotel keeper who refused accommodations to a man because he was a follower of any one religion "is not likely to be overburdened with sensible guests." The *Chicago Tribune* concluded that any social prejudice against Jews could be traced to women, "for there is not one man in a hundred who cherishes any feeling against any other man or woman on account of race or religion."

Other papers were more ambivalent, stressing the financial power of the Jews or their vulgarity, even while denying the validity of Hilton's order. The *Washington Nation* was worried that if the insult was believed to be the beginning of persecution in America, "the Rothschilds would withdraw from the syndicate and oppose American credit in Europe . . . for the Jews are as clannish as the ancient Scots." The *Fitchberg Sentinel* argued that as long as "the scrawl of a Jew on the back of a piece of paper is worth more than the royal word of three kings, it will be in vain to try and limit them to two dollar hotels." The *Springfield Union* was even more equivocal in its defense of the Jews. Although firmly declaring that it was ridiculous to shut hotels to Jews when they had just been opened to "colored men," the paper conceded that rich New York Jews had filled Saratoga hotels to the annoyance of those "prejudiced against the chosen people not on account of their religious beliefs

... but because of their vulgarity." The *Philadelphia Times* dismissed the whole episode as a quarrel between two men whose only claim to distinction was money and whose only craving was for notoriety.

There were even a few published defenses of Hilton. The *New York Times* ran several letters to the editor stressing the unpleasant character of the Jewish parvenu. Hilton's views, they argued, were the same held by most "respectable Gentiles" that the Jew is disgusting, obtrusive, gaudy, insolent, unclean, and afflicted with "petty avarice." The Jewish race would not have been hated by every race with which it has had contact "unless there was something inherently disagreeable in the people itself." Similar views were expressed by the *Harrisburg Daily Telegraph,* which declared that the Jew had brought a stigma upon himself as a "boor and an upstart."

Most commentators, however, were firmly opposed to Hilton. Despite this, and despite an effective Jewish boycott of the Stewart department store (also administered by Hilton), the policy of exclusion was not withdrawn. Gradually, it spread. Two years later a similar story broke when Austin Corbin, proprietor of Manhattan Beach, announced that Jews were not welcome. He was evidently upset by the large numbers of Jews who came with families and picnic lunches, rather than buying food and beverages from him. Corbin claimed that Jews were driving away the better class of customers since they were "a detestable and vulgar people." This time the public appeared to be more divided by the "attempted ostracism." The *Herald* pointed out that, unlike the Saratoga case, this affected the mass of middle-class people. Many hotel owners and private citizens were interviewed. One admitted that there was widespread prejudice against Jews, "although it is not as deep-seated as the Jewish prejudice against Christians. They refuse to allow their children to marry Christians. Why should they complain if Christians refuse to associate with them?" The *Herald* found that "the clannishness of the Hebrew was one feature that militated against them." Several of the hotel men, however, disagreed with Corbin. One insisted that Jews were the "money-makers, the money-holders and the money-spenders." An innkeeper who believed that most Jews were well-behaved and welcomed them added, nevertheless, that there was a class of Jews obnoxious not only to "Americans," but to "the cultivated and refined people of their own race."

Most of the New York newspapers again supported the Jewish position.[8] The *Herald* felt that Corbin's act was particularly mean. The Jews were superior citizens. The usual litany—the lack of Jewish criminals and paupers, the thrift and charity of the Jews—was recited. The *Sun* concluded that no true Christian wanted to punish Jews. "The whole genius of American institutions is opposed to tyrannical exclusion." At any rate, "a man might as well oppose Niagara" as to try to keep down the Jews. The *Commercial Advertiser,* true to its class attitudes, argued that Corbin had attacked a large group of people "who are no better and no worse than any other class or race." Coney Island would continue to attract the rude and boisterous as "noisy as the worse Jew from Division Street" and the refined, "among whom there are none more cultivated or elegant than the educated Jew." The *Evening Post* was more seriously disturbed. If a class of people could be excluded from one public place, it could be excluded from another. Eventually, it could be excluded from all public places and from the United States itself. There must be equality before the law or we must "give up the radical doctrines of our political system. . . ." Today it might be the Jew, tomorrow someone else. This was a rare and interesting attempt to relate private and public discrimination.

The German press was particularly outspoken against Corbin's activities. The *New Yorker Zeitung* blamed "our better classes so called" for permitting demonstrations like of Hilton and Corbin. The more radical *New Yorker Volks Zeitung* felt sorry for the poor Jews who had escaped the "hepp, hepp!" cries of Europe, only to find the worst kind of banishment in civilized America. Religious prejudice was at the bottom of this. "One of the principle traits of Americanism is its Christian hypocrisy." This led to attacks on the Jews "notwithstanding all the cant about their boasted tolerance." The paper castigated the leaders of American society, "The railroad thieves, the Wall Street speculators" who didn't like Jews.

Some other New York newspapers were considerably more ambivalent.[9] The *Evening Mail* felt that the Jewish race would eventually gain recognition for its great qualities while "those whose manners brought odium may be driven into more retired places for their manifestations and held in check by the better classes of their own people." The *Times* was annoyed that "the perennial Jewish controversy is upon us in all its original silliness and virulence." Most Jews, the paper noted wryly, would oblige Corbin by staying away, leaving him to detect vulgarity in other races. On the other hand, the paper conceded that Jews were not in the habit of doing things by halves "and when they take to imitating a certain class of American society they decidedly distance the originals." It was the very people whose own loudness and tawdry displays were most exaggerated by "the coarser type of Jew" who complained most noisily about "Hebrew vulgarity."

The *Brooklyn Daily Eagle* was even more equivocal. The *Eagle* felt that there had never been a time in the history of America when there was less inclination to persecute any race or religion: "such is the manly temper of our times." Although Jews had distinguished themselves in "every department of human effort," this had nothing to do with the livelihood of hotel keepers. They claimed that Jews were "clannish," which was even more annoying at summer resorts where people relax and the young go to meet each other. "The fact that those of the Jewish faith intermarry only among themselves" took them out of the stock of eligibles and led them to be regarded as intruders. This distinction was made by Jews themselves and it "leads to others." Leading Jews should encourage "the rights of others in their social intercourse" if they wished to avoid problems.

Other periodicals opposed Corbin's pronouncements far more vigorously.[10] *Puck,* a consistent supporter of Jewish rights despite its unflattering cartoons, wrote of "Corbin's boomerang." He had tried to suppress the Jews. "This little feat has been attempted in many countries for many centuries but at latest accounts it had not succeeded." It went against all the principles of America. There were Ludlow Street Jews who might be "nasty," but there were also Jews on Fifth Avenue. "When the admission to a public place depends on the shape of one's nose, liberty lies bleeding." The *Nation* noted wryly that Corbin's main complaint appeared to be that Jews sat at tables too long, smoked cheap cigars, and didn't drink enough; "so that, apparently, a little more fondness for the promenade, greater extravagance in the consumption of tobacco and a decided disposition to get drunk would go far to redeem them in his eyes." *Harper's Magazine* felt that Jews were not excluded because they were vulgar, "but because they are Jews." This was blatant race prejudice, "a relic of barbarism," unworthy of American Christians. The whole issue stemmed from the crucifixion. "Men of no Christian principles whatsoever flout better men today because other men murdered the founder of Christianity."

Despite the fact that there had undoubtedly been exclusion of Jews from hotels before the Hilton and Corbin incidents, most newspapers and magazines appeared genuinely shocked. With few exceptions, the general view was that this was contrary to American ideals. Jewish contributions to civilization were often cited in response to exclusion. Unless one supposes a universal hypocrisy, this social proscription was not a practice the public knew much about. Initially, the opposition to such exclusion, at least in the press, was virtually unanimous. Many of the Jews' defenders did concede the presence of the supposedly objectionable traits that were the targets of the hotel men. Some urged Jews to ignore those hotels which barred them or to reform "vulgar" characteristics. As time went on, exclusion from hotels, fashionable and otherwise, and justification of such practices, became more acceptable. By the 1880s social ostracism was widely recognized, and by the 1890s it was considered a given factor in social relationships. The Seligman incident may not have introduced anti-Semitism to America, as some observers have suggested, but it did bring to the fore the image of the Jew as arriviste parvenu.

According to the *New York Mail* in 1880, the first thing that visitors to Long Beach noticed was the preponderance of Jews. One hotel was "thronged with Israelites. The women wear fine clothes and big diamonds and the men dispute their bills. . . ." When the Jews first came "it was an evil day for Long Beach." Just as oil and water could not mix, "no more will Jews and gentiles." Such sentiments led to "numerous announcements of summer hotel-keepers . . . refusing to receive Jews." A New York legislator then introduced a bill prohibiting distinctions in public places. The *Nation*, in May 1881, hoped that he would not press the measure. The worst advice to Jews would be to "push" more. Jewish energy ought, instead, to be "devoted to cultivation of the arts of which social success depends, and the art of making one's way into circles where one is not wanted is not among the number." *Puck*, at the same time, featured a cartoon captioned "A Hint to the Hebrews—How they May Make Themselves Independent of the Watering Place Hotels." It showed the "Hotel de Jerusalem" right off the beach, with a large-nosed guest thumbing his nose at the signs on the beach—"No Jews Taken," and "Look Out for the Jew."[11]

By September 1881 *North American Review* featured an article entitled "Jewish Ostracism in America," by Nina Morais, a member of an established Philadelphia Sephardic family. Despite his temperance and patriotism, the Jew was a victim of social prejudice that stigmatized him as objectionable. He was perceived as a shrewd dealer who wore diamonds and "flashy clothes." He was uncultured, obsessed by money, "the finer features he cannot appreciate. In a word, he is foreign—outlandish—a Jew." Ms. Morais conceded that most rich American Jews did not display culture commensurate with their wealth. With his "mercantile aptitude," the Jew rose too rapidly, "bewildered by the privileges which the almighty dollar would purchase" and having little contact with American culture. The real source of the prejudice, she felt, however, was the "abysmal ignorance of the Christian world regarding the Jew." The supposed exclusiveness of the Jew was only an excuse. People urged intermarriage, but this would "remove prejudice by doing away with the object." Eventually, she hoped, Christians would realize that the Hebrew race is "celebrated for its culture."[12]

Alice Hyneman Rhine wrote an article called "Prejudice at Summer Resorts" for *The Forum* (1887). Newspapers ten years before, she reminded her readers, had denounced Hilton and assumed such prejudices "could only have a momentary existence." But the predictions proved to be incorrect. Hotels, and even boardinghouse owners, had followed the Saratoga example, and it was now considered the "genteel thing" to refuse to accept Jews. The excuses were that Jews lacked "social refinement," and were at once "ostentatious and parsimonious." This was a reflection of Christian ignorance, which had its roots in the Jews' "terrible responsibility for the crucifixion." Actually, the picture of Jewish ill-breeding "represents the newly rich of all creeds." In fact the real "money kings of America," the great monopolists, were Christians. Most Jews were kindly, forgiving people, "too sensible" to show displeasure. Ms. Rhine predicted that, with their versatility and capacity, Jews would acquire refined dress, "modulated tones of voice," and drawing room etiquette. She was pessimistic that Christian attitudes would improve with greater Jewish refinement, however. She concluded, "For the obliteration of a prejudice so unjust the Israelite can only look forward to a time when a broader culture shall prevail among his Christian fellow-men."[13]

By 1893 Theodore Seligman, son of Jesse Seligman (and nephew of the Joseph Seligman in the Hilton incident), was blackballed when he sought membership in the Union League Club, of which his father was cofounder. Since the Seligmans were a respected and extremely wealthy German Jewish family, "race feeling" was the openly discussed reason for the exclusion.[14] The *New York Herald* labeled the action as "Indefensible. Anti-Semitic Prejudice Unchristian and Unworthy of the Nineteenth Century." Dr. Charles Parkhurst, the well-known reformer, charged that the blackballers would have excluded Moses! The *Evening Post,* however, commented that prejudice kept Christians and Jews apart all over the country. "In fact, there is no social phenomenon of the day more familiar to all New Yorkers." The *Post* regretted the failure of Christians to associate with even well-bred Jews, but added that people should not try to fight their way into private dwellings where they were not wanted.

As the *Post* reflected further upon the causes of anti-Jewish exclusion, it became involved in an interesting exchange of views with the *New York Sun.* The *Post* felt that prejudice was brought on by the Jews themselves in their "failure to cultivate the social arts . . . and neglect of the importance trifles which go to make a social acceptableness." Foremost among these was "abstention from small and tempting advantages." In effect, the accusation was that Jews were obnoxious parvenus. The *Sun* responded that "such a generalization applied to a whole race, the most ancient in civilization, is manifestly false." Through history, numerous Jews were distinguished in social tact and grace. Yet social antipathy to the Jews had survived through the centuries. The *Sun* accepted the widely held upper-class view that antagonism resulted from the self-separation of the Jews. The paper agreed with anti-Semites that Jews would not become socially acceptable "until they had abandoned the rites and prejudices which separate them from the rest of mankind and tend to perpetuate their own characteristics." Unlike other immigrants who quickly became Americans, losing their "race identity," Jews retained this identity undiminished. The "Jewish face and character remain the same as they were in the days of the Pharoah." Although, in reality, German Jews like the Seligmans were thoroughly assimilated, the *Sun* concluded that prejudice depended on "whether the Jews will sacrifice their Judaism to their desire for social acceptableness. As long as they keep by themselves, they will be left to themselves socially."

Six years later the *Sun* again concluded that Jews provoked fear and enmity by striving to perpetuate their special characteristics. Whether deliberately or not, the *Sun* misinterpreted a rabbi's explanation of the concept of mission or "chosenness." It warned that if Jews persisted in such assertions "they must be prepared to accept the consequences . . . continued and unconquerable anti-semitic prejudice." Here was a frank endorsement of a widely held American view—assimilate or be damned—carried to its ultimate conclusion. On the other hand, the *Tribune*, which appealed to a similar class audience, came to quite opposite conclusions. The Jew-hater followed a logic that "requires the Jew to remain aloof and distinct and then . . . curses him for so doing." The *Tribune* argued that "no man becomes more fully and loyally naturalized and more completely identified with his adopted country than the Jew." To exclude these "indomitable people" was to "affront the spirit" of the times.[15]

For the most part, periodicals tended to oppose anti-Semitic incidents in the United States and to support equality of treatment. Their defense of Jews, however, often reinforced the paradoxical perception of the Jew both as quintessential parvenu who pushed himself into places where he wasn't wanted and as clannishly aloof and unwilling to assimilate. The general acceptance of these images is confirmed by the social ostracism of the Jew, which was a general practice by the 1890s. Everyone agreed that a denial of political rights was un-American, but social exclusion had become tolerable. In the general uneasiness about the lack of culture and breeding among the American elite, the Jew provided a convenient scapegoat. The criticism of the Jewish parvenu was, in effect, also a criticism of American social values. Perhaps the Jews themselves, some periodicals concluded, had caused this "American" form of anti-Semitism.

Reaction to Famous Jews

One interesting barometer of the image of the Jew was the treatment accorded by the press to Jews who had reached some degree of prominence, either in America or on the world scene. In most cases, these men were admired rather than censured, adding to the positive image of the Jews.

Judah Touro was probably the earliest American Jew to present the picture of the Jew as unselfish philanthropist, one of the strongest positive Jewish roles. His contributions to save a local Presbyterian church led to favorable comments in *Niles*, as did his efforts on behalf of the restoration of the Newport synagogue. When he contributed $10,000, along with Amos Lawrence, to the building of a Bunker Hill monument, a poem by Oliver Wendell Holmes was read at the 1843 dedication, proclaiming "Christian and Jew . . . though of different faith, each is in heart a man." Touro's obituaries in 1854 contained lavish praise. The *New Orleans Delta* commented that humanity had lost "one of its truest friends." The *Bee* remarked that Touro was "a local and national hero, an exemplary Jewish philanthropist." Bertram Korn has suggested that Touro "contributed a benevolent portrait of 'the Jew' which contrasted forcefully with the distorted folk-image."[16]

Certainly the most flamboyant and controversial of the early Jews was

Mordecai M. Noah, politician, journalist, playwright, prophet, and person-ality, a genuine original. Early observers decried his "political corruption and want of veracity." *Niles Weekly Register* chided the "judge of Israel" for his "ridiculous" proclamation of a Hebrew settlement in New York. He was nothing more than an agent for foreign land speculators, "Jews themselves, perhaps, who have no sort of objection to advance their own wealth at the cost of their fellows." If they made money, one could expect a proclamation "that our brother-editor is self-declared to be at least, the immediate forerun-ner of the expected messiah!"[17]

The *New York Herald,* another long-time opponent of Noah, reported in 1840 that he delivered a discourse at the Crosby Street Synagogue on the subject of Sunday schools. The Jews were starting these schools to improve the morals of "the poor children of the tribe of Judah." The *Herald* was "glad to see such a sinner as Noah endeavoring to balance his accounts for the many lies and rogueries he has committed as a politician." If he succeeded in reforming "the morals of the old clothesmen in Chatham Street," he would deserve to be rewarded. "Go on Noah, God knows you are not too old to reform. . . ."[18]

In general, however, by the 1840s Noah was perceived as a grand old man and an interesting character. By 1844, *Niles,* a vigorous early opponent, was approvingly citing a letter from M. Noah, "whose enthusiasm upon the subject of Jewish restoration had been exhibited during his whole life." When Noah died in 1851 both the *Commercial Advertiser* and the *Evening Post* carried complimentary obituaries. The *Advertiser* noted that, although not a profound thinker, "he was a ready writer, with a good stock of practical knowledge and considerable humor." The *Post* added that he wrote with "unusual vivacity of manner" and "his cordial good nature gave him a large circle of warm friends."[19]

Later memories of Noah were even more affectionate. George Foster, who had written most unflatteringly of Jews in general, described "Major Noah" as the "patriarch of the Press," in his book *New York Naked.* At the end, "the old King of Israel" was over seventy, but his eyes had not lost their bright-ness. His death was mourned, "for in the attributes of husband, father and citizen, no stain of reproach rests upon his name." A memorial article in *Lippincott* magazine in 1868 remembered the gentleman "of the stock of Israel." The author recalled the elderly Noah assisting a "noble . . . pa-triarchal" rabbi who had come from Palestine to seek help at a time of famine. The writer concluded that Noah's "memory to me is pleasant . . . how happy would I be could I see his influence for the general weal yet alive and with us."[20] The reaction to a man of such controversial character was, of course, mixed. Opposition tended to be based upon his political activities, rather than his Judaism.

Judah Benjamin, in view of his important and visible position in the

Confederacy, was the frequent target of anti-Semitic remarks. Earlier, as Senator from Louisiana, he had been praised by the novelist Joseph Holt Ingraham in *The Sunny South* (1860). The young heroine of the book meets the friendly and talented Senator Benjamin. His election is a "practical illustration of the free institutions of our happy land, where theological disabilities are not known." Jews possessed an element of inherent greatness, "the blood of David and Isaiah, of Abraham and Solomon . . . their princely lineage is not extinct." Perhaps America would one day have a Jewish President, and that might well be Benjamin.[21] The passions aroused by the Civil War, however, led to far less flattering views of Benjamin. Anti-Semitic remarks were directed against him by Senator Henry Wilson and by the governor of Ohio. An article in *Harper's Magazine*, "Some Secession Leaders" (1863), characterized Benjamin, "Were you to meet him on Pennsylvania Avenue, you would rather take him for a peddler of jewelry or an old clothesman than for the . . . politician and brilliant orator he was."[22] Of the top Confederate leaders at the end of the Civil War, for whatever reason, only Benjamin felt the necessity of going into exile in England—much of the blame both for the war and for the South's defeat had been placed upon him.

By the 1880s, comments about the ex-Confederate leader had mellowed. Reporters often interviewed him in England where he was quite successful. Their reports were generally admiring in tone. The reporter for the *Philadelphia Record* in 1885 noted that both of Benjamin's parents had been "devoted adherents to the grand old religion of their fathers." Benjamin had always "retained his respect for his race," though married to a gentile, and never "identified with the Jewish church." Once, in Senate debate, he was taunted about being Jewish. " 'The Senator,' he said in his usual silvery way, 'will please remember that when his half-civilized ancestors were hunting wild boar in the forests of Silesia, mine were the princes of the earth.' "[23] (Another version of this undoubtedly apocryphal story was attributed to Disraeli.) When Benjamin died in 1885, the obituaries were long and, in spite of occasional speculation as to whether he had converted on his deathbed, generally fair.

August Belmont, the American representative of the house of Rothschild, was generally considered a Jew by the American press even though he had married into an aristocratic gentile family and severed all connections with the Jewish people. Although he was an Episcopalian, his appointment as American minister to The Hague was widely publicized as an honor given to American Jews. The Jewish newspaper, the *Asmonean*, indignantly rejected such an interpretation. Nevertheless, Belmont was not allowed to forget those origins he had worked so hard to surmount. In 1868 the treasurer of Pennsylvania wrote Belmont, "We are willing to give you the pound of flesh, but not one drop of Christian blood." Belmont responded that the treasurer was a disgrace to his state and his reply to a simple business communication "must raise the blush of shame on the cheek of every citizen. . . ." The *American Israelite,* reporting this exchange of letters, noted that the house of Rothschild would have been better served by a genuine Jew as its representative. When the mistreatment of Romanian Jews came to public attention, the *New York Times* suggested that such men as "August Belmont and other citizens of Hebrew origin who have risen to wealth and position in this country might cooperate" in solving the plight of Romanian Jews. Through his marriage, his snobbery, his horse racing, his art collection, and his political influence, August Belmont was able to win the acceptance in society which normally took three generations. The press, though certainly not hostile to him, was, however, unwilling to let him forget his origins.[24]

In 1893 *Frank Leslie's Illustrated Weekly* ran a series of sixteen articles on notable Jews in America. Written by a Jew, this series was extremely complimentary and informative about Jewish leaders who were not well known to the general public, such as Nathan Straus, Rabbi Solomon Schindler, and other judges, lawyers, businessmen, and rabbis. The author predicted a similar success for the new group of Russian immigrants.[25]

Foreign Jewish leaders, however, were the sources of far more comments than American Jews whose accomplishments were minimal compared to outstanding figures like the Rothschilds. Benjamin Disraeli was a popular topic for articles. Although he was a practicing Anglican, the press always considered him a Jew (with some justification, in view of his constant stress upon his Jewish ancestry and his writings glorifying his "race"). Disraeli was often cited as indicative of how far Jews had come in the present "enlightened" age. American articles about him were almost invariably laudatory, particularly stressing his brilliance. An *Atlantic Monthly* piece, for example, praised him as a descendant of the "pure sephardim stock; they were Hebrews of the Hebrews." Although Disraeli practiced Christianity, "so far from repudiating his race, he has always gloried in it. . . . He has made people understand that they do not insult him by calling him a Jew—they only pay him a compliment." An 1882 *Century* article anonymously contributed by Emma Lazarus discussed whether Disraeli was a representative Jew. He did possess the facility "which enables this people not only to perceive and make the most of every advantage of their situation . . . but also with marvelous adroitness to transform their very disabilities into instruments of power." The picture generally presented of Disraeli added to an image of the Jew as a man who accomplished great things in the modern world.[26]

Above all, American periodicals were fascinated by the Rothschilds. Populists, and other opponents of international capitalism, used the name "Rothschild" as an interchangeable symbol for international banker. In that context, the Jew was an iniquitous figure. Most of the American press, however, tended to blanket the family with a kind of "super-folklore." In a society in which money was king, there was a particular, and generally not hostile, attraction to the mythic Rothschilds.[27] In the early part of the century *Niles Weekly Register* took particular notice of the Rothschilds. In 1829 *Niles* reported a rumor that they had purchased Jerusalem. This was not improbable since they were "wealthy beyond the desire even of avarice." They might gather a large nation that could reach unimaginable heights under their direction. In 1835 *Niles* burst forth with a paean of praise to "the wonders of modern banking." The Rothschilds were "sprung from the poetic, that ancient, that mysterious race, from which we all derive our religion and half our civilization." Now they can be seen, "holding a whole continent in the hollow of their hands" and governing the Christian world. Baron Rothschild, "the true King of Judah," possessed "more force than David—more wisdom than Solomon." *Niles* was thrilled that "an accomplished and beautiful daughter" of the family had married an American and was planning to live in New York.

In many ways the Rothschilds came to symbolize the essence of capitalism, not in the manner of the buccaneering "robber baron," but with a reassuring stability that passed the fortune on from generation to generation in a never-ending chain. The power of the family was frequently acknowledged without rancor.[28] The *Philadelphia Times* declared in 1856, "Whoever may be king in Europe, Rothschild rules!" He was not the autocrat of Europe by money alone, but because of "Jewish genius . . . strong endurance, an indomitable will." As for Hebrews, "this is their age of action. All that is brilliant and dazzling will come from the Hebrew race." *Harper's Weekly* in 1882 featured "The Rothschilds." Their rise was a "remarkable chapter in the personal romance of business." Their founder was known for his integrity. He was "scrupulously upright," but "formidable." *Illustrated American,* in an 1891 series, "A Tale of Great Fortunes," stated that the rise of the Rothschilds was due to "thrift and patience and the watching of opportunities." There was no war, no political movement in Europe "but the Rothschilds, have had a hand in it." The *Nation* in 1900 hoped that the Rothschilds would use their power on behalf of oppressed Romanian Jews. They could prevent the Romanian government from borrowing money. "If the Jewish bankers will teach the Christian rulers a few lessons in elementary humanity by cutting off their financial supplies, it will be an application of the 'money power' which even the Byzantines might condone."

Many articles featured anecdotes about the Rothschilds or gossip about family activities.[29] Puncturing the pretensions of others or the awesome quality of the Rothschild fortune were favorite themes, as in an 1883 tale. Old Baron Rothschild was playing cards at the home of a marquis. The marquis accidentally dropped a louis on the floor and held up the game to search for it. The Baron, remarking that "a louis lost . . . is worth looking for," rolled up a thousand franc note, lighted it and held it to assist the Marquis d'Alegre in his search." Rothschilds marriages and deaths were conscientiously covered by many newspapers. The *New York Tribune* was especially fond of gossipy stories about various family members. An 1878 Rothschild wedding provided the occasion for a *New York Times* editorial. Jews had "never known so golden a period as the latter half of the nineteenth century." England's top leaders attended the wedding. "There can be no question that the Rothschilds have had a great deal to do with the rise of their race in public estimation."

Most observers stressed the positive contributions of the Rothschilds.[30] The *Spirit of the Times* in 1835 took note of Rothschild's friendship with Solomon Herschel, a noted rabbi. Rothschild was reported to have speculated at his own risk and presented the rabbi with the profit. An 1848 article on "The Late Mr. Rothschild," in the same publication, quoted several of his aphorisms about business as good examples for developing American capitalism. The family charities were the subjects of constant comment. *Harper's Weekly,* in 1857, reported that little homemade gifts had been "placed in an honorable eminence amidst the raid of glittering treasures" at a Rothschild wedding. They were the gifts of children at a Jewish charity school that had been aided by the family. "We love to think that in her girl's heart, the young Baroness Alphonse will value these little offerings of gratitude far higher than the costly contributions of the jewelers." The death of one of the Barons Rothschild in 1869 caused the *Overland Monthly* to comment on his generosity in trying to prevent famine in Russia and in founding hospitals, a synagogue, and in "many acts of charity among his own people." In a touching rite, any poor person who came to the house on the day of his death would be given coins and "an enormous sum of money was thus distributed." *Munsey's Magazine* in 1892 summarized the prevalent picture of the Rothschilds. No family had ever existed "whose history has been so prominent and so romantic." The integrity of the founder was legendary. On his deathbed he blessed his sons and enjoined them "to remain faithful to the Law of Moses." He was a noble, kindhearted man who could not refuse a beggar. Modern financial conditions, the author concluded, made it unlikely that "another such family of financiers will again rise."

The Rothschilds had come to stand, in many minds, for the positive virtues of modern capitalism. They used their wealth wisely and charitably, and exemplified the family virtues Americans prized. This image was more widely disseminated than the negative one of conspiratorial international financier. On balance, the Rothschild image added to the positive picture of the Jew, although it did reinforce illusions of enormous Jewish wealth.

Moses Montefiore was undoubtedly the most admired Jew in American periodicals.[31] His life exemplified the positive image of the Jew as unselfish philanthropist. As early as the 1840s *Niles* approvingly noted his efforts on behalf of the persecuted Jews of Damascus. In the 1870s the *St. Paul Pioneer Press* ran a long editorial on the virtues of Montefiore. In 1883 and 1884, when Montefiore amazingly celebrated first his ninety-ninth and then his hundredth birthday, articles of praise poured forth. *Harper's* acclaimed Montefiore as a man dedicated "not only to the race of Israel but to the cause of human need in every creed of clime." He and his wife were devoted to such philanthropy as a hospital in Jerusalem, aid to the Jews of Vilna, and an attempt to rescue Romanian Jews. Now, in his hundredth year, he retained the "full power of mental forces and all the quickness of his humane sympathies."

The *New York Times* featured several homages to Montefiore. On his ninety-ninth birthday the paper wondered "if generous giving is conducive to long living." He had pursued a "noble ideal of human life" will all the zeal characteristic of his people. In all his life "he has never failed to identify himself with his race, never forgotten he was a Jew . . . while there were distressed Jews to relieve or oppressed Jews to plead for." His life "does more to abash the people who would like to revive the persecution of his race . . . than all the literary and political agitation that could be done in a generation." When he reached one hundred in 1884, people paid homage in Baltimore, Rochester, Petersburg, Washington, and Cincinnati. In New York a huge crowd heard Henry Ward Beecher extol him as an example of the ideals of the Bible, "the true uses of wealth and position." Montefiore towered over all in goodness, philanthropy, and humanity. "If Judaism is to prevail . . . let it prevail by bringing forth such heroes of goodness."

Other papers agreed. The *Pioneer Press,* honoring Montefiore, noted that the Jewish record was one of "race solidarity," which led to "phenomenal success." If there was "some mixture of craft" in their natures, it was balanced by goodness and "intellectual strength." The *New York Tribune* editorial declared that Montefiore was justly entitled to veneration as a biblical "just and righteous man." He was a "living representative of the ideal Hebrew." Even the greatest bigot had to respect a man who not only clung to his faith, "but who had adorned that faith by deeds of rare charity and philanthropy." He was indeed a "worthy son of the old Hebrew patriarchs. . . ."

Montefiore, thus, provided one of the most potent positive images of the Jew. The charitableness of the Jew was generally recognized, and was the counterbalance to the negative picture of the compulsive amasser of treasure. At least Jews like Montefiore contributed to the good of society, utilizing the wealth they had accumulated. Pointed contrasts were often made to the behavior of many American millionaires who performed no such socially useful function. Ambrose Bierce summarized the reaction to Montefiore in a poem to commemorate his centenary, which concluded, "Jews and Gentiles in a hundred tongues,/Extolled his deeds and spake his fame aloud."

Baron de Hirsch was another philanthropist who was accorded continuous coverage. Although periodicals praised his efforts to train and resettle Russian immigrants, many of the articles about the Baron had a certain ambivalence. An article in *Life,* which described him as "shrewd and able," was typical. He expended huge sums of money to establish intimacy with the Prince of Wales and the Duke of Orleans, "but even with their help he could not overcome the prevalent prejudice of European society against a Jew." As a consequence, he turned to charitable works "and especially to the ameliora-tion of the conditon of the people of his own race" in backward countries. There had long been an issue of what to do with vast accumulations of wealth in private hands. "His example is respectfully recommended to . . . American gentlemen."[32] Newspaper obituaries also invariably discussed his extensive charitable works and his efforts at social climbing. In this way, Hirsch could stand for both parvenu and philanthropist, two common, and not necessarily mutually exclusive, perceptions of the Jew.

The *Atlantic Monthly* in 1895 featured an interesting article on James Darmsteter, "A True Israelite," who was very different from the wealthy philanthropist usually cited as the ideal Jew.[33] While the virtues of the latter were measured in monetary terms, Darmsteter's were a matter of intellect. He was a French Orientalist and philospher, "in all and through all, a Jew of Jews." He had emerged from four thousand years of travail to express living Jewish ideas. "He had not even assimilated by the way the Western inheri-tance of distinctively Christian thought and feeling." His father had been a poor bookbinder, and his mother was from the Brandeis family, which had given birth to "so many of the doctors of Mosaic law." He was aided in the development of a unique intellect by his struggles and by "the spirit of solidarity" of the Jewish community. His death, shortly after the completion of a great work on the Prophets of Israel, was deeply regretted. This article was unusual, not only for its praise of a Jewish intellectual, but also in its approval of his resistance to "enlightened" (i.e., Christain) ideas. It marked, perhaps, the beginning of a new image of the Jew as intellectual.

In general, there was amazement at the supposedly significant role played by Jews in Europe. It was assumed that Jews held dominant positions. However, this was given as a fact, albeit wildly inaccurate, rather than as a cause for censure. The *New York Times,* for example, remarked in 1878 that there was probably no city with as many influential Jews as Vienna. They ran the banks and press and were prominent in music, government, and restau-rants. "The richest men are Jews, the prettiest women are Jewesses." This "new Jerusalem" was delightful and "owes much of what it is and what it yields in pleasure to its large Hebrew element." *Atlantic Monthly* concluded, in a review of a book about "Eminent Israelites," "When we view the Jews as a class, those of their qualities which strike the eye are such as command respect and often esteem."[34]

The coverage of prominent Jews did tend to bolster the positive aspects of the Jewish image—intelligence, business ability, philanthropy. These virtues of famous Jews stood in sharp contrast to the picture of the old clothesman or pawnbroker. There was some ambivalence, however, because the noble, philanthropic Jew was also presented as a powerful figure in control of much of the world's economy.

Economic Images

The perceived economic role of the Jew was a major source of ambivalence. As has been shown in chapter 3, the most consistently negative image of the Jew was the man whose God was money. Often this view was strengthened by reports on Chatham Street as a center of activity for the Jew who would sell you anything to make a quick, and not always legal, profit. This particular picture of the Jew could be found from the beginning of the century to its end. In the latter part of the century, it was more commonly expressed than the negative religious stereotype. Related negative perceptions included Jews as permanent aliens, so involved in their quest for wealth that they remained exclusive and unassimilable, and as quintessential parvenus. Yet, it was also true that the developing American economy was in need of hard-driving entrepreneurs. Jewish "vices" could also be seen as important virtues in the American environment.

Early in the century (1820), *Niles Weekly Register* discussed the reasons for discrimination against Jews. "The must be some moral cause to produce this effect," *Niles* argued. "They create nothing and are mere consumers. They will not cultivate the earth, nor work at mechanical trades, preferring to live by their wit in dealing, and acting as if they had a home nowhere." Although *Niles* insisted that "this had nothing to do with their rights as men," it did provide a major theme in the commentary about Jews thereafter. In 1842, for instance, the *National Anti-Slavery Standard* quoted without comment an assertion that the "unrelenting persecution" of Christians had left Jews with nothing but gain to pursue, an often-cited mitigating consideration. The money they earned had enabled them to purchase the right to live. Now, however, "the same all-absorbing thirst of gold that formed the leading principle of the life of . . . Rothschild, animates the merest Israelitish urchin." They directed all their energies to that end "with an intensity, unscrupulosity, and perseverence unknown to . . . Christians."[35]

As Jews moved into cities and became involved in the second-hand clothing trade, such comments increased.[36] The *Spirit of the Times* remarked cuttingly in 1845, "Why don't we have a Society for Ameliorating the Condition of the Jewed? That is a question which one who buys his clothing in Chatham Street asks us to propound." An 1858 *Leslie's Illustrated* article, which was widely resented in the Jewish press, noted the presence of many Jewish criminals on Chatham Street. They did observe Passover since one might pick a Gentile's pocket or even plunge a knife into his heart, but one would not touch any but unleavened bread or eat beef or mutton (?).

Although the author concluded with a discussion of Jews as charitable and law abiding, "among the very best citizens of the United States," the Jewish press was not mollified. In California, Hinton Helper reported that adventurous Christians who needed convenient ready-made clothes were pursued by Jews, those "erratic and money-loving descendants of the ancient biblical patriarchs" who refused any useful occupation. The Speaker of the California House agreed that Jews "did not invest their money in the country. . . . They all intended to settle in their 'New Jerusalem.'" He favored a tax on them to prevent them from residing in the area.

This basic picture of the Chatham Street Jewish love for money continued throughout the century.[37] A *Harper's Weekly* article in 1859 commented on the "fantastic signs" one could find there. One was "the Original Jacob." You could harldy believe he was the Jacob you have read about since "the only ladder he dreams of is the ladder to riches." In 1867 the *Atlantic Monthly* described Chatham Street as a place where "Israel predominates" with its "traditional stock in trade of cheap clothing and baubles that are made to wear, but not to wear long." The *New York Tribune* in 1883 described the manner in which a Chatham Street Jew operated with a country bumpkin. If he detected a man who might be induced to buy, he "promptly seizes upon his prey . . . and a few minutes later sends him away clad in raiment of which the less said the better." The *Christian Union* in 1883 warned working women to beware of Jewish employers who "would cheat a poor woman out of her earnings any time they could do so with safety." This picture of Jewish merchants and peddlers was summarized in a sardonic verse about "industrious Israelites" who refused to work, "But peddle healing salve for wooden legs."

The supposed money-making capabilities of the Jew was not always considered a cause for condemnation, however. The Jew had succeeded by utilizing capitalist skills. Could this be criticized without disavowing capitalism itself? In 1837 the *Boston Journal* remarked that Jews had been "reproached with their avidity to acquire riches." Actually, this was the result of their hard work, business qualifications, and knowledge of trade, rather than of any "morbid wish to increase their hoards." The building of a synagogue in Syracuse in 1851 prompted a local paper to comment, "The Jewish population comprises some of the most industrious and frugal of our citizens. . . ." It hoped that the new temple would induce "others of the same creed" to settle in the city. In similar terms, the *St. Louis Republican* in 1855 noted that there were a number of Jews in the city who were actively engaged in business. "No other portion of the population gives less trouble." *Harper's Weekly* described the Jews in 1859 as "among the foremost merchants of the world." In large American cities they were proving their "industry, shrewdness, energy and success."[38]

That success could be considered both a credit to the Jews and a benefit to society. The *Shoe and Leather Reporter* in 1860 compared the Jew to his competitor. The Jew saved, which got him through hard times. When the feckless "American" failed, he blamed the Jew rather than his own lack of foresight. The Jew has "by economy added to the strength and material wealth of the country . . . Jew traders of the South and West have done much by their accumulated savings to form a reserve in hard times." The *True Pacific Messenger* in 1861 noted that, because of the "indomitable energy of their race," Jews were among "the most useful and respectable merchants." Their industry had helped in "banishing shameful prejudices." One commentator remarked on the great increase in Jewish merchants in New York from 1800 to 1863. It was the "high standard of excellence of the old Israelite merchants of 1800 that had made this race occupy the proud position it does now in this city and nation." Another recalled the positive effect of the presence of Jewish traders in Savannah. "The devotion of a whole race . . . to trade and commerce . . . brought about results alike favorable to them and to the world."[39]

Once Jews started to come into this country in ever-increasing numbers, the arguments in favor of the beneficent influence of wealth-producing Jewish businessmen receded from the press. Destitute immigrants did not fit this picture. For quite a while, however, the accepted stereotype of the Jew as money-maker was not necesarily a derogatory one in a capitalist-oriented press.

The picture of the charitable Jew, on the other hand, was a favorite one throughout the century.[40] *Niles Weekly Register* was fond of stories about Jewish philanthropists. In 1832 a rich Copenhagen Jew was reported have made substantial bequests to Jewish and Christian schools and charities. "This is no solitary instance of Hebrew liberality. En passant: is there any apprehension of such 'foreign capital' endangering the liberties of a country?" An 1845 report of the funeral of a Prague merchant who had freely aided all denominations noted the presence of many Christians. "Everywhere the spirit is passing into dishonor which would have spit upon the Jewish gabardine of a man like this."

Other commentators agreed. The *New York Evening Mirror* remarked that it was "the noble and truly Christian munificence of such Hebrews as Judah Touro," that "is shaming down the disgraceful prejudices." An 1855 article in *International Magazine* described how the author had been cheated by a Christian and helped by a Jew who aided hundreds of young writers by paying more than their efforts were worth. Hebrews, the author concluded, were not only outstanding in intelligence, but "in defiance of the prejudices and disabilities . . . are of the most honorable portion of mankind." The *New York Tribune* in 1880 discussed a large donation by Jews to the starving Irish.

The Hebrew was always "generous with his money for all wise educational and charitable purposes." He retaliated to hate with liberality—there was "no finer revenge than his."

Through the years the *New York Times* contained many editorials on the subject of Jewish charity. A long 1877 feature was headed "The Jews Care for Their Poor—Munificent Private Benevolence—A Glorious Record." It pointed out that there were many poor Jews, but they were supported by the "widely liberal charity" of some of the wealthiest and most enterprising merchants who, "by their noble deeds," proved their reverence for the dictates of the Bible. An 1883 description of the "Traits of New York Jews . . . Busy People Who Help Others as Well as Themselves" noted that the Jew was an industrious, benevolent man whose "religion is charity." This positive Jewish quality of charitableness was stressed to the end of the century. It helped to mitigate fears of the onslaught of poverty-stricken Jewish immigrants. The expectation was that they would be taken care of by wealthy Jews. As the Rev. Charles Eaton remarked, "in the practical exemplification of principles of charity, they far surpass the Christians." As in the literary images, the strongest negative and positive pictures of the Jew rested upon the assumption that he was an accumulator of money. This was not necessarily a bad thing to be in America. The ambiguity depended upon the way he was perceived as using his wealth—merely to accumulate more or to unselfishly share his good fortune with others.

Jewish Character and Contributions

Opinion was also divided on the quality of Jewish character. The Jew was frequently chided for his exclusiveness. The *Boston News* in 1860, provoked by a judge's decision to allow Jews to open businesses on Sunday, editorialized that it was certain that the Jew "never becomes a citizen, his posterity never amalgamates with the great mass of people. . . . The Jew and his offsprings are Jews and will be to the end of the chapter." Even the Irish were more valuable since they worked hard and faced danger. The *Boston Post* responded that this "maligned the Jew" who was "eager in the pursuit of gain" only "within lawful limits." The *Boston Pilot,* a Catholic paper, in 1881 expressed the belief that the refusal of Jews to intermarry had "cost them dear in money, pain, blood." Until they mixed and married and extended their occupations into "general manufacturing and agricultural interests instead of confining themselves . . . to dealing with money," they would not be permitted to live in peace. "We admire the Jews for their strong and grand qualities, but we deplore, for their own sakes, the narrow lives they mark out for themselves."[41]

Similar views were expressed in the 1890s.[42] *The Independent* deplored the tendency of the Jewish religion to stay "in the narrow limits of racial con-sanguinity." *Life* remarked that Jews chose to "cling to one another and to the traditions of their race." Christians whom they reproached with excluding them could respond, "we might have learned that from you." In the *American Hebrew* symposium on the causes of anti-Semitism, several respondents ex-pressed similar opinions. The Rev. W. H. P. Faunce believed that the "clan-nishness of the Jews" was the inheritance of centuries of persecution. The Rev. Ensign McChesney commented that "the Jews are historically an ex-clusive people" who look upon others with prejudice. President E. N. Capen of Tufts noted that Jews maintained their "race peculiarities. They do not assimilate like others aliens . . . They can never be Americans pure and simple." The only real solution, Edward Atkinson believed, was "breaking down of Jewish barriers by which even cultivated Jews separated themselves." As Robert Wiebe has pointed out, ethnic minorities in the nineteenth cen-tury were told to play by the rules of the game, which laid out the terms of assimilation they were expected to follow.[43] Any refusal to play was consid-ered dangerous. Was the Jew who insisted on his "peculiar" religion, his different sabbath, his intragroup marriages, challenging the rules?

When the issues of social exclusion of Jews flared up, the press openly discussed the Jew as parvenu. That particular image remained in the back-ground even when no such issue arose. Many of the participants in the *American Hebrew* symposium referred to Jewish social vices as causes of prejudice. The Rev. Robert Collier, for example, remembered staying at a place where Jews were "loud and pushing, with but the scantest sense of that courtesy which has grown to a fine instinct in our people who are well-to-do . . . their money had grown ahead of their manners." Another "friend" blamed only those Jews who had abandoned their faith and "become utter materialists." Such vulgar Jews caused great suffering for "high minded, cultivated, refined Hebrew ladies and gentlemen." Washington Gladden, the famed social gospel minister, felt that Jews had been debased by accepting the maxims of economic competition so prevalent in society. Rev. H. Heber Newton noted that the lower strata was pushing into the higher ranks and demoralizing them. Jews did not do this any more than Christians "but possibly in a more obtrusive manner." Henry T. Finck conceded the presence of many refined Jews who, for the most part, no longer even looked Jewish. The problem was the "vulgar manners of the common Jew." As these became wealthier, they grew more overbearing, selfish, and ill mannered. The Rev. J. R. Day admitted the Jew was generous to his own kind, but these gifts were clannish. He could end prejudice by becoming more American and less ostentatious. He should "go to Gentile churches more frequently. Cultivate the American idea: move forward into nineteenth century thought." The Jew set himself apart. The remedy was to "discourage everything exclusively

Jewish," except for worship. America was indeed a "melting Pot," but it was obvious who was expected to be melted away until "disagreeable" characteristics had disappeared.

If Jewish vices were the subject of some commentary, Jewish virtues were often seen as larger than life. Few groups were so impressively endowed with outstanding qualities in the press. Many articles focused on Jewish contributions to Western civilization. An 1868 article in *De Bow's Review* was both typically Judeophile and proof that hostility existed before the supposed social pressures of the Gilded Age. The article derided those who thought that money was the only touchstone of Jewish success. Jews were famed for erudition as well, and their attainments were the result of "their wonderful aptitude, their keen insight. . . ." Further honors awaited American Jews. "Yet," the author conceded, "there still courses through the veins of all societies . . . a hidden but strong undercurrent of prejudice against the Jew." Still, the conclusion was hopeful: "Henceforth the Israelite has only to confront the opposing tides with the self-confidence and moral courage of his ancestral archetypes and he will not only breast the surges, but in time dissolve it as a bubble."[44]

Other journals also took note of Jewish progress and achievements.[45] An 1871 *New York Times* editorial on English Jews noted that, in the past forty years "their acquisitions have soared far above the mere lust of gold. . . . They are pre-eminent in commerce, prominent at the bar, powerful in politics," and they accomplished this all by themselves. *Harper's Weekly* in 1873 declared that the phenomenal progress of the Hebrew race was "ominous indeed to all their persecutors." They had continued to preserve their industry and moral vigor and their intellectual advances "through every period of oppression, always the benefactors of barbarous Europe, its teachers as well as capitalists, the Israelites are in our day almost the masters of European civilization." *Harper's New Monthly Magazine* reported seeing Meyerbeer in 1877 and feeling, "How much we owe to the Jews and how mean Christendom is." There was the usual list of great Jews in industrial activity, art, philosophy, and politics of the Christian world. Despite this genius, the Jew was still hounded by prejudice. "Honorable men will be careful how they heedlessly use the name of a race to which the religion, the literature, the art, the civilized progress of humanity are so greatly indebted. . . ."

These Jewish contributions could provide an effective response to anti-Semites. The *New York Sun* refuted the bigoted views of Goldwin Smith in 1880 with a discussion of the "solid and brilliant achievements . . . credited to contemporary Israelites" that were "out of all proportion to their numerical importance and social opportunities." In *Harper's Weekly* in 1881 Eugene Lawrence protested that the treatment of "The Persecuted Jews" was the result of their extraordinary success. Even New York owed its prosperity to them, for, "they bring with them wealth or they create it." "The Mission of the Jews," according to an 1894 piece in *Harper's New Monthly Magazine,* was to be the "chief bearers of spirtuality . . . intellectual and emotional sensibility." This would help balance the stolid character of the Saxon through mutual intercourse. This author even rejected the accepted view that Jewish bankers made and unmade wars. There was a need for the "cosmopolitan spirit of humanitarianism," which it was the destiny of the Jews to carry. In a lecture about Moses, Henry George concluded that the spirit of Mosaic law had caused the Jew to maintain an "intensity of family life," a real "love of independence," and, despite exile and torture, "the highest exaltation of thought." The result was the "intellectual vigor that has over and over again made the dry stuff bud and blossom."

This quality of Jewish intellect was also the frequent object of praise.[46] The *Brooklyn Daily Eagle* in 1874 reported a Congregational minister's description of the Jewish people as "of the highest culture and purest intellect." In *The Children of the Poor* (1892) Jacob Riis remarked of Jewish children in the public schools that, when they competed with Christian children, "they distanced them easily . . . taking all prizes. . . ." James Reynolds of the University Settlement was quoted in *Atlantic Monthly* in 1898 commenting that the overwhelming quality of the Jews was "their intellectual avidity. Much has been said about their desire for gain. But . . . the proportionate number of those with intellectual aims is larger than that of any other race. . . ." Combined with their idealism, this produced "a character full of imagination, aspiration and appreciation." These intellectual qualities were referred to more frequently in the latter part of the century as characteristic of the Russian Jews.

All of these fine traits might serve to make the Jew into an outstanding citizen. This was the reverse of the view that the Jew was a permanent alien who could never be assimilated. A New York story in 1854 that there was not one Jewish applicant for relief that year inspired several editorials on the subject of the Jew as citizen.[47] The *Washington Sentinel* remarked that, despite all hardships, the Jews had retained "those better traits that dignify and adorn civilized man." In this country they could not be found in prisons or poor houses and they took care of their own. They "set an example worthy of all imitation, They are among the best, most orderly, well-disposed of our citizens." In an anecdote about a barefooted Jew boy," the *New York Sunday Dispatch* noted that the Jewish nation was "devoted in kindness to the members of its own individual family" and possessed a pride that "keeps them above charity." All this made them ideal citizens.

Even during the slight upsurge of anti-Semitism during the Civil War, the loyalty of Jewish citizens was a constant theme.[48] *The Independent* in 1861 praised "our fellow citizens of the Hebrew race and faith" who were the embodiment of "wealth, intelligence and culture." They were "prompt in declaring their loyalty to the United States and in devoting their treasure and influence to the defense of the Union. . . ." The *Daily Alta California* remarked in 1862 that Jews were "staunch supporters of the Federal Government and the Union which has given them liberty." They were widely respected and were "an element in our midst which will contribute essentially to our future rise. . . ." In the same year, the *Chicago Tribune* commented on the recruitment of a largely Hebrew company, which was rapidly filled. "Our Israelitish citizens have gone beyond even their most sanguine expectations. Their princely contribution of itself is a record which must ever redound to their patriotism."

Later comments reiterated the values of "the Jew as a Citizen," the title of an 1872 editorial in the widely circulated *Philadelphia Evening Telegraph*.[49] The Jew was credited with middle-class virtues associated with enterprise. "The peculiar advantages it offers to his characteristic abilities render America his favorite home." America should be pleased "for the Jew as a citizen is be highly esteemed." The Jew was never an applicant for public charity. "The Jew is also law-abiding. No other element is so orderly in character and so observant of the law." It was true that the Jew was "perhaps more innoculated with the love of money-getting than is the average Christian." However, though "sharp," he was also "honourable," "sober and industrious" and "open handed" in charity. All this made Jews "a good element in society."

Other observers agreed with this estimate. In 1878 Mayor Ely of New York noted that "the Jews form ten percent of our population and contribute less than one percent to the criminal classes." The *New York Herald* praised New York Jews for their "qualities of good citizenship." They were "peaceful, charitable, industrious, intelligent. . . ." In the 1890 *American Hebrew* symposium The Rev. Howard Crosby saw the Jews "as a people of remarkable virtue. In family life they are models, and as citizens they are maintainers of peace and order." Robert Ingersoll, the famed atheist, felt that Jews were "more industrious, more temperate . . . intelligent . . . kind to their wives and children . . . kept their contracts and paid their debts." The only solution to unreasoning prejudice was for all people to give up the superstition of religion. The idea of the Jew as the ideal citizen continued to the end of the century, but the advent of the unruly Russian Jew subjected it to severe strain.

The paradox, of course, was that one might find the positive and negative image of the Jew only a few pages or a few issues apart in the same publication. It has often been said that philo-Semitic writings are merely reverse sides of anti-Jewish sentiments. In the case of the impossibly noble Sheva-like figure, this might have been true. Positive images in magazines and newspapers, however, do not generally fall into this category. They presented Jews as contributors to world civilization. In America, Jews were seen as valuable citizens—law-abiding, temperate, and loyal to the only nation that was fair to them. The Jews were also leaders in culture and intellectual activities. The two positive characteristics that were most appealing to America's image-makers were the strong family ties and widespread charitable activities, which assured that no Jew was ever a burden to American society. Even the generally acknowledged money-making proclivities of the Jew was not always a reason for condemnation. In a society that accepted capitalism as the key to its growth and greatness, the Jew was often admired as a successful capitalist who could increase the prosperity of America.

Postscript—The "Jew" and the "Sheeny"

American Jewish newspapers and letters to the editor seemed to be more concerned with the casual and frequent use of the word "Jew" in a pejorative sense, rather than with the rare virulent anti-Semitic article. Such usage began at an earlier time than is usually supposed. The *Monthly Chronicle of Interesting and Useful Knowledge* suggested in 1839 that "Jew" was "an extraordinary compliment . . . whenever you meet a body who takes care of the main chance . . . you call him a Jew . . ." In 1858 the editor of *Harper's Magazine* discussed a letter that decried the tendency to use the word *Jewish* as a "stigma of selfishness and meanness." One reason for this practice, the editor believed, was that Jews, under the disadvantages of prejudice, had developed sharpness and "a retaliatory hatred of the Christians. . . ." They extorted all they could. They lived to accumulate money and became naturally a byword." After this dubious defense, he concluded that "however many Jew knaves a man may remember . . . he cannot readily recall a Jew fool." In 1866 *Harper's* was guilty of the same usage that had disturbed the earlier letter writer. "You know people who 'Jew you down' . . . and you all know that the children of Abraham have always been, and still are, notorious for jewing folks down—hence they are called Jews."[50]

Newspapers and periodicals frequently received indignant letters from Jewish readers on the subject, like the one in the *New York Times* in 1865 complaining about describing a petty offender as a Jew.[51] The editor replied that he did not know if it was proper to give the religious persuasion of any perpetrator, but it was "inadvertent," and there was little to gain by "parading of casual grievances." The *Times* was plagued by this issue, as an 1874 editorial suggested. "One of the funniest things in the world is the rage into which the Jewish papers throw themselves when reporters describe any culprit brought before the courts as a 'Jew.'" The *Jewish Messenger* had rebuked both the *Times* and the *Herald* for that practice. The *Times* responded that all you were saying was that "he is descended from a very ancient and honorable people." No insult was intended—"any Jew who is ashamed of the name of God's chosen people, does not deserve to be a Jew at all." The paper returned to this sensitive issue in 1877 with a discussion of the verb "to jew," found in the "standard dictionaries of the English language." Though this did contain "footprints of prejudice," the sensitivity to the use of the word *Jew* in a descriptive sense was "unreasonable." Jews were "chosen by one God to proclaim Him to the world . . . Let them sit as serene as Mordecai. They who have outlived the Pharoahs may outlive philology."

Other periodicals received silmilar complaints. The *Nation* in 1872 described the correspondence between the publisher of a dictionary and a "respected Israelite gentleman." The latter objected to the "intolerant definition" of "to jew" as "to cheat." The publisher replied that he would omit the world in the future. The *Nation* disagreed. The word was now obsolete "except as a colloquialism which oftenest is in the mouth of low and mean men." It was part of the language historically used by "persons who really knew the Jew as an accomplished bargainer and merchant, a man justly sharp at a bargain amid enemies. . . ." The Jewish population had no need to conceal this. The *New York Tribune,* while expressing some understanding at the "sensitiveness on the subject," concluded that "the matter does not seem to us to deserve the attention which Hebrews often give it."

The *New York Sun,* in two 1870 editorials, considered the interesting question, "Can a Man Be a Jew and an Irishman?" The Republicans had nominated Sigismund Kaufmann for lieutenant governor in order to win the German vote. The question was whether he was a "Teuton or a Hebrew." The *Sun* asked if he really claimed to be both "just as a Jew born in Dublin might claim to be an Irishman." A Jewish reader responded that "Jew" was not the name of a nation. Mr. Kaufmann was "a German by nationality and a Jew by religion." The *Sun* felt that this correspondent had overlooked the fact that "the Jews are not merely a church; they are a race, and as such they are distinct from Teutons." Although contrary to modern accepted definitions of race, the paper's discussion was not necessarily unfriendly. It went on to declare that Jews had the "glory of being the oldest distinct race in existence, and of maintaining an unbroken, indestructible continuity through calamities and persecutions. . . ." Despite some modern fusion, it was still demonstrably true that "A Jew is a Jew . . . a Teuton is a Teuton." Implicit in this discussion, which did not appear to be motivated by ill-will, was the idea that the true nationality of the Jews would always be Hebrew, rather than that of the nation in which they dwelled. This might have grave implications for their assimilation into American life.[52] While most Jews today are comfortable with the idea of a Jewish peoplehood as well as religion, these fears led to the rather pathetic insistence by Jews of that era that Judaism was "merely a religion." That was one reason for their strenuous objections to the designation in the newspapers.

The newer word, *sheeny,* was more obviously derogatory, and, therefore, more bothersome. One bit of Arkansas doggerel ended: "Ireland grows the

Shamrock/And sheeny grows the nose." The use of the word *sheeny* was discussed in the 1890s. *Life* remarked in 1891 that, although it was not a "particularly pretty word," it was not wise to demand its exclusion from the dictionary. *Yankee* once meant "sharp fellow" and was used as an epithet. As the Yankee type gained respectability, the term "gained in grace." In the same way, "sheeny" "may gain in grace . . . or . . . it may become obsolete because the thing it expresses no longer exists. . . ."[53]

While the unthinking and uncomplimentary use of the words *Jew* and *sheeny* were most unpleasant to American Jews, the fact that Jewish journals seemed preoccupied with ending this annoyance in the press indicates the relative absence of more serious forms of anti-Semitism. It is also significant, as Jonathan Sarna has pointed out, that American Jews felt free to fight against even the most petty anti-Semitism, vigorously responding to perceived slurs. This was a striking contrast to the historic Jewish response in Europe.[54]

The image of the Jew that a reader would get from the American press was incredibly complex. The very same publication that vigorously opposed anti-Semitic manifestations, such as the Saratoga incident, might engage in casual anti-Semitism, or even occasionally publish overtly anti-Semitic articles. Famous Jews were extolled, humble ones sometimes denigrated. The picture might include the Jew as an avaricious moneygrubber who would commit acts of the most questionable legality to accumulate wealth. He was unwilling to mingle (while at the same time pushing himself where he wasn't wanted) and was, thus, unassimilable. Just as widely accepted, however, was the totally contradictory picture of the Jew as industrious, honorable, charitable, family-centered, law-abiding and intelligent—the ideal citizen. The Jew who profited by America's capitalist success-oriented ethos was, in one sense, an ideal American. As Washington Gladden remarked in the *American Hebrew* symposium, the Jew is "very much like the average American, only more so." The puzzling aspect was that these very different images could all be found, sometimes side by side.

A segment in the *California Mail Bag* in 1872, "Our Hebrew Brethren," typified this confused reaction. Some Jewish peculiarities could well be imitated by Christians. They were never beggars, prostitutes, or paupers. They were very religious, "an apostate Jew is as rare as a white blackbird." Their family life was exemplary—"a bad, ungrateful son is almost unknown; a disobedient, erring daughter is rarely heard of." They were great bankers, but never farmers, laborers, or explorers. "Ever since the allotment of Christ's vestments they have dealt in clothing, old and new." The section concluded that, although the author did not wish to be a Jew, "we do wish we were rich as a Jew; and although they did kill Christ, we think the statute of limitations should bar any further prejudice against them upon that point, so long as they are good citizens and mind their own business as they do in San Francisco." The total picture was a mixture of distaste and admiration. As one paper remarked in perplexity, "It is strange that a nation that boasts so many good traits should be so obnoxious."[55]

5
Political and Ideological Images

ANTI-SEMITISM IN EUROPE IN THE SECOND HALF OF THE NINETEENTH century was primarily public and political. In this manifestation, Jews were perceived as menaces to a well-ordered society. They were permanent unassimilable aliens, international conspirators who used their dominance in banking and finance to gain power for their own nefarious ends. European governments were often parties to, or even agents of, the anti-Semitic movement, which had reached considerable proportions by the end of the century.

Anti-Jewish sentiment in the United States, on the other hand, largely took the form of private, social discrimination. There was no organized anti-Semtic movement. Dislikes were too diffused to allow much heat to focus upon Jews. Blacks, Catholics, Mormons, and Chinese, among others, were more obvious targets for political action than the Jews. The role of the government was benevolent or, at the very least, neutral.

Political issues did arise during wartime and, early in the century, over remaining vestiges of Jewish disabilities. The press frequently discussed foreign discrimination against the Jews and, almost unanimously, rejected the European anti-Semitic movement as unworthy of the enlightened spirit of the age. Nevertheless, there were some people who accepted the ideological image of the "International Jew." These included some rural and urban radicals and alienated members of the old aristocracy. In the nineteenth century most periodicals rejected their fears and retained the ideal of America as a land of freedom to which the world's persecuted peoples could flee. There was something "unamerican" about organized anti-Semitism. Nevertheless, the image of the dangerous "International Jew" did hover in a shadowy existence, ready for revival in the twentieth century.

American Political Issues

There were only a few occasions in which political issues concerning Jews arose in America. The first period in which anti-Semitism might have been expected was the American Revolution. But, as Richard Morris has noted, Jews were looked upon as old settlers, rather than as aliens. "It is astonishing how little antisemitism was stirred up in America as a result of the Revolutionary crisis," particularly in comparison to contemporary England where Jews were "humiliated and physically attacked in the streets." According to Morris, "the tie-in of Jews with usury and sharp financial dealings was rarely made in America of Revolutionary times."[1] When Ezra Stiles reported that the governor of Rhode Island and two judges sat with the president of the congregation at a Jewish religious service, he was casually describing an event that had no parallel in Europe. After the war, comments about the role Jews had played commonly stressed their loyalty in fighting beside their Christian countrymen.

The conflict between Jefferson's Democratic Republicans and the Federalists grew bitter enough to arouse the kind of passion that often leads to anti-Semitism. In his preface to the American edition of *The Democrat*, James Rivington wrote that the Democratic clubs came out of agitation by Paris agents, "This itinerant gang will easily be known by their physiognomy; they seem to be like their vice president of the tribe of Shylock. . . ."[2] The reference was clearly to the vice-president of the New York society, Solomon Simpson, merchant and president of Congregation Shearith Israel. This outburst, however, was not taken up by the Federalists generally, and the Jews had no special role in the bitter controversies of that period.

The most notable "Jewish" issue in early American history was the struggle over Maryland's "Jew Bill," which tried to remove political disabilities from the Jews of that state. Most of the American press supported this change.[3] This was particularly true of *Niles Weekly Register*, probably the most influential periodical in early America. Its subscribers included presidents, congressmen, and even foreign monarchs. Although *Niles* often criticized Jews for "abhorrent" traits, it advocated equality and decried anti-Semitism. An 1819 editorial on the subject was entitled "Rights of Conscience." It noted with approval that a committee of the Maryland House had urged extension of political privileges to Jews. If there was only one Jew in the state, "the Constitution ought to be altered in his favor. The day of the fire and faggot has passed away." Later, it endorsed a speech by H. Breckenridge before the Maryland Assembly. He denied that Jews, "the chosen people of God" who had brought "the blessings of Christianity," were in any way inferior. They had been wickedly persecuted which had "a most unhappy influence on their character." If the Jew was like his enemies described, "these enemies had made him so." Christians had been "taught from early infancy to entertain an unfavorable opinion of them." American Jews, the speaker concluded, had been treated far better and "have the same proportion of estimable individuals" as Christians. They were as attached to the country and had been devoted to the Revolution for freedom.

The most typical expression of the deeply ambivalent attitude of *Niles* came in an 1820 article. It reported another attempt to "exonerate this persecuted sect from the odious restrictions which our incomprehensible constitution imposes on them." Jews were denied rights everywhere because "their interests do not appear identified with those of the communities in which they live . . . they will not sit down and labor like other people—they create nothing and are mere consumers . . . preferring to live by their wit. . . ." This caused hostility, "But all this has nothing to do with their rights as men;—let us do our duty and place them upon an equality with ourselves. . . ." This is a vivid illustration of the distinction many Americans made between private and public anti-Semitism. *Niles* continued to follow the issue closely. In 1826 it was able to report exultantly that the Maryland Bill was finally passed, bringing about the "political liberation of persons held in servitude for conscience sake. . . . Jews are freeman. . . ."

Many newspapers held the same point of view with less equivocation. The *Philadelphia Freeman's Journal* regretted the "illiberal principles" exhibited by the Maryland legislature. The denial of rights to Jews "ought not to be in this country, the asylum of the oppressed." The *Charleston Southern Patriot* charged Maryland with having caught "the spirit of German governments," a spirit that was "the dishonor of our age." If this clause of its Constitution was not eliminated, the people of Maryland could not boast of living in an advanced liberal age.

Despite these comments, opinion was not unanimous on the issue. It took seven years for the bill to be passed. Its original sponsor was defeated for reelection by a man who capitalized on anti-Jewish sentiment. One speaker told the Maryland legislature that "he did not think it proper or expedient to grant the rights and privileges which we enjoy to a sect of people who do not associate with us, and who do not even eat at our tables." This disapproval of supposed Jewish exclusiveness was often used by opponents of Jews in America. Another objected that the bill would "encourage the Jews to come and dwell among us." Even in this early period, George Houston, an "Israelite," complained that people saw Jews as "bent on acquiring wealth without regard to the means employed to obtain it. . . ." This led some Americans to see Jews as a people "who ought to be debarred all social intercourse." It is interesting that this remonstrance was written in 1823, well before such attitudes were thought to have been a problem.

The restrictions in the North Carolina Constitution were less publicized, but gave rise to a similar reaction.[4] In 1835 Governor Branch pleaded for the removal of any constitutional religious test directed against Jews, the "favorite people of the Almighty" who included men "as talented, as virtuous, as well qualified to fill any office . . . as any other citizen." Another exponent of change felt that there was no hostility against Jews. "The only class against whom there was any excitement in the public mind was Roman Catholics. . . . " The newspapers were virtually unanimously critical of the North Carolina limitations. There must, however, have been more animosity than had been conceded, because the legislature failed to act. As late as 1858, the *Wilmington Journal* noted a petition on the subject presented by a Jewish congregation. The editorial admonished, "The invidious distinction in our state constitution against the members of this religious denomination is not in accordance with the liberal spirit of the age. . . ."

As might be expected, the pressures and passions engendered by the Civil War brought out more overt feelings of anti-Semitism. Bertram Korn has described this in *American Jewry and the Civil War*. Although, as Korn himself comments, he has been criticized for exaggeration, he does convincingly demonstrate a definite upsurge of anti-Jewish feeling during the War.[5]

Even before the war, the passions were rising. Abolitionists were disappointed at Jewish inaction on the slavery question. They had hoped that "the objects of so much mean prejudice and unrighteous oppression as the Jews have been for ages" would be stronger "enemies of CASTE and the friends of UNIVERSAL FREEDOM." Jews, alas, were no nobler than any other group in society. When Morris Raphall, a New York rabbi, offered a biblical defense of slavery, the *New York Tribune* was particularly upset. "As Senator Wade said of his co-religionist, Judah P. Benjamin, he is 'an Israelite with Egyptian principles.'" However, to be fair, the paper noted that, despite oppression and persecution, only a few Jews were "perverted . . . thousands of the children of Abraham . . . are among the most faithful and consistent upholders of the inalienable Rights of Man."[6]

During the war, both North and South indulged in some scapegoating of Jews.[7] There were Southerners who accused Jews of being "merciless speculators, army slackers and blockade runners." The *Richmond Southern Illustrated News* blamed Jews for much of the ills of the South, but "what else could be expected from a Jew but money getting . . . for them money has been country. . . ." Such comments, however, were not commonplace in Southern journals.

More such statements could be found in the North. Senator Henry Wilson of Massachusetts was particularly noted for his anti-Semitic remarks. Several were quoted in the *American Israelite*. Wilson accused Judah Benjamin of plotting to overthrow the government "of his adopted country which gives equality of rights even to that race that stoned prophets and crucified the Redeemer of the World." It was a contest between the "Jew-brokers, the money-lenders . . . and the productive toiling men of the country." The *Dutch Zeiting* of Peoria believed that nine-tenths of the Jews were defenders of slavery. Where they were no longer slaves themselves, "they make themselves tyrants." The *Detroit Commercial-Advertiser* carried a vicious diatribe by its New York correspondent claiming that gold speculators "of foreign birth and exclusively of the people who look up to Abraham as their father" were sowing distrust for the government. These "hooked nose wretches" chuckled about a battle lost by the Union "as it puts money in their purse." A *New York Times* article about Senator David Yulee of Florida claimed to find "treason in embryo" in his earlier conduct. He and an Irishman tried to obtain government subsidies for a railroad of which they were the contractors. They succeeded, but it was "because his Jew heart did not get all it craved that he urged the secession of Florida—and like the base Judean, threw away a pearl richer than all his tribe." The *Patterson Press* commented that the vast majority of gold speculators were Jews. (According to the *Jewish Messenger,* less than five percent were Jewish.)

"The Lounger" in *Harper's Weekly* was notorious for his uncomplimentary remarks. In an open letter to a German Jewish trader, he complained that the man had no "sympathy for this country. You are here solely to make money. . . ." He was "the enemy of all who will risk war to save the nation," since money was his only concern. Judaism was, of necessity, "entirely divergent from the stream of civilization on this country." This is why "the country you left did not regret your coming away; the country in which you trade will not mourn your departure."

The most sensational event involving Jews during the Civil War was General Grant's Order no. 11, removing all Jews, including local residents, from his area of command.[8] Grant had been plagued by cotton speculators. Although only a small portion of these speculators were Jewish, Grant identified the entire illegal traffic with Jews. A few Republican papers supported the general's actions. The *Washington Chronicle,* for example, condemned Jews as the "scavengers . . . of commerce." Many journals, however, vigorously opposed Grant's actions. The *Cincinnati Enquirer* considered the order a "gross and flagrant" injustice. There were good and bad Jews, but "a more law-abiding class of citizens we do not know." The *Philadelphia Public Ledger* was indignant at the singling out of "some of the most intelligent, educated . . . and patriotic men" in the country. In Europe, where they were persecuted, they might "retaliate by fraud against oppressive power," but in America they were reliable. The *New York Times,* which generally supported the administration, was pleased that Lincoln had set the order aside, redeeming the nation from "the disgrace of a military assault" upon rights guaranteed to Jews by the Constitution. It would not be as easy to efface "the affront to the Israelites." Certainly most of the swindlers were not Jews, "We have native talent that can 'beat the Jews.' "

Despite the vigorous defense of the Jews by most papers, the image persisted of the Jews as the main profiteers of the conflict even after the war was over.[9] A *New York Herald* story about Southern Jews in 1865 noted, "they take care of number one." In the war the Jew grinned, stayed far from the fight, "picked up the Christian's valuables, and then bought and occupied the Christian's houses." All the old family homes, according to this reporter, were "owned and occupied by Jews."

As Bertram Korn has remarked, all the anti-Semitic outbursts of the war, including the Grant Order, were minor compared to the total expressions of hatred, suspicion, anger, and grief brought forth by this most terrible conflict. The passions of war led to the most sustained expressions of the negative image of the Jew. It is noteworthy that, even at this time, there continued to be numerous forceful defenders of the Jews.

The Role of Populists and Other Radicals

While most of the major image makers stereotyped the flaws of Jews in terms of Chatham street clothing dealers and the like, the rural radical tended to picture the Jew as the epitome of the exploitive moneyed interests. Even early in the century there had been a tendency on the part of agrarian politicians to blame economic ills upon the Jew. It could be found in the works of William Cobbett, which were read by Jacksonians. John Higham has remarked that these anti-Semites "were alienated and often despairing critics of the power of money in American society." The "International Jew" thus became the hobgoblin of the rural imagination, intertwined with the insidious influence of the Eastern cities. These rural Americans lived in areas of low Jewish density where the enemy "was a remote and shadowy figure rather than a daily reality."[10] The same people who believed the negative stereotype of "The Jew" without question often readily accepted the few Jews who did live in their local communities.

As Irwin Unger has remarked, farm folk and small-town Americans knew the Jew, if at all, "largely as a storekeeper or peddler." The Jew was often a mythic figure, sometimes favorably identified with the Old Testament, but sometimes associated with the "folk image of the usurer." In addition, Jews were aliens, not part of the "producing classes," often "detested" middlemen. While the Jewish banker, unlike the storekeeper, was beyond the immediate experience of the average American, he learned about that evil figure from Greenback leaders who warned of international Jewish banking houses. The Jew was identified with the money power of Wall Street, that center of nefarious forces. Although Unger believes that anti-Semitism was not pervasive nor the exclusive ailment of the agrarians, he does feel that it was significant "because it was symptomatic." A good example was Brick Pomeroy's *The Great Campaign,* which attacked Jews as men "who do not pay attention to farming . . . but who from their peculiarities are skimmers, gleaners, gatherers who can scent a dollar as far as a Yankee politician can a carpet bag."[11]

An even more extreme example of the views described by Unger was an 1879 speech to a Greenback Labor Club by Elizabeth Bryant, describing how the "passion for gain" had extinguished all else in Jews who knew that "wealth constitutes power." Their dispersion had been voluntary and organized so that "without a country . . . owing allegiance to no government . . . he today controls the money power of the world." The Jew was attempting to enforce a money system based on gold, his symbol of wealth. He never engages in farming or labor, "but wherever on the globe commerce exists there hovers the Jew with his bag of gold" carrying "the curse of usury." Americans had to recognize the crisis created by the presence of the Jew-enemy "in our midst" and redeem their liberty before the "prairie, our rivers . . . our majestic mountains . . . all, all are mortgaged to the Jew."[12] This was one of the purest examples of ideological opposition to the menace of the "International Jew."

Nonagrarian radicals of the era often perceived issues in a similar light. *Irish World* in 1877 featured a cartoon of Rothschild dressed as Shylock and brandishing a knife. The accompanying article charged that the effort to depreciate silver "has been projected by the great Jew bankers of the world. . . ." The low prices and destruction of trade would cause them to realize huge profits. Their plot could succeed because "these rich Jewish capitalists . . . have access to Secretaries of Treasuries and Finance Ministers and to people who manipulate the press of the world."[13]

Populist leaders in the 1890s also made occasional references to Jews as part of the money conspiracy. "The conspirators are drawn mainly from the money changers of old—the Jews." G. T. Washburn, a prominent Populist, warned that the gold trust "under the generalship of a European Jew, is capable of anything." Mrs. Lease, the famed Populist orator, declared, "The capitalist press rejoiced in the power of Grover Cleveland, the American agent of Jewish bankers and British gold. . . ."[14]

Several publications written by Populists demonstrated hostile feelings toward Jews.[15] Ebenezer Wakely asserted that Jewish control of the world's economy harkened back to the Bible, where Moses "permitted the Jew to exploit the Gentile race." According to James E. Goode in *The Modern Banker,* Jews were in control of most of the banks, which were creations of "the cunning brain of the Jew." Even before his demogogic phase, Tom Watson claimed that Jefferson would be astounded if he returned to find his party "prostituted" to "red-eyed Jewish millionaires," the new "chiefs of that party."

One of the most widely read writers who favored Bryan's cause was William H. "Coin" Harvey.[16] His novel *A Tale of Two Nations,* which sold several hundred thousand copies, depicted Jewish bankers bribing senators and bending Washington's monetary policy to suit London. Victor Rogasner, the main character, is the nephew and representative of the scheming Baron Rothe. With "the fire of his race . . . the fire that came when David gazed upon Bathsheba," he falls in love with an American girl and plots the ruination of his noble rival, a young Nebraska congressman, patterned on William Jennings Bryan. The Jew is rebuffed by the heroine who declares that despite his shrewdness and devious ways "inbred through generations," he is "repulsive to me." He learns his lesson through his "fair Jewess" girlfriend who cares for him in his misery, but a new agent of Baron Rothe arrives to subvert the American economy.

Coin's Financial School was Harvey's runaway best-seller; over a million copies were sold. In it he referred to a "Jewish Shylock clutching his gold." In *Coin's Financial School Up-to-Date,* Harvey attempted to make amends for his earlier anti-Semitic remarks. The two protagonists of the book cross State Street where one notices a "big Jew firm," and asks Coin what he thinks of Jews. Coin's "defense" of the Jews reveals a deep-seated ambivalence:

> The Jews are the brightest race of people that inhabit the earth, and they treat each other with the greatest fairness . . . You never saw a Jew beggar, and they are seldom found guilty of crime . . . There are good as well as bad among all races . . . Among the Jews many became money changers; it seems to be natural with them, probably on account of their excessive shrewdness . . . But . . . this should not prejudice you against them as a race . . . .

Ignatius Donelly's *Caesar's Column* was a fictional version of the Populist nightmare and a warning to America.[17] This popular novel sold over 250,000 copies. The hero leaves a rural paradise of Uganda to visit New York of the future in which the aristocracy is almost totally Hebrew. This is a consequence of the survival of the fittest in which the weaker Jews had been destroyed by Christian persecution and those who survived were tougher and meaner than any Christian. The Jews were "the great money-getters of the world," risen from peddlers to merchants "to bankers to princes." A revolutionary organization plots the overthrow of the oligarchy, but its brains too is a Russian Jew. His face is "mean and sinister; two fangs alone remained in his mouth; his nose was hooked; the eyes were small, sharp. . . ." The terrible revolution brings ruin and slaughter everywhere, but the cunning Jew flees the carnage with $100,000,000. "It is rumored he has gone to Judaea; that he proposes to make himself king in Jerusalem, and, with his vast wealth . . . revive the ancient splendors of the Jewish race. . . ." The hero also flees the nightmare to the good life in rural Populist-run Uganda.

Donelly's views, however, were more deeply ambivalent than was shown in the one novel so often cited by critics of the Populists.[18] In an earlier period, 1876, he had vigorously opposed prejudice in his paper, the *St. Paul Anti-Monopolist.* "Give the Jew a chance," he advised his readers, "A great nation . . . has room in it for all the race elements of the world." Later, in the *St. Paul Representative,* he noted that there were Jews "that are an honor to the human race," as well as those who were a disgrace. At least the Jewish plutocrat had the excuse of thousands of years of persecution during which Jews had preserved the knowledge of "the one true God." Plutocratic Christians were, therefore, worse. "Karl Marx, the Jew reformer, faces Rothschild, the Jew plutocrat." He concluded that he did not want anything he wrote to be misconstrued to "pander to prejudice against any man." *The Golden Bottle* also reflected Donnelly's more tolerant views. In an anticipation of modern Israel, the hero, dictator of the world, restores Palestine to the Jews "from whom we derived our religion and so much of our literature." The "poor afflicted Hebrews" poured out of lands of hatred and persecution to start a nation which would be "illustrious and honored in the world." In 1899, in the *Minneapolis Representative,* he spoke out forcefully against incidents in New York in which "cannibals" pulled the beards of old Jews. The growth of European anti-Semitism led him to editorialize, "The Jews are not all plutocrats. A large majority of them are the poorest people in the world. The half-starved workers of the sweatshops of London, Berlin and New York are mostly Hebrews." He could not understand how "a Christian people, worshipping a Jew, the son of a Jewess, should entertain such terrible bigotry against the people of his race." It would seem that Donnelly was far more tolerant when he wasn't in the midst of the passions of a silver campaign and when he saw the consequences of prejudice. Certainly these remarks, written by the same man who wrote *Caesar's Column,* strongly indicate that it is an oversimplification to assume inevitable Populist anti-Semitism.

There are many other examples of Populists criticizing anti-Semitism and advocating tolerance.[19] The *Farmers and Laborers Journal* of Kentucky, an organ of the People's Party, opposed "senseless twaddle about 'Jew bankers.'" Jews, the paper declared, were not responsible for the economic system of America or for legislation passed by the government. If Jews were bankers, it was due to "sagacity, energy and executive ability." William Jennings Bryan repudiated accusations of anti-Semitism directed against his campaign. "Our opponents," he noted, "have sometimes tried to make it appear that we are attacking a race when we denounce the financial policy advocated by the Rothschilds." Instead, he was attacking, "greed and avarice which know neither race nor religion." Bryan concluded, "I do not know of any class of our people who . . . can better sympathize with the struggling masses in this campaign than the Hebrew race."

There is no doubt that in their intense hatred for the "money power," some Populists accepted anti-Semitic stereotypes and identified Jews with the evils of society. Even those who criticized the nation for its lack of devotion to true democratic ideals sometimes strayed from these ideals and engaged in scapegoating. Throughout history, many men have found it possible to combine a desire for justice with this particular social injustice. There is doubt, however, that the Populists did this any more frequently than other groups in society. The Populists, in their credulity, may have helped to reinforce the image of the Jew as usurer and international banker. It is not fair, however, to say that the Populists were responsible for modern American anti-Semitism. In fact, they were as ambivalent on the issue as the rest of society.

Anti-Semites and Judeophiles

There was a very small group in America that could accurately be characterized as ideological anti-Semites. By the 1870s the number of overtly anti-Semitic articles and books began to increase noticeably. They sounded many of the same themes that appealed to similar people in the twentieth century. Goldwin Smith's anti-Semitic diatribes in British publications were beginning to attract interest in the American press even before he came to this country. It is important to remember, however, that most of these authors constituted a "lunatic fringe." With the exception of Smith, they were totally ignored in the American press, and certainly could not be considered part of any "movement."

H. P. C. Worthington's pamphlet *Hell for the Jews* appeared in 1879 as an answer to a defense of the Jews by Henry Beecher and others. The real issue, according to Worthington, was whether the Jews would "govern, own and control the future of America." The Jews may have given the world Christ, but they rejected him and were doomed to Hell. Eventually, at the rate they were reproducing, everything would be "drowned into insignificance by the rich perfume of little baby Jews." At this point, the author lapsed into total incoherence. Yet, it is interesting that even he felt the need to "abjure all prejudice."[20]

The best known anti-Semitic pamphleteer was a Greek immigrant printer, Telemachus Timayonis. There is no evidence of any real popularity or importance given to his work. In fact, his views met with "almost universal indignation," according to the *Evening World* of Boston. In *The Original Mr. Jacobs* (1888) he argued that, "with treachery and fraud . . . serpent like," the Jew was taking possession of everything. The Jews owed loyalty to no country. Above all, they hate Christianity, leading them to bleed and crucify Christian children from the Middle Ages to the present. To guard against the Jewish menace, stringent laws should be passed "forbidding Jews to enter the country." *Judas Iscariot* (1888) continued in the same vein. "A Jew can have no hope of salvation unless he robs a goy." They were traitors, "a state within a state." The proof that the Jew is naturally a murderer is that his first ceremony was a bloody operation that often proved fatal to Jewish infants! There is no evidence that these books had any substantial audience. It is interesting, however, that they were considered respectable enough to contain an ad for Van Houten chocolate on the inside cover.[21]

The work of Goldwin Smith, a well-known English anti-Semite who became a professor at an American university, was far more important. His writings were often published and seriously discussed in major American periodicals and newspapers.[22] The *North American Review,* which published numerous sympathetic articles about Jews (despite its association with Henry Adams), ran a long article by Smith in 1891. He contended that the world-wide "anti-semitic revolt is, in fact, one of the great features of the age." The problem was that the Jews were "a parasite race," detached from their own country, who asserted "themselves for the purpose of gain into the homes of other nations, while they retain a marked and repellent nationality of their own." Their isolation was maintained by the Talmud, which preserved their purity, and, by circumcision, "the seal of tribalism." The Jew was detested because he absorbed the wealth of a nation and "when present in numbers he eats out the core of nationality." In Western society "of which wealth is the ruling power," the financial skill and aid of his kinsmen made the Jew "the master of wealth." (Smith wrote a similar article for *Nineteenth Century.*) In succeeding issues the *Review* carried two responses by Jewish authors who argued that American Jews were "diligent, thrifty and law-abiding."

The *Catholic World* ran a series from 1891 to 1893 by Manuel Perez Villamil that presented an extremely anti-Semitic interpretation of the Jewish role in Spanish history.[23] Since the articles were published without comment and no critiques of any kind were printed, they may well have represented the views of the editors as well. According to Villamil, there was an inevitable conflict between Hebrew and Christian due to the Jews' "cunning and guile" and their "perfidy and conspiracy." They also committed "apalling crimes" like the 1491 crucifixion of a Toledo boy. Laws against the Jews were required "to preserve social and religious unity . . . against the transgressions of the proscribed race . . . the cause of so much evil and disorder recorded in history." Their Talmud taught them to curse Christians and "to plunder them either by fraud or violence." Even today Jews sacrifice little boys. The conclusion was, "No act of disloyalty, treachery or conspiracy took place in which they were not involved."

Despite the publication of a few anti-Semitic articles and pamphlets, from the earliest part of the century to its end, most journals and periodicals were opposed to overt expressions of anti-Semitism, whether in this country or abroad. (This does not mean that the same paper or magazine would hesitate to publish an article that we might consider blatantly anti-Semitic.) Some of the defenses of Jews had a curiously ambiguous quality. The *New York Sun* in 1849 published an article on the secret of success in America, averring that "all are equally encouraged and protected." A Jew wrote to complain that the doctrine did not work here as shown by employment advertisements, which stated, "No Jews wanted here." (Note the early date of this practice.) The *Sun* replied that this was an incorrect interpretation of what it had meant. Governments and institutions treated all with equality. Those who battled with other races were "pitiable and shameful." Obviously, "the spirit of our institutions and government is often more liberal and generous than many of the individuals who enjoy its blessings and who ought to imitate its example."[24] This distinction between private and public discrimination was precisely the difference between American and European anti-Semitism.

The 1880s, in response to an upsurge in European anti-Semitism, brought an increase in articles condemning that prejudice.[25] The *Atlantic Monthly* in 1880 noted that, despite the many good qualities of Jews, "inherited prejudices are not easily expelled from the moral system." If the prejudice had been based solely on religion, it would have died. Its real cause was that Jews "are the greatest traffickers in the world's most indispensible commodity, money." Christian oppression was responsible for other "peculiarities of the race" like "the filthy habits of their lower class." This was a common, if dubious defense. *Puck* compared the actions of Germany to those of Hilton and Corbin. It was about time Jews "had a little rest from persecution." Americans did not torture, but "we make ourselves decidedly disagreeable in a small civilized way." *Century* in 1882 explained that "not all of Christendom has come out of barbarism yet." The Jews were not only no worse than any other group, but in fact had a larger number of eminent men than other races. In the following year *Century* published a rueful exposition of the "Jewish problem" by Emma Lazarus. In America prejudice took the form of social boycott. Even supposedly refined Christians used the word "Jew" as a "term of opprobrium . . . to denote the meanest tricks." The real "insatiable thirst of the Jew," she assured her readers, was not for money, but "for knowledge."

The issue of anti-Semitism continued to occupy the press in the 1890s.[26] An 1890 editorial in the *Chicago Evening Journal* was headed "Still Pounding the Jews." America's record was better than Europe's, but still "far from creditable." Educated people complained that Jewesses talked too loud and that Jews were not up to society's standards. The paper commented sardonically, "It should be a matter of general thankfulness that the Jews . . . have ceased to offer . . . a Christian child in sacrifice . . . and are satisfied now with talking too loud and with a free use of oil on the hair." In 1893 the *Detroit News* ran a series on "Why is the Jew Hated?" Merchants had protested anti-Semitism at a local club at the same time trouble broke out in Berlin. This universal prejudice must have deep causes. Certainly, it was not the result of inferiority since the Jew in the United States "is more law-abiding than the Christian . . . is less burdensome to the poor funds; his family relations are purer; he is healthier"; and has made great intellectual contributions. Modern civilization owes him more than any other breed, "Why then does the world hate him?" The paper invited Jews in the interests of science to discuss what characteristics of theirs "set the Christian's teeth on edge all over the world." Perhaps the victims were responsible for their own mistreatment—this became a familiar theme in later periods.

New York newpapers vehemently opposed the organized anti-Semitic movement growing in Europe in the 1890s. This was shown by their reaction to Hermann Ahlwardt, an Austrian agitator, who came to the United States in 1895 to stir up anti-Jewish antagonism. The papers unamimously concurred with the *Herald*'s headline, "Ahlwardt Unwelcome," when the hatemonger arrived. The *Herald* asserted that American Jews had achieved much in culture and science and contributed their share "in promoting the stability and advancing the prosperity of the United States." There was no room in America "for fanatics who come with the avowed purpose of pitting . . . race against race. . . ." The *Sun* dismissed the charge that Jews were not productive members of society. Certainly, the paper insisted, "his charges are not applicable to the Jews of New York . . . a large majority of whom are engaged in productive industries . . . Why Ahlwardt we have Jews here who are beer brewers! And we have heard that some folks regard their brew as the best."

When some young Jews threw rotten eggs at Ahlwardt, the *Tribune* combined stereotyped thinking with a defense of the Jewish people, showing how Judeophile rhetoric and anti-Semitic ideas could be interrelated, as John Higham has suggested. The "characteristic Hebrew thrift should have prevented any such demonstrations. The rotten eggs might have been better employed." Ahlwardt actually compliments them by his charges and maligns the "Aryan race," which was made to seem "so contemptibly weak that it cannot maintain its ascendency over vastly inferior numbers." Jews had once been compelled to make their living through usury, so they developed a "natural aptitude" for it. However, though "their power of making money may be abnormal, their love for it is not greater than their fellows." If New York had indeed become the New Jerusalem, it was because "the Hebrew in a free and fair contest . . . proves himself the stronger and abler man."

Papers and periodicals around the country tended to agree. The *Indianapolis Journal,* for example, felt that American Jews "rank in the common estimation as among the safest, soundest, most conservative and at the same time more progressive members of the community." The *New Orleans Picayune* informed Ahlwardt that, under America's liberal laws, Jews were "rapidly amalgamating." Only persecution had kept them a "peculiar people." The *Review of Reviews* summed up Ahlwardt's odyssey. When he came to New York, he could hardly find one person "saying anything but pleasant things about the industrious, charitable and intelligent race," despite their "representative faults."

At the end of this period, both the *Times* and *Tribune* attacked antiSemitism as a manifestation of jealousy over superior Jewish business acumen and prosperity. It was "just another form of anarchism." Actually, Jews, "far from beggaring the people among whom they live, diffuse and develop prosperity." This is a clear example of seeing the Jew as the exemplar of capitalist virtues, making his opponents radical expropriators in the eyes of the conservative press.

Often the journals that decried anti-Semitism disseminated the very stereotypes that led to prejudice. However, there was little reference to the European-type fears of an imminent Jewish takeover in the nonradical press. Only extreme anti-Semites like Goldwin Smith pictured the Jew as a parasite who might ultimately sap the strength of society. Ahlwardt's hostile reception is evidence that such charges were not taken very seriously at this time. Anti-Semitism in the American press was largely the casual and unfeeling kind, rather than a deliberate or malicious effort to undermine the position of Jews in America. Nevertheless, the images depicted by the anti-Semites were present and available for later use by more dedicated anti-Jewish forces.

Judeophile writings were even more commonplace than anti-Semitic diatribes, as shown by complaints by Jewish authors. In 1856 Morris Raphall remarked, "Much has been written these last years—not always wisely—upon the singular gifts and achievements of the modern Hebrew race," most of it by "philo-Jewish writers." Later in the century, in 1894, Abram Isaacs entitled his article "The Glorification of the Jew." It had become difficult, he noted, "to keep pace with the stream of books . . . and countless articles" praising the Jew. In 1897 he protested that the Jew was treated "with superlative praise or superlative condemnation."[27]

Isaacs's complaints can be verified by the spate of philo-Semitic articles, lectures, and pamphlets that appeared, particularly in the last third of the century.[28] They were generally kindly and well meaning despite some elements of condescension. Their strenuous protests against anti-Semitic ideas points up the continuing presence of the latter as well. James Parton's 1870 article, "Our Israelitish Brethren," was one of the earliest and best-intentioned of these noncritical pieces. Christians owed unlimited reparation to this "interesting and unoffending people who had been despised, a wrong that "all Christians have done to all Jews all the time." In time-honored liberal fashion, Parton argued that if a Jew played "a scurvy trick," one should kick a Christian for it! In their lack of bitterness, "the Jews are the only Christians." They needed only a fair chance "to develop more shining qualities." One need only compare the Jews just entering from lands of oppression with those in America for a generation. "America can boast no better citizens, nor more refined circles."

The best known of the philo-Semitic works in the United States was a lecture by Senator Zebulon Vance of North Carolina, "The Scattered Nation." It was written between 1868 and 1873. Over the next fifteen years the lecture was repeated hundreds of times in every important American city before Christian and Jewish audiences. Vance presented the Jew as "the most remarkable man of this world." Their social life was outstanding, lacking prostitution, pauperism, and crime. They were educated: "I have never seen an adult Jew who could not read, write and compute figures—especially the figures." (Note the presence of this stereotype even in a friendly observer.) Forced into trade, they became great merchants, but also left marks in learning, law, science, literature, and song. They asked only to be left alone. Although Americans prevent physical persecution, "there remains among us an unreasonable prejudice of which I am heartily ashamed," in a country that fought a war to help African "barbarians." Here, "educated and respectable" Jews, kinsmen of the Son of God, were "ignominiously ejected from hotels and watering places as unworthy of the association of men who had grown rich by the sale of a new brand of soap." Where the Jew was persecuted, he refused to have patriotic ties; where he was protected, "he has been a faithful and zealous patriot." Jews were not even the sharpest Americans—they could not live in New England and compete with the Yankees. The Jew was what we made him. If gentiles stopped all prejudice, Jews would end exclusion and forgive them. This friend of the Jews concludes with a hope for eventual total assimilation, a common goal of many sympathetic observers.

Johanna von Bohne, who described herself as a "Protestant lady," wrote *Jew and Gentile* in 1889 as a reply to the anti-Semitic tracts published at that time. She listed the usual "Jewish virtues" of intelligence, industry, "indomitable perseverance," prudence, and family pride. The Jew was no coward, or he could not have kept up the "unequal struggle during eighteen centuries of persecution." She also refuted the popular belief accepted even by many defenders of the Jews that America's wealth was in Jewish hands. A few of the wealthier New York millionaires possessed more than all the Jews of America combined. She was one of the few to remind readers of the "misery of the poor Jew of the Ghetto."

An 1891 article in the *North American Review* by M. Bourchier Sanford was forthrightly entitled "In Favor of the Jew." Many Jews, the author asserted, were untainted by the "stain of meanness and cunning" that oppression had caused. Contrary to widely held fears, "A revengeful spirit is not a racial characteristic, gratitude is." Nor were bad manners especially Jewish, "Jews who have had advantages of education and association compare favorably with our cultured classes . . . Jewish pupils are the brightest and most docile" (a most revealing compliment). On a hopeful note, Sanford believed that the public schools would ultimately end prejudice on both sides and lead to intermarriage. It was already true that "among cultured Jews the racial features are generally less strongly defined." Like Vance, he regarded this as a desirable goal.

A great deal of space in American periodicals was given to reviews and summaries of the pro-Jewish works of Anatole Leroy-Beaulieu. The *Review of Reviews* in 1893, for instance, offered a series extensively recapitulating his ideas. The Jews had, in proportion to their numbers, "more men and women of first rate ability" than any nation. This was the result of their "marvelous adaptability and plasticity." Far from constituting a state within a state, "the Jews readily amalgamate with any nation they have settled among, if only they get a chance to do so."

Madison Peters was a Protestant minister who was well known for his Judeophile lectures in New York churches. His "Justice to the Jews" and "The Jew as Patriot," both incorporated into a later book, attempted to refute popular misconceptions about Jews. There were many poor Jews throughout the world, "Capital and Jew are not synonymous terms." Even if the Jew was a middleman—merchant or peddler—that role was "as important a cogwheel in the machinery of society as the railroad." You would find "vulgar, loud-mouthed, money-inflated offensive snobs" among gentiles as well as Jews. In the history of America and its wars, Jews had "the best record of any race or religion." Despite this, the Jew did not receive the treatment he deserved. "He is caricatured in the comic papers; in our social, professional and even political clubs the Jew is blackballed . . . the Jew is excluded from society." Evidently, despite the publication of so many philo-Semitic works, social discrimination continued to flourish.

Mark Twain's 1899 essay, "Concerning the Jews," is a most interesting example of the ambiguities often found even in works or obvious good will. In an era of growing European anti-Semitism, Twain discussed possible explanations for this universal hostility. The Jews were good, law-abiding citizens, although they did have "an unpatriotic disinclination to stand by the flag as a soldier—like the Christian Quaker." They also engaged in such "discreditable ways" as shady business practices, although they certainly didn't have a monopoly on these methods. The real reason was that the Jew was superior in any field he attempted—the Christian could not compete with him. "You will always be by ways and habits and predilections substantially strangers—foreigners—wherever you are, and that will probably keep the race prejudice against you alive." In spite of this, the contributions of Jews in all fields were out of proportion to their numbers. "All things remain mortal but the Jew; all forces pass but he remains."

There were many objections to portions of Twain's comments. *Overland Monthly* published "A Rabbi's Reply to Mark Twain," which charged the author with "malice and prejudice" and cited numerous examples of Jews as patriotic soldiers. Later, figures of Jewish war efforts in America were presented to Twain. He apologized for his initial comments in a highly publicized little piece, "The American Jew as Soldier." "The slur that the Jew is willing to feed on a country but not to fight for it," was untrue and "ought to be pensioned off right now and retired from active service," Twain concluded. Twain's confusions vividly illustrate the tenacity of the stereotype, even among those who were the most favorably disposed.

Judeophile articles greatly outnumbered anti-Semitic ones. In these the virtues of the Jews were often presented as larger than life. The Jew appears to have had more vehement defenders than any other ethnic group. The defender would often find himself making the same underlying assumptions about the Jew as the attacker, but arriving at very different conclusions. Many modern observers have pointed out the ubiquity of stereotyped images of the Jew. This was an era in which virtually every ethnic group was catalogued in the same way. Nevertheless, it is also true that political, ideological anti-Semitism was not a real factor in American life in the nineteenth century and that, in the press at least, friendly commentators greatly outnumbered hostile ones.

Treatment of Foreign Issues

The American press rather extensively covered issues involving Jewish persecution in other countries. Generally, their reaction was strongly favorable to the Jews. It was safe, easy, and self-righteous to condemn "barbarities" against the Jews by nations that were less "progressive" than the United States. The general approach was that, if Jews were reprehensible, persecution had made them so. Organized anti-Semitism in other countries was almost universally castigated. The implication was clear that things like this were not done in America, causing a higher quality Jew in this country.

Niles Weekly Register provided early conscientious coverage of Jews throughout the world.[29] *Niles* noted that Jews tended not be "honest laborers," but rather "mere consumers," as a result of a persecution that "reflects no credit on the professors of Christianity." The journal remarked, with equanimity, that prejudices in Europe were "driving many of the Jews to seek refuge in the United States." It also approved attempts to improve conditions for Jews, including the possibility, endorsed as early as 1816, of reestablishing Israel as a nation.

The *North American Review* also evinced an early interest in Jews in various parts of the world.[30] The persecution of Jews in countries like Italy was "inconsistent with the liberal spirit of the times." The only reason America's religious liberty did not attract more Jews was "the proverbial astuteness of us New Englanders, with which not even the Jews dare venture into competition." Despite mistreatment, Jews "bear these indignities with wonderful patience."

In 1840 Jews in Damascus were arrested, tortured, and murdered when they were accused of committing the ritual murder of a priest. Protest meetings were held in New York, Charleston, and other cities expressing "abhorrence" at the "bigotry," "intolerance," and "barbarities" of the Damascus Blood Libel case. The American press supported the American government in its protest. Later, a reporter described meeting a "princely" old Jewish merchant from Damascus. The author could not forget his nobility and fine face, "I do not believe that Father Abraham himself was a finer looking or more dignified personage."[31]

The debate on the Jewish disabilities bill in England was closely followed by most of the press.[32] A long editorial in the *New York Times* in 1852 set forth the attitude of most of the periodicals. "No more accurate judge for advancing civilization could probably be chosen than the political condition of the Jews." After centuries of persecution, the advance of the world is marked by the improvement of the condition of the Jews. "The sharp schooling in money-getting finds its account in the control they now wield over the motive power of the age we live in—capital." They now produce statesmen, scholars, poets and musicians as well. "The world at last does homage to the genius of the chosen and rejected people." Now it was time for complete political emancipation.

The Swiss Treaty, in which the American government accepted prohibitions against American Jews in some of the Swiss cantons, became a serious issue in 1857. Many newspapers objected to the government's insensitivity on this issue.[33] The *New York Herald* commented caustically that Americans should not find fault with Britain for refusing Jewish emancipation since the Pierce administration had ratified a treaty with the Swiss government in effect disqualifying Jews from citizenship. The actions of the American government, the *Chicago Daily Journal* concluded among others, was a "disgrace." These protests did not succeed in obtaining the abrogation of the treaty, however.

The most sensational issue of this period was the Mortara case of 1858. The seizure of a Jewish child from his parents by papal officers, on the grounds that he had been secretly baptized by a servant, brought forth a storm of protest in Protestant countries. American secular and Protestant journals were nearly unanimous in condemning papal actions.[34] The incident also presented an opportunity to engage in anti-Catholic propaganda, extremely common in America at the time. Political attacks on Catholicism were far more widespread than similar attacks on the handful of Jews. Most of the press deplored the kidnapping as a violation of the rights of private conscience, and an attack on the family unit. Many papers expressed "indignation" when Secretary of State Lewis Cass rejected a petition urging the American government to take action. Of the secular journals, only the *Boston Semi-Weekly Courier* seemed hostile in telling Jews to be content in America where they had the same rights as other citizens. Religious animosities could only be rekindled by "this extraordinary assumption of theirs that the private wrong of Jews in every foreign country is to be redressed by the Government of the United States. . . ." As Bertram Korn has pointed out, this was one of the earliest versions of the modern accusation of "dual loyalty," often directed against Jews in a later era. The Catholic press, naturally, defended the papal actions, and occasionally utilized traditional anti-Jewish epithets. As a whole, however, the American press supported Jewish rights in the Mortara case and expressed compassion for the Jewish parents. The *Chicago Presbyterian Expositor* felt that the public indignation would not have occurred at an earlier time. "Was there ever a time before when the civilized world could have been aroused to defend the religious rights of a single Jewish family?" This appreciation for such rights could lead to great changes, the paper believed.

The persecution of Romanian Jews in the 1870s and '80s often elicited outrage in the American press.[35] Vivid reports of horrors led the *New York Times* to urge more action. Civilized nations should not "fold their hands and look on." If their own government refused to protect these people, the advanced countries "should step in and do their work for them." Interestingly, while the editorial pages of the *Times* remained sympathetic, the correspondent who covered Romania after 1878 presented a picture of Jewish parasites, "this filthy race," who "eat up the substance of a country like a swarm of locusts." Most journals were more clearly on the Jewish side, endowing the issue with class undertones. Romania, *Harpers' Weekly* noted, wanted to restrict and expel the Jews because they were successful and hard working. This was an example of "the conspiracy of the idle against the industrious, of the ignorant against the studious." No nation could prosper with such practices. In fact, the *Nation* concluded in response to the suggestion by the American ambassador that the Jews emigrate to the United States, if they left, "they would leave behind them nothing but an ignorant peasantry and an idle and licentious aristocracy. Usury would probably come to an end, but so would industry." In 1885, in response to a new round of Romanian persecution, the *Chicago Daily Times* echoed these sentiments. The mistreatment was due to the Jews accumulating wealth "as they do in most places," which aroused the envy of the Romanian proletariat. The latter felt that "the proper method of dealing with the people who save their money is to kill them . . . economy is crime." The Jew, these papers seemed to feel, was being punished for possessing capitalist virtues.

Measures directed against Jews in Germany were also the subject of much discussion from 1879 to 1881.[36] Again, American opinion tended to oppose anti-Semitism vigorously, while often expressing preconceptions about Jews and their wealth. As distant a paper as the *Ogden Journal* declared outrage at the "fanatical hatred of the bigoted masses and the avaricious jealousy of the great." The *New York Tribune* commented that there had been no such complaint in Germany of Jewish ignorance and bad manners as in America's fashionable watering places. The real motive in Germany was that a larger proportion of Jews were educated, wealthy, and influential. If the German race could not hold its own against a small minority of Jews, "it deserves to go under." The *Times,* as usual, stressed the upper-class view of anti-Semitism as a lower-class resentment of the industrious and thrifty by the idle and stupid. "Because one class, the Jews, are guilty of making money, certain other classes, less able or less energetic, rise up and demand that they be deprived of privileges which . . . every citizen enjoys." Henry Ward Beecher, a friend of the Jews and the wealthy, inquired whether, because Jewish bankers had fiscal ability, the solution was to "decapitate them . . . Can we remedy the bottom of society by pulling down the top?" The *Nation*'s defense of the German Jews included an interesting commentary on the preoccupations of Western society, "If they are materialistic and self-seeking money-hunters, it is because they follow, not lead, the tendency of the age." An 1881 issue of the *American Israelite* included comments from around the country about the German anti-Semitic movement. Only one Christian journal justified the persecution. The *Troy Times* had the typical reaction. It concluded, "The Germans should be happy to assimilate such an element. A little more tincture of Jew would be a good thing."

Few issues stirred the American press more than the Russian persecution of the Jews, particularly in view of the many refugees who came to this country as a result.[37] Some journals discussed the growing hostility to Jews in Europe as exemplified by expulsion and oppression in Russia. The *Nation* in 1893 related this anti-Semitism to "the socialistic feeling which is now in the air. . . ." Its most marked feature is a vague hostility to the rich in trade and manufactures . . . and the Jews are made to stand for wealth in general and take the blows intended for it. . . ." In his "Israel Among the Nations," in *The Forum*, W. E. H. Lecky worried about the "strange and unforseen development" of the late-nineteenth-century anti-Semitic movement. Here was the "thrifty and sober Jew" in the midst of "idle, drunken and ignorant populations." As a result of perseverance and industry, he was prominent in occupations that excited animosity. Although Jews possessed great capacity for assimilation, "charm and grace of manner seem to have been among the qualities they most slowly and most imperfectly acquire." They were prone to extremes of "arrogance and obsequiousness." However, Lecky concluded that these defects would eventually diminish as the result of their pride, ability, and reverence for learning.

The most sensational of all foreign issues concerning the Jews at the close of the century was the Dreyfus case, which was closely watched and widely reported in the American press.[38] It was clear that the overwhelming majority of the American public and press sympathized with Dreyfus. Protest meetings were held throughout the nation. Such disparate groups as the New York Municipal Assembly, the Central Republican Club, the St. Louis Merchant exchange, the New York Daughters of 1812, and the San Francisco Chamber of Commerce expressed dismay or urged boycott of the Paris Exposition. The Protestant and secular press was virtually unanimous in opposition to this newest example of foreign injustice, and even a few large Catholic papers were pro-Dreyfus. *Harper's* declared that the public outcry meant that "now no nation can deny to one Jew even, the means of justice, and escape the condemnation of her sisters." A long article in the *Atlantic Monthly* reflected some of the ambivalent feelings so prevalent at the time. While the United States could be grateful it was not like France, the author remarked, it was well to remember, "If all the Jews of continental Europe were suddenly transported to this continent, we might find the national digestion, powerful as it is, badly nauseated." In spite of this distaste, the author opposed the "raging torrent of anti-semitism," reminding his readers that "if Judas was a Jew, so also was Christ."

The possibilities of the return of the Jewish people to the Holy Land was another issue often discussed.[39] In an earliler period this had been an integral part of the religious beliefs of Protestant fundamentalists, and remained so. The idea of the restoration of the Jewish people had interested both *Niles* and the *North American Review* in the early years of the century. It also was a central consideration in Melville's *Clarel*. The idea gained increasing popularity with the publication of George Eliot's *Daniel Deronda,* which received much favorable publicity in this country. In an 1883 article in *Century,* the poet Sidney Lanier declared that the mission of Daniel Deronda was not chimerical. Jewish restoration to Palestine was "so noble and captivating that to fail in it appears finer than to succeed in most of the promising projects of this world; and one almost wishes one were a Jew." The Rev. William Blackstone, chairman of the Conference of Christians and Jews, submitted a memorial to President Benjamin Harrison asking that Palestine be given back to the Jews. The signers included such luminaries as the chief justice, J. P. Morgan, John D. Rockefeller, Cardinal Gibbon, and all the New York newspapers with the exception of the *Sun.* Despite occasional doubts that the Jews would ever manage the necessary farming, many periodicals covered the Zionist movement with great interest. In fact, there was a more positive response by the secular press than there was in the American Jewish community at the time. Many of the journals were attracted to the idea as a method of absorbing prospective hordes of Russian refugees.

American periodicals tended to be fairly consistent in their support of Jewish positions on international issues. The ideals of American democracy required them to oppose blatant persecution. This also enabled them to stress the superiority of America to backward nations where "barbarities" were still carried out in "this enlightened age." Such practices were invariably condemned as "medieval." Without any particular pattern, some publications would casually, seemingly not realizing their significance, include anti-Semitic justifications of foreign practices in an attempt to be "fair." Although many journals accepted notions of Jewish wealth and power, most firmly supported the persecuted Jews safely distant from America. The issues sometimes seemed less clear when it might mean that these Jews would come to America. The significance of the condemnation of foreign oppression was that it established the idea that political and ideological anti-Semitism was the product of decadent, backward nations and, thus, un-American.

America as a Haven for the Oppressed

One of the most important ideals operating against ideological hostility to the Jews was the pride many Americans felt in their nation as a land of opportunity for oppressed people of all nations. They were particularly fond of the contrast between the tyranny of "backward" Europe and the glorious tolerance of generous America, the savior of the downtrodden. No group seemed to be more oppressed than the Jews. Periodicals and newspapers frequently congratulated Americans on welcoming those whom the benighted nations of Europe had mistreated. This self-image prevented anti-Semitism from achieving the same respectability in the United States that it enjoyed in much of Europe at this time.

Niles Weekly Register formulated this generally accepted view of America's role very early in the century. America was portrayed as saying to people of all nations and religions: "Come and partake with us of the blessings of independence, and in due time be to us as our own kindred. Come and help us to . . . establish manufactories, and extend commerce . . . by your labor, intelligence and capital . . . Bring with you a love of liberty, habits of temperance and industry." Hannah Adams, in her popular *History of the Jews,* echoed that idea, proudly reminding her readers that the United States was the "only place where the Jews have not suffered persecution, but have been encouraged . . . in every right. . . ."[40]

In the same period, there were several suggestions to Jews to settle in the United States on their own land. Mordecai Noah's plan for an agricultural settlement on Grand island in the Niagara River near Buffalo, in particular, excited a great deal of interest.[41] The *Albany Gazette* noted that it had often wondered, "Why the Jews do not emigrate more frequently to the United States; why should they suffer from the intolerance of other governments, when an asylum so desirable can be found in this country?" The United States would also benefit from such an emigration especially if great Jewish bankers would come, "circulate a few millions . . . and give a spur to internal commerce. . . ." This was an ideal country for Jews where they could live without fear of mobs and persecution "and who knows but Divine Providence who to this day protected the Children of Israel as a nation, may finally lead them to this country. . . ." The *Commercial Advertiser* also felt that, as the Jews advanced, "they cannot but turn their attention to this happy land where perfect freedom awaits them." A new generation, born in an enlightened America "would be free from those errors generally imputed to the Jews, and participating in the blessings of liberty, would have every inducement to become valuable members of society." The only opposition to the plan was based upon criticism of Noah, a controversial figure, rather than upon distaste for Jewish emigration. It is interesting that, in this early period, the value of Jewish immigration to America was stressed as much as the importance of American freedom to the Jew. This flowed naturally from the assumption of great Jewish wealth, which could help provide the country with needed capital.

Articles about the dedication of synagogues often stressed the freedom of religion that Jews had found in America.[42] In 1841 the *Charleston Courier* was hopeful that in America "the dark clouds of sectarian prejudice seem everywhere to be fast fading away before the widely spreading lights of right, reason and philosophy." In 1851 the *San Francisco Evening Picayune* welcomed the building of a synagogue and was glad that Jews "have chosen to cast their lot with us under a government that gives them the fullest protection in the exercise of their faith" and equality of opportunity. In the same year Pomroy Jones, in his *Annals and Recollections of Oneida County,* described the synagogue of the "descendents of Abraham" who had fled to America "to enjoy the right of worshipping God according to their own law and to escape the exactions of tyrants."

America's tolerance was a beacon to the world. In an article about the Jews of the East, the *American Literary Magazine* noted that one such merchant had only limited knowledge about the United States, but he did know about "the existence of religious liberty in these United States—where the Jews . . . enjoy . . . all the rights which other men possess. Often did he speak about our glorious country." An 1852 *New York Times* editorial, about "Jewish Disabilities" throughout the world, gloated that "a certain sense of exaltation on the part of the American people" was justified. "Here at least the Israelite enjoys full equality and protection." No wonder so many Jews emigrated to the New World, "considering the peril and repression they flee from and the genial kindness with which they are received." Some prejudices might linger among Americans," but they would end if people understood that "the traits we dislike in the Hebrew character are precisely those produced by the same unreasoning antipathy that flowed forth so vehemently among our progenitors."[43]

Eliza Woodson Farnham felt that living in America had already changed the character of the Jew who "does honor to his name here." Since the pressure that kept him down elsewhere had been removed, "he eschews old clothes, and rarely if ever . . . attempts to get a greater advantage in trade than his neighbors." The Rev. Dr. Cox of New York agreed. He boasted that America had set an outstanding example as "the only Christian nation . . . that has never endorsed the persecution of the Jews. On the contrary, we have cherished, respected and protected them." Here, they were "characteristically good citizens," because they had been treated so well. "They love this country with reason, it is their occidental Palestine."[44]

Various newspapers commented approvingly that, as a result of its freedom, Jews had assimilated in America.[45] In 1869 the *New York Herald* endorsed a San Francisco society to encourage the entry to European Jews to the United States. In this great, free land, Jews prospered. "In no country of the world . . . have they found so much of a home as they found here. . . . Let our rich Israelites bring their oppressed brethren to this new land of promise." The *New York Times* in 1870 noted that Jews had generally prospered in all civilized nations "without becoming identified with any," but now, "in the midst of our glorious American civilization," Jews continued to prosper and were good citizens as well. "The resistless power of amalgamation which is building up on this continent out of diverse elements a strong and great people has touched also the chosen race and is urging them into harmony with the modes of thinking that prevail around them." In a similar vein, an 1876 *New York Tribune* editorial remarked that, remembering his past and contrasting it with his present, the Hebrew "could appreciate his repose and liberty here." That was why, in this country, "the Hebrews are so thoroughly amalgamated . . . that they scarcely have achieved for themselves a distinctive character." The strongest point in the Jew's favor was his evident willingness to readily assimilate. The subsequent entry of Eastern European Jews shook this assumption.

The upsurge of persecution in Europe put the image of America as a haven for the oppressed into sharper relief.[46] The *Memphis Appeal* reported an 1880 speech by Louisiana congressman, P. K. Ewing. The Jews, he declared, begged to be rescued from bondage and inhumanity and given a chance in this "great and glorious land of liberty. Oh America! My country, thou friend of the friendless . . . 'lift up thy arms and take these wanderers in.'" *Frank Leslie's Illustrated Weekly,* discussing Russian exiles in 1882, maintained that America would benefit from this addition. "Instead of their presence being tolerated, it will be welcomed. . . ." (Later, *Leslie's* was far less sure about this.) A Christian newspaper in the 1880s urged Jews not to apologize for the humble new immigrants. America could find room, work, and homes for them. "They will add to our strength, to our wealth, to our . . . moral forces . . . We welcome them . . . we offer them our liberties and our opportunities. Let them come!" The *National Baptist* felt that since the Jew had been ostracized in Europe, it was not strange that he had lost his noble instinct and had become what he was made, "covetous, grasping, usurious. . . ." It would take years of justice and liberty to eliminate the traces of oppression. But, under freedom in this country, higher traits had already appeared and would continue to develop. Joaquin Miller expressed similar sentiments in poems published in many magazines. "The Jewess" was urged to "come where stars of freedom spill their splendor." In "To Rachel in Russia," the oppressed Jews were urged to escape to America: "Rise up and come where freedom waits . . . come where Kings of Conscience dwell/Oh come, Rebecca to the Well!"

In the 1890s, when stories of anti-Jewish repression had become more commonplace and pressures for immigration restriction were building, there was considerably less allusion to America's role as a haven for the oppressed. Such ideals did, however, continue to serve to some extent as a countervailing force to the ever growing restrictionist movement. The continuing attraction of these ideals can be seen in a 1902 story in *McClure's*, "The Promised Land," in which a restrictionist congressman learns about the true meaning of America. He is told, "The United States is the refuge to which the oppressed of every land are looking. They don't come to overturn our institutions." When the immigrant ship arrives, it is the Jew who gives thanks with a fervent prayer from the Scriptures.[47]

The image that Americans had of their nation as the only hope for freedom, a country with a mission to end the intolerance of the Old World, had a great impact upon the attitude of the press toward the Jews. Hostility toward the Jew ran counter to the perceived superiority of American institutions. The potency of this American self-image would not be severely tested until the Russian Jews came flooding into the United States.

Political and ideological anti-Semitism was not characteristic of nineteenth-century American society. Virulent anti-Jewish attacks, so much a part of the European scene, were anomalies in the United States. Even the Populists, often characterized as committed anti-Semites, were more often afflicted with the typical American ambivalence. In fact, organized anti-Semitism seemed to many to be a product of inferior, foreign societies. By the end of the century the *Jewish Messenger* firmly believed that anti-Semitism was totally on its way out in the United States since it was incompatible with "The American Way of Life."[48]

6

Eastern European Jews

THE MILLIONS OF JEWS WHO FLOODED IN FROM EASTERN EUROPE altered the American perception of the Jew in many significant ways. The German Jew was easily assimilated. His sanitized and protestantized Reform Judaism was far from mysterious. He was a paragon of middle-class virtues. The newcomers, on the other hand, were obviously poor, adherents of strange religious rites, exotic in dress and speech. Although many of the older religious stereotypes continued to have some potency, the impact of the Eastern European Jew was far more profound than a mere complication.

Generally as hard working and upward striving as their German co-religionists, the newcomers were also law abiding and did not require Christian charity. Their strikes tended to bring forth more sympathy than other labor disturbances. A great deal of compassion was expressed for obvious victims of Russian barbarities. There was fear, however, that the persecutions had destroyed the abilities of the immigrants to function in a society that required comprehension, cleanliness, and order. At times the newcomers appeared anarchistic and oblivious to society's need for the rule of law. Some seemed to regard their bizarre religious "laws" as superior to civil authority. The language used in describing Jews from Eastern Europe was, in itself, significant in its preoccupation with "savages," "dwarfing" of personality, and "Oriental" qualities.

Robert Wiebe has pointed out that in nineteenth-century America "the line between acceptable and unacceptable . . . ran hard, and all those who crossed it . . . were expected to divest themselves rapidly of all traits that a current absolute judged alien."[1] Whenever a favorable image of the Russian Jew was presented, the writer tended to endow him with middle-class virtues.

Even before the era when the Eastern European Jews arrived in any considerable numbers, there was a generally unflattering awareness of their differences. The *North American Review* in 1845 described these most religious Jews as the "lowest" of all in morals. This was caused by the "gross immorality of many Talmudic precepts."[2] Even in America "Polish" Jews maintained these Jews as "brutes" who didn't even speak their own language, but conversed in a "miserable German . . . and a worse Hebrew which are as commingled and polluted as to render the mixture unintelligible to any but each other." In the United States they were "despised and disbelieved."[3] The Eastern Jews, when they first arrived, were described as inferior to other Jews. But in time-tested ways, they were seen as dishonest and money mad.

By the 1870s the press was discovering the more exotic aspects of the Polish Jews for the first time. In 1872 an early-day Craig Claiborne came upon what must have been one of the first restaurants serving the food of Eastern European Jews. Although the people spoke an "impossible language," the waiter was a cockney. The venturesome food critic overcame the waiter's obvious reluctance and was served such unfamiliar fare as a beet soup "which set our teeth on edge" and a "Moldavian" dish of beef with "incompatible raisins floating in a sea of gravy." Finally, the critic settled for "delicious" fried fish, causing him to muse, "Might not the children of Israel as they passed through the Red Sea . . . have tarried by the shore and prepared fish exactly in this way?" The delighted waiter concluded that the author might eventually be "fully educated up" to other traditional dishes.[4]

A sensational murder case brought the strange community of Eastern European Jews to the attention of the New York press. Nathan Rubinstein, a Polish Jew, was accused of murdering his cousin. She had become pregnant at the very time he was expecting his wife to rejoin him from Poland. The press reported the case in detail, focusing on its exotic aspects.[5] When the police searched Rubinstein, they found over $3,000. In conformity with the old literary stereotype, he was reported to have exclaimed, "my monish, my monish; give me my monish!" The peculiar religious practices of this odd community was a subject of frequent comment. In his observance of rites, the defendant had been "rigid to a fault." He would not eat "butter, meat or leaven bread." He turned his face to Jerusalem to pray after the guilty verdict. He swore that he was innocent in the Polish Hebrew dialect" and unloosened his hair, which was an oath "of peculiar sacredness" among strict Jews who never cut their hair. These various misstatements were indicative of the lack of any real contact with these newest immigrants.

The 1876 death of Rubinstein in his cell led to further speculation about the strange practices of these odd Eastern Jews. He had died of insufficient nourishment and "filthy habits." Although he was covered with vermin, he had prayed zealously, wearing "twillin," straps that "bound him in a painful position for hours at a time." The *Herald* indulged in the wildest conjecture. Perhaps religious authorities as "fanatical" as Rubinstein himself may have decided to avoid scandal "according to their creed" and appointed Rubinstein "an instrument of God's wrath." Americans knew so little about the precepts of Orthodox Jewry that the newspaper could seriously advance the notion that rabbis had convened and ordered a murder! The *Tribune* more moderately attributed the extraordinary interest in the case to the fact that the victim and her murderer "belonged to a class of Israelites, few in number, holding peculiar views and regulating their lives according to the Talmud and tradition. . . ."

The *New York Times* followed up with articles about the "curious mode of life" of these newest Jewish immigrants.[6] Generally, "their contempt for state laws and their reverence for the decisions of their rabbis are indulged" since they lived together with little contact with the larger society. This was the beginning of a continuous concern with the Jew as an unassimilable perpetual alien. A *Times* reporter was one of the first to describe the non-decorous, crowded service that became characteristic of the East Side. The congregation consisted of peddlers and "others of that ilk." The ventilation was terrible and "foul odors were strong and varied." The singing of the service's leader "was not unpleasant to the ear, but the inharmonious howls made in response were simply terrible." This was a typical response to the lack of order apparent in Orthodox Eastern European services in startling contrast to American Protestants or Reform Jews.

These early perceptions of the Eastern European Jew tended to focus upon his distinctiveness. Images of lack of cleanliness, basic inability to accept American law, dishonesty, and permanent alienation resulting from a fanatic religion existed before the advent of great masses from Eastern Europe. Their arrival would both reinforce and moderate these uneasy perceptions.

The real flood began in the 1880s. At that time the press was stirred up and outraged by the Russian persecution of the Jews. The few exceptions were mainly the result of sporadic attempts to be "fair" and present the Russian side of the story. Unquestionably, the extensive coverage substantially increased public consciousness of events in Russia in the 1880s.

Even sympathetic articles, however, often revealed basic misconceptions about the role of Jews in Russian society. The *New York Tribune* was typical in its ignorance of the poverty of Russian Jews and its assumption that they were moneylenders and wealthy merchants.[7] The Russian found the Jew abhorrent for ancient reasons: "he has imperceptibly got the money bags of the nation in his hands." In addition, "indolent and intemperate" peasants were in debt to Jews and committed atrocities out of the "rage of an unthrifty, impoverished class against their wealthy, arrogant and successful rivals." The Russian women who envied the silks and satins flaunted by wealthy Jewesses "out rival the hags of the Paris Commune in malevolence." The ambivalent nature of this defense is apparent.

The *New York Times* presented a mass of contradictory articles.[8] The Paris correspondent, who had earlier endorsed blood libel accusations, defended the Russian persecutions. He felt that the Jews had brought their troubles on themselves by zealously "spoiling the Egyptians." Maudlin sympathy should not be wasted on "these pariahs" who prove that "Shylock was not the mere creation of a poet's fancy." The London correspondent, by contrast, wrote of the "heart rending crimes" directed against "thrifty and hard working Jews." Editorials explained the "unreasoning, ineradicable" antipathy of the "dull and sluggish" Russian as a function of class differences. It resembled American workers hatred of the Chinese. An improvident class of men was filled with jealousy for those who "by intelligence, frugal habits and a parsimony peculiar to themselves . . . are able to grow richer every day." Later, the *Times* was astonished to learn that Russian Jewish immigrants were not moneylenders, but included almost every kind of artisan and even farmhands!

A large protest meeting held in New York's Chickering Hall in 1882 against Russian pogroms led to extensive editorial comment in support of Russian Jews.[9] The *Evening Post* vehemently condemned "brutality on the part of a barbarous populace" with the wicked connivance of the Russian government. In a rare suggestion that emigration to America might be a desirable solution, the paper added that the protest would assure the oppressed "that there is safe haven here and charitable hearts to aid the unfortunate." The *Commercial Advertiser* suggested reprisals against Russia if it refused to end the persecutions. Other journals throughout the country voiced similar sentiments. The *Cincinnati Commercial* felt that Russian Jews were industrious and inoffensive. American Jews were among the nation's best citizens, and "there is room in America for the class of people now being driven out of Russia by inhuman persecution."

There were a few dissenting voices defending the Russians against the depredations of Shylock.[10] The *Weekly Witness,* a widely circulated evangelical journal, claimed that the Russian Jew, living in a separate exclusive community, had grown rich through a lack of scruples. Those who suggested, out of pity, that the exiles should come here, should remember that these Jews would never be productive, but would go into "clothing, dry goods . . . and money." When a panic came, "every one of them runs straight to the bank to demand his 'monish'. . . . Were conditions the same as in Russia, it is not likely that his treatment would be any better here." *Century Magazine* published an explanation from the Russian point of view, supposedly in order to open discussion on the issues. The Russian author called the Jews parasites, "sucking out the country's blood." The article concluded with a charge, which had echoes in the twentieth century, that Westerners did not realize how "loathsome" and dangerous Jews were because of the Hebrew control of the press. Such comments, however, were far less common than condemnations of the Russians.

The persecutions of the 1880s succeeded in making the press more aware of the presence of Eastern European Jews. Compassion often mingled with anxiety. The *Tribune* was again representative in the ambivalence of its response.[11] Initially, the paper praised English Jews for aiding homeless but affluent Russian Jews to migrate. Later the *Tribune* conceded that most of the refugees were penniless and would probably come to this country. Here they would succeed due to "exceptional energy, thrift and skill in trade," and lack of prejudice. Americans had no reason to be envious of Hebrew success. "The American is just as pushing and sharp as his Jewish brother, and is not likely to let the trade of his country slip into Hebrew hands as it has done elsewhere." In this way, the Jew was endowed with the capitalist virtues also possessed by Americans. A bit later, the *Tribune* was far more cautious, reflecting what Robert Wiebe has characterized as the fear of "any congestion of aliens." It was suggested that the immigrants should be promptly sent to the "waste lands or even the small communities of the West." They might be mixtures of virtuous martyrs and arrogant usurers, but as foreigners without funds, they would "add fresh weight to the huge load of pauperism, disease and crime which our cities have to bear."

Within a month, the *Tribune* had become aware that the refugees were poorer than expected and unlikely to go West. The lower-class Russian Hebrew, it declared, was not a "picturesque or poetic object of compassion." Rather, he was dirty and "tyranny has given his wits an unpleasant edge and poverty an offensive savor to his manners." Still, he would earn a living and was by nature neither drunken or criminal. That was more than could be said for some other immigrant groups. A later story, however, reported that there had been complaints against lazy Jewish immigrants lounging in Battery Park. "Their filthy condition has caused many of the people who are accustomed to go to the park . . . to give up this practice." Perhaps this kind of conduct explained why no country wanted these immigrants. By September 1882 an editorial headed "No More Russian Hebrew Refugees" concluded that they should be sent back to Russia.

By the following year, however, the *Tribune* had become reconciled to the presence of the Eastern European Jew. A long feature, "The Jewry of New York . . . Tens of Thousands of Slavonic Jews East of Grand Street, . . ." was quite sympathetic. Unlike earlier Jewish arrivals, they isolated themselves and pursued industrial occupations. (This was one of the few times that this essential difference in occupations of Jewish immigrants was acknowledged.) The synagogue was eloquently described as a place of refuge for the poor peddler who had tramped throughout the week for meager profits. When he enters the congregation, "he puts away from him all the sordid cares" of the week. "For one day he belongs to his God and his God belongs to him."[12]

The *New York Times* was equally inconsistent in its treatment of Eastern Jews.[13] In 1881 the paper approved of the efforts of "israelite" residents to assist their "persecuted brethren" in coming to America. Early arrivals were described as "active, energetic and healthy" and, although penniless, "intelligent . . . industrious." The *Times* warned that the American people were not "fully alive to the importance of this influx." Jews tended to appear three times as numerous as they were since they clustered in the same occupations, "all" in business. Only 250,000 of them had arrived, but there were three million more in Russia. If America permitted unrestricted asylum, "the possibilities in the way of Semitic acquisitions seem almost unlimited." Unlike average American Jews, these immigrants were Orthodox and found it difficult to adjust outside of Jewish centers, leading them to flock to New York. Although they were intelligent, they lacked the physique for manual labor. By 1884 an official of United Hebrew Charities was quoted characterizing penniless immigrants as "idle and shiftless," too lazy to keep a job.

Other periodicals and newspapers throughout the country were more consistently sympathetic to the refugees. *Harper's Weekly* remarked that, "with a little aid just now," they would soon "become self-supporting." Papers in Cincinnati, St. Paul, and Minneapolis backed humanitarian appeals on behalf of the "half-starved" refugees, while expressing surprise that Jews could indeed be poor.[14]

Some journals were decidedly less compassionate. *Frank Leslie's Illustrated Newspaper* vividly illustrated the shifting perceptions as ever more Russian immigrants arrived.[15] A March 1882 story welcomed victims of persecution whose hard work, thrift, and excellent character compared favorably with "the best this country has received." By August the tone had altered considerably. Russian immigrants were "filthy," accepted "no restraints of morality," and preferred "to be cared for and do nothing." Such undesirables would find that this country had no place for able-bodied paupers "even if they are religious martyrs." *Judge* added caustically that observation of the newest arrivals from Russia would lead one to admire the Pharaoh who "was able to extract honest, useful labor from such unpromising material."

By the early 1880s it was clear that Russian immigration was creating a new image of the Jew. This new Jew was a radical departure from accepted stereotypes: poor rather than rich, dirty, unwilling to work—a parasite on charity funds. The Jew had always been conceded his willingness to labor long hours (even in dishonest activities). later it would become obvious that these newer Jews were also hard working, but laboring men rather than bosses. Clearly the journals were of two minds about these strange new Americans.

By the mid-1880s there was a definite rise in interest in the new immigrants as a source of exotica. In 1885 the critic of the *New York Sun* viewed "A Quaint Hebrew Drama," *Bar Kochba*, which would "well repay the interest of every thoughtful and discriminating student of the drama." The language of the play was not really Hebrew but "a hybrid Russian mixed with Polish, Massouric and Old Hebrew and at times resembling German." The Yiddish language was a continual source of amazement to the press. *Harper's Weekly* was equally taken with the "mongrel tongue known in Europe as jargon which appears to be a chaotic mixture of Teutonic, Sclavonic [*sic*] and Hebraic." *Harper's* declared that the acting was excellent since "with the Russian Jew the dramatic profession is practically a matter of heredity." The audience was good natured, but "remarkably strange in appearance to an Anglo-Saxon," with the familiar German-Jewish face scarcely to be seen.[16]

In the 1880s a new, although contradictory, picture of the Eastern European immigrant was taking shape. The *Times* in 1885 illustrated this characteristic ambiguity in its coverage. One article asserted that Russian laws against Jews resulted from the idea that Jews were "parasites not producers." Yet a story appearing one month later concluded that the departure of the Jews would harm Russia by depriving it of "the most thrifty, energetic and intelligent of her population . . . a more orderly, well-behaved set of people would not often be seen."[17]

The resumption of active anti-Semitic measures in Russia in the 1890s led to an alarming increase of Jewish immigrants to America. This not only resulted in extended coverage by newspapers and periodicals, it also raised disturbing questions about the desirability of these peculiar newcomers.

Journals like the *Illustrated American, Harper's New Monthly Magazine* and *Littell's Living Age* worried about the Jewish tendency to become a "nation within a nation," as they were in Russia.[18] The Russian hated the Jew because the Jew lived only to squeeze out money from society. The refusal of the Jew to serve in the Russian army was typical of "his behavior in regard to all his obligations to the state and every community except his own." A condemnation of "immoral" Russian persecution concluded that "it was not the Jews' fault that they became a race of money lenders." Long Christian mistreatment had caused "the imperfection of modern Jews," but was it fair to expect America to bear the brunt of their rehabilitation?

It was not common to find old stereotypes in the pages of the same newspapers that vigorously condemned Czarist tyranny. The *Tribune,* for example, followed a story about the hardships suffered by "loyal and industrious" Russian Jews with an article claiming that the public read only the Jewish side of the controversy because "almost all the principal newspapers of Europe are either owned, controlled or influenced by Hebrew gold." The Jew exploited the Russian "with all the ingenuity of his race." A later, sympathetic feature on the plight of Russian Jews, nevertheless, concluded that while other immigrants intermarried, worshiped, and ate with Americans, the strict Jew would not. "He is contemptuous toward the people of his adoption."[19]

A combination of the older view of the Jew as an aloof, self-segregated Shylock and the more modern notion of the all-powerful international banker frequently found its place in New York newspapers, even in sypathetic articles. A *Sun* editorial condemning Russian barbarity asserted that the persecution could be averted by "the great Hebrew bankers . . . the real masters of Europe. . . . They have it in their power to paralyze Russian credit and Russian commerce and it is obviously their duty to assert that power."[20] The ultraconservative *Sun* had thus incorporated a viewpoint usually associated with the Populists.

The pervasiveness of the old stereotype was apparent in a human interest story in the *Times*, "Not the Hebrews of Fiction—Sorrows of Cloakmakers." An observer on the East Side, the author noted, would find "no richly-fed men extravagantly attired, gleaming with diamonds . . . rubbing their hands and computing their ill-gotten gains." This was obviously the image in the minds of many people, although the reality was the "timid atmosphere of poverty." The ancient pictures of the calculating money-mad Jew could be frequently found sprinkled among stories about life in the ghetto. Even a bittersweet little tale about a young man who came from Russia to marry his sweetheart, spending all his hard-earned money on her, only to be jilted at the ceremony, concluded that his hurt lessened when the ring and thirty dollars were returned.[21]

This persistence of the classic stereotype, even among educated and sophisticated people, can be seen in a speech given by Charles W. Eliot, president of Harvard, to Jewish residents of Boston. Eliot was widely known as a proponent of unrestricted immigration and ethnic self-identity. His 1902 address entitled "The Duty of Jewish Youth toward Their Persecuted Brethren" argued:

A great factor in the prejudice against the Jew is due to the fact that he has been a money lender . . . I therefore suggest to the young Jew when he becomes prosperous that he no longer lend his money to individuals. Let him invest his money by lending to municipalities, states, corporations. . . . A vast service to the race will be done in removing a cause of enmity.[22]

The older image of the Jew was a reflection of long-held European stereotypes, rather than of American experiences. The resumption of oppression of the Russian Jews in the 1890s complicated the picture. On the one hand, America, with a two-hundred-year-old tradition of welcome to Europe's downtrodden and a distaste for official repression, felt compassion for the ill-treated Jews. On the other, many Americans found these desperately poor, exotic immigrants repugnant. The desirability of the "new immigration" in general had become a real issue. Sympathy struggled with distaste on the pages of newspapers and magazines, and the perception of the Jew underwent profound revision.

Several journals were unreservedly friendly. An 1890 article in the *Arena*, "The Jewish Question in Russia," protested the "absurd and revoltingly unjust conduct of the Russian government." Far from being exploiters, the Jews lived in "extreme wretchedness," many "literally starving." There was no

Jewish issue in England and America where the Jew was free to engage in legitimate pursuits and was neither better nor worse than other citizens. The *Forum* came to similar conclusions. As a result of Russian brutality, Jews were anxious to come to America, even to what appeared "to us to be a miserable existence" of extreme poverty. Emigration was claiming "the best element among the Jews." Eastern Jews were "singularly free from the kinds of vice that do most to enfeeble and corrode a race." They were moderate, took care of their children, and were less addicted to alcohol than Christians.[23]

Others were less sanguine at the thought of floods of destitute immigrants pouring into the United States. Benjamin Harrison, president at this time, reflected their concern. In a message to Congress in 1891 he worried that great numbers of these "unfortunate people," forced out of Russia were likely to come to America in "proportions which make it difficult to find homes and employment for them." The president conceded that Jews were never beggars, were law-abiding, and cared for their poor more than other groups. He felt, however,that "the sudden transfer of such a multitude, under conditions that tend to strip them of their small accumulations and to depress their energy and courage is neither good for them nor for us."[24]

Papers and magazines throughout the country were less sensitive in their expressions of fear and hostility. The *Cincinnati Times-Star,* owned by Charles Taft, felt that the immigrants were in desperate need of "enlightenment" about American democracy. "There is no more relation between the American Hebrew and the Russian Jew than there is between white and black." Another Cincinnati paper remarked that the Russian Jews were "a source of danger," the "least desirable of all Jews." Detroit papers expressed alarm at the presence of a "pauper and lawless class." In an 1891 article in *North American Review,* Henry Cabot Lodge argued that the Russian Jews planned to enter the "congested ranks of middlemen." The place to stop the entry of such a "revolting" group was "not at Castle Garden, but in Russia." The *Illustrated American* believed that "the inroad of the hungry Semitic barbarian is a positive calamity." *Leslies's* argued that legislation was essential to "enable this country to prevent itself from being an offal-heap for all Europe," although it expressed more sympathy for Jews "fresh from starvation, tyranny and persecution," than for "hang-dog, thieving" Italians. *Life* reported that Baron Hirsch, with the "well-recognized shrewdness of his race," picked the "fool" United States as the dumping ground for "all the shiftless, incompetent, lazy, ignorant and diseased objects of his charity, whom he couldn't locate in any other country."[25]

The 1901 *Reports of the Industrial Commission on Immigration* showed the continuing ambivalence at the turn of the century. John Commons, who wrote the main body of the report, noted that the Jew's "physical strength does not fit him for manual labor; his instincts lead him to speculation and trade. . . ." The positive side, for a believer in the Protestant work ethic, was that, unlike Italians, Jews had definite aspirations for advancement. They sacrificed to keep their children in school, where the latter were remarkably successful. A former Commissioner of Immigration added that one could find no Jews in almshouses. The Jew was an able bodied worker who "is of value to this country the moment he lands." Another commissioner complained that these emigrants were paupers who engaged only in "light" work like tailoring. They would not do any productive labor, but became middlemen, "and the middleman is always a drain on the producer." Another testified that Russian Jews "speak the Jews' jargon only" and were controlled by superstitious rabbis. He favored the Lodge Bill to restrict immigration by literacy tests, which would bar two-thirds of the Jews since, "I would not recognize the Hebrew jargon as a language."[26]

In similar fashion, public opinion veered between antipathy and sympathy. Some periodicals clearly believed that American traditions required the admission of refugees. *Puck* effectively satirized the superficial expressions of compassion for the exiles, coupled with unwillingness to take action on their behalf. The "Labrador Pemmican" was "aghast at the barbarity of the Czar" who drove away "honest hardworking people." It suggested that they would find lack of prejudice and warm climate in "the vast fertile plains of Brazil." The "Chilean Daily Nitrate" and the "Mexican Vaquero" were equally appalled and equally willing to suggest sojourns in North Dakota or Patagonia. The same combination of rhetoric against persecution and fear of the admission of its victims was common in the United States.[27]

No newspaper was more involved with the problem of Jewish immigration than the *New York Times,* whose concern bordered on the obsessive.[28] When news of Russian anti-Semitic decrees of 1890 first became known, the *Times* sounded the alarm. Readers were reminded that, after the anti-Jewish attacks of 1882, thousands had flocked to New York "and a sorry lot they were . . . filthy and ungrateful and riotous. . . . It is well to remember how our hospitality was abused." The tone of editorials and articles became more strident in 1891 as Russian immigration multiplied. These "undesirable" exiles simply "drop where they are dumped from a ship and wait to be succored." They were a "burden to any community." If this immigration had diffused itself, it might have been absorbed. Instead, the *Times* warned, Russian Jews persisted in forming "a segregated community . . . a source of weakness and danger under institutions like ours." The paper concluded, "there are enough Jews in this country already." A fever pitch of emotions was aroused by an outbreak of typhus aboard an immigrant ship. It was ascribed to "neglect of fundamental laws of sanitation." It was the duty of Americans "to protect themselves against such persons as these." They may have been persecuted, but they were "repulsive in every way."

The epitome of the class (and/or racist) attitude of the *Times* was shown when a group in New Jersey complained of being put to work at sewing machines rather than receiving the farms promised to them. According to the paper, this proved that they were unwilling to work for a living and expected their fellow Jews to take care of them. Their complaints alienated anyone who might have felt sympathy for their plight. In a revealing example of nineteenth-century social Darwinism, the article concluded that any man "who complains of the nature of work . . . or the equality of bread ought to be told, 'Root hog or die.'"

One month after this, however, Harold Frederic, the *Times* London correspondent and a well-known novelist, began a series of reports on conditions in Russia. (American Jews funded his trip.) His perceptive and accurate accounts ran weekly for four months and were later collected in a book, *The New Exodus*.[29] The *Times* reader was presented with a radically different picture of the Jews. Even the editorial policy appeared to change at that time. Frederic attacked descriptions of Jews of the Pale as prosperous usurers. "I have not seen anywhere in Europe . . . a more terrible poverty. . . . The sober truth is that it has been the Jew who has been exploited." In spite of brutal persecution, the Jews "remained a simple and devout people, clinging doggedly to their despised faith, helping one another . . . and keeping up the virtues of temperance, family affection and chastity." Their isolation had indeed harmed them, developing narrow-mindedness and ignorance of the rest of civilization. Of all Jews, only the Russians had produced no real culture. This would seem hopeless "were it not for the startling recuperative power in his race. The grandsons of these bearded refugees now fleeing in dumb despair . . . will be recognizable cousins of Heine and Mendelsohn," the author assured his readers. Other articles showed that Russian Jews were not revolutionaries, but were law-abiding and top students when given a chance—in short, desirable immigrants. Public gaze at the time was shifting from events inside Russia to the streams of refugees. There was growing nervousness in the United States where "humanitarian sympathy takes on sternly practical limitations." Frederic felt, however, that America had "room enough for all newcomers who promised to be good citizens." He was sure Russian Jews would qualify:

> The woe-begone outcast in cap or caftan, wandering forth dismayed into exile, will take heart again. His children's children may shape a nation's finances or give law to a literature, or sway a Parliament. At the least, they will be a living part of their generation; they will be freemen, fearing neither famine nor the knout.

When Jewish charities, for the first time, requested outside assistance in December 1891, the *Times* responded sympathetically. The unfortunate exiles were "peaceable, honest, temperate, willing and earnest. . . . They will in the end make a desirable class of citizens." In its newfound tolerance, the

Times noted, "The Russian Hebrew had proved an extraordinary person in his adoptiveness." A supporting statement by the first Christian contributor, Judge John Dillam, decried reports that some Jewish refugees had been sent back as possible public charges. Such regulations "have no rightful application to your fugitive people who in their necessity come . . . to this land of freedom. . . . Let us receive them with welcome and hospitality."[30] At least temporarily, the claims of America's liberal tradition seemed paramount.

By 1893, with the Frederic series receding into the past and the depression approaching, the *Times* had reverted to its original views.[31] The paper again advocated excluding the "least desirable, worst class" of Jewish immigrants whose ignorance was particularly deep and "whose characteristics may be studied at the anarchist meetings in the East Side in this city." An immigration inspector was quoted approvingly in his description of a "swarthy race with long, dark, unkempt hair. The clothes they have on are invariably old and dirty. . . ." In short, a "stolid, stupid horde . . . dumb cattle," were invading our shores. When Adolph Ochs, a Jew himself, took control of the newspaper in 1896, its policies did not change. It continued to favor exclusion of a class that tended to "live together and live as they have lived in the past." The image of a large, unassimilable mass of poor immigrants, with strange and inappropriate life-styles, remained threatening.

None of the other New York newspapers was nearly as obsessed. The *Tribune,* with rare lapses, was far more sympathetic to the plight of the Russian Jews.[32] In fact, the *Tribune* often ascribed their difficulties to supposed American-like bourgeois characteristics. The Jews' crime was "less their race and creed than their wealth and intelligence." These immigrants were not really destitute. "They lack industrial skill, but readily adapt themselves to their new conditions, are frugal and persevering and seldom become a public charge." One headline asserted, "The Hebrew Immigrants—They are Nearly All Desirable Persons."

In endowing Russian Jews with middle-class virtues, the *Tribune* seemed genuinely unaware of the lower-class origins of the vast majority. Most Russian Jews, after all, were not merchants whose success was resented, but workmen who eked out a miserable livelihood. This positive view derived from accepting anti-Semitic stereotypes, but reversing their import. An interesting article, "The Jew Workman in England," illustrated this tendency to absolve the Jews of working-class "vices." Unlike the inert mass of unthinking workers, the Jew did not accept "a station in life," but was "always pushing his way forward." Unlike the British worker who tried to place limits around his trade, the Jewish immigrant accepted innovation with his "abundant store of restless mental energy." To some this might seem like a picture of the "pushy" Jew. To the *Tribune,* however, this was the embodiment of the proper conduct for an Americna worker in 1899.

Other papers also tended to be friendly, if less actively concerned. The

World opposed "know nothingism." It did concede that the new immigrants were distinctly inferior to earlier groups. "Their character is, like their bodies, often dwarfed and distorted by generations of oppression." (This idea of the "warping" or "dwarfing" effect of persecution was widely accepted.) In spite of this, however, the paper urged their continuing admission. "Human nature is not a thing of fixed character." In America's superior environment, aided by education, they would improve. To shut them out would be an act of "national cowardice."[33] This faith in the ability of our society and institutions to eliminate undesirable characteristics is a good example of what Eric Goldman has called, "Reform Darwinism."

The ever-increasing migration of Eastern European Jews did far more than merely complicate the image of Jews in America. It added a whole new dimension, even though elements of the old stereotype persisted. This was the era of rising restrictionist sentiment culminating in the formation of the Immigration Restriction League and the American Protective Association. Jews were not the focus of their concern. They directed their vituperation against all "new immigrants," and the latter group, particularly, saw Catholicism as the greatest danger. A profound moral struggle was taking place between the idealization of America as the haven of the oppressed and the obvious distaste for the strange newcomers. Only by disguising the real nature of this immigration, as the *Tribune* did, were the papers able to reconcile these two attitudes. As Barbara Solomon has noted, by 1898 most Americans were still not interested in the restrictionist cause. However, by the early twentieth century immigration limitation became widely accepted and was "destined to change a basic tradition of the United States."[34]

Except for the mass-circulation newspapers, most of the press made some attempt to describe the peculiar customs of the new immigrants. Generally, the stories were sympathetic, although there was a tendency to overstress the "quaint," "exotic," and "Oriental" and an inordinate preoccupation with cleanliness. Attitudes were frequently an unpredictable mixture of friendly interest and antipathy.

The *Times* commented in 1895 that a man who had not been in New York in fifteen years would be bewildered by a walk on the East Side. He would find a very different group, an immense beehive in which thousands, speaking only Yiddish, crowded together in poorly ventilated rooms in a "semi-Oriental city." The people of this "unique race" were human, "intensely so," and their very strangeness "lent an additional charm." More often, however, the charms seemed less apparent to the *Times*. An article on East Side vendors described rotton food that "would make the average citizen turn his nose up in the air." These people who "claim to have been driven from Poland and Russia," had created "the eyesore of New York and perhaps the filthiest place on the Western continent." Cleanliness, a middle-class obsession at the time, was unknown to them. "They cannot be lifted up to a higher plane because they do not want to be."[35]

Generally, the tone of the *Tribune,* while somewhat patronizing, was almost invariably kindly.[36] An article about life among New York's tailors demurred from the popular impression of rampant filth. "Contrary to the usual impression, the rooms of the tailors are surprisingly neat" and clean. Yet the same paper contributed to the caricature of the "dirty" Jew in a fascinating article on the Jewish settlement in Brownsville. There, ruled by "primitive customs," low-class people lived packed together. A typical resident had a "matted untrimmed beard . . . a greasy threadbare old coat." The numerous children were "invariably unwashed." However, the men were "keen witted and diligent workers."

Other *Tribune* articles were more unequivocally friendly. One described the "curious ceremonies" at Jewish weddings, which were of "Oriental origins." Another visited East Side cafés where the "intellectual aristocracy" met to discuss the issues of the day. "Life is a struggle for a livelihood part of the time and a feverish search for knowledge for another part." Even the candy store was analyzed as a "new social center" for the boys. The paper lectured sternly that, unless there were a healthier moral surroundings, the boys would succumb to evil influences and go on to such horrors as "Bowery concert halls, beer parlors and poolrooms." The East Side markets were most engrossing to the *Tribune,* as to other journals. Here, even the lower classes were so exacting in their standards that only the best-quality meat and produce were sold. (One wonders if the reporters of the *Times* and *Tribune* had been to the same markets.) A most revealing section described the reaction of a woman who found this area gratifying to her vanity. "You walk in and say in a queenly fashion that you want an umbrella . . . the best in the store and and every member of the family will . . . make you feel like the most bloated kind of aristocrat. . . ." You might step into a shop and pay fifteen cents a piece for two handkerchiefs without any haggling, "which brings blessings upon your head and gives you a fine sense of superiority."

Like other New York papers, the *Evening Post* often shifted between approval and condemnation.[37] An article on the caliber of Jewish office holders described them as "east-side Hebrews of the lowest class." On the other hand, feature articles by Lincoln Steffens were quite sympathetic. People in the Jewish quarter preserved their "distinctive customs and practices almost inviolate." Their children, however, acquired English rapidly and assumed responsibilities normally given to elders. Humbler Jews were born musicians, natural gamblers, abstemious and earnest admirers of education. . . ." The intelligence of the children meant that the ghetto would lose most of its "Oriental characteristics" in the next twenty-five years.

No newspaper penetrated the East Side culture more deeply and with less condescension than the very upper-class *Commercial Advertiser*. From 1897 to 1901, under the supervision of city editor Lincoln Steffens and through the reporting skills of Abraham Cahan and Hutchins Hapgood, the paper ran a feature on Jews almost every Saturday.[38] The Saturday supplement presented an unequaled picture of East Side ghetto. Sketches of its cultural life showed that "refinement and intelligence often shone through distressing poverty." There were stories about the fun and pathos of a Yiddish comedy; the literati of the slums; the popularity of Shakespeare; a Yiddish adaptation of Hamlet; the scholarship and poverty of a rabbi immersed in research; the "high thinking" in the East Side café; and other demonstrations of the combination of "proletarianism and intellectual seriousness," so bewildering to the "Anglo-Saxon." The poems of Morris Rosenfeld were first published in English in the *Advertiser*. His life of "privation, of struggle" and his personality, "tender, simple, suffering and sad," were described. There were several stories about Russian Jews in the old country, including a delightful little gem by Cahan, "Imagining America: How a Young Russian Pictured It." In 1901 Steffens left the paper, and it returned to its earlier massive indifference to Jews.

Some of the national magazines, like the *Nation* and the *North American Review,* while including features about Jewry in general, virtually ignored the presence of Russian Jews. Others reflected the same upswing of interest as the New York newspapers.[39] *Harper's Weekly* was constantly positive in its descriptions. "A Friday Market in the Jewish Quarter of New York" featured preparation for the Sabbath. Contrary to stereotype, "perhaps nine-tenths of the people earn a scanty living with their needles and sewing machines." Intemperance was rare and piety common. "Swarms of children" were at play and the "babble of the little ones blended pleasantly . . . without a dissonance." There was "endless love" and "devotion to family," charmingly illustrated in several vignettes. In an atmosphere of freedom, poverty-stricken Russian Jews promptly attempted to become American. They were aided by the companionship of the tenements, "and this fellowship is so strong that it rises above many of the miseries and disadvantages of the crowded life."

Other periodicals were equally compassionate, if not always as consistent in their coverage. The *Century's* two part series "The Jews in New York" conceded that the prevalent thrift could at time harden into "avarice and greed," but, it asserted, "none respond more willingly to the elevative forces of modern civilization." Jews were prudent, diligent, and lawful. A wedding reminded the author that, among Jews, "chastity is the cornerstone of the family institution" and "family life exemplifies many of the sweetest qualities of human nature." *Atlantic Monthly* published several of Abraham Cahan's short stories and his 1898 article "The Russian Jew in America," which stressed good citizenship. A 1900 discussion, "Our Immigrants and Ourselves" by Kate Holliday Claghorn, reported that a study of "even the most poverty-stricken and forlorn" of the Russian Jews showed them to be "a temperate, moral and industrious people." In spite of the "unwholesome tenements" and "universal filth," Jews had a lower death rate than well-to-do natives in uptown districts. (This was the subject of widespread commentary.) Their vitality was caused by moral habits. Their family affection was strong, and they were not found in prisons or charity institutions. Since they first came, one could note remarkable advancement:

> The casual visitor to the East Side today will see apparently the same old patriarchs with side curls and velvet cap, the same mothers in Israel with wigs awry and infants multitudinous that he saw yesterday. But this is a human stream in which, while it looks the same, the individual elements are always changing. The old man in the gabardine one saw last week has now put on the garb of America and moved uptown with his family. The one you took for him has just landed from the immigrant ship. Next week he, too, will be gone . . . .

The reader was thus reassured that the Jew would not remain in an indigestible mass, but was, in fact, a believer of the "American way of life."

Some of the reformist magazines at the turn of the century made a conscientious effort to inform their readers about the exotic newcomers. A 1900 article, "In the New York Ghetto" by Katherine Hoffman, ran in *Munsey's Magazine*. She assured its readers that, while the first generation kept Jewish customs with "vivid picturesqueness," their children adopted American ways. As among the poor in all religions, "ancient forms are followed with a literal exactness infrequent among the more liberally educated . . . of the same faith." Amid dust, the odors of the tenements, and the roar of the city, children sat and studied Torah. Limiting Hebrew immigration would be unfortunate, she concluded. "If it were not for the new arrivals coming in with ancient beliefs and habits, the Ghetto would soon have nothing to lift it out of the sordid and squalid into the poetic and dignified." Both the *Outlook* and *The World's Work* published several perceptive articles about immigrants, accompanied by excellent photographs. Both also carried discussions by American Jews seeking to explain the Russian newcomers to American readers. Americanization, one remarked, meant to the ordinary immigrant, "dejudaizing himself without becoming a Christian." Another reassured his readers that American civilization had "improved the moral qualities of the Jew, refined his character, and brought out such elements as intellect, honor, frankness, dignity, a high regard for labor."

The most positive comments about Jews concerned love for learning and intellectual accomplishments. Virtually all the New York press and many of the magazines lauded this quality in the Jewish people.[40] The *Times* carried a book supplement feature, "Good Taste Shown by Russian Jews." Even the poor East Side resident could "claim citizenship in the world of letters," a goal "his race has always so signally cherished." The *Evening Post* noted that, unlike the Jews, the ignorant of other nationalities tended to regard educated people with distrust. Jews were proud of learned leaders and "no matter how ignorant they may be themselves . . . they crave education for their children." The *Post* described "Jew Babes" waiting on line at East Side libraries. "The Jewish child has more than an eagerness for mental food; it is an intellectual mania." Many had graduated from City College or the Normal College. "The city may be proud," the *Post* concluded. Of all the money spent by New York, "none is better expended than that required for the training of these bright, studious and patriotic graduates." The *Herald* pointed out that many of the now penniless exiles had been educated people in Russia "whom our carelessness has confused with the devouring hordes of South European peasants." (The *Herald,* generally favorable to Jewish immigrants, was hostile to Italian newcomers.)

As might be expected, the *Tribune* was most enthusiastic about the intellectual capacities and aspirations of the Jews. This enabled the paper to fit the Jew more easily into the middle-class image it had created. "It will astonish many people that the average small boy of the ghetto has none of the commercial instinct which is ordinarily taken as a sign of his race," the *Tribune* informed its readers. Instead, there was an "intense craving for knowledge." The rapidity with which these children learned was "a constant source of surprise." Teachers at the "Hebrew Grammar School," P.S. 22, described their students as "industrious, ambitious and easily managed." The principal stressed that they were "intensely patriotic . . . enimently respectful to teachers." The implication was clear that one did not have to worry about lower-class laziness, vices, or rebelliousness from these people. They were seized by a laudable "relentless American spirit." In another generation, "their language will be an anachronism," the paper predicted without regret. The culmination of these laudatory articles was an extreme Judeophile editorial prompted by a picture of the 1901 City College graduating class, which "might almost have been mistaken for a picture of the Young Men's Hebrew Association." City College had come to be known as "Jews' College," a term that the *Tribune* certainly did not regard as a reproach. Especially in the "humbler walks of life," there was no question that educational standards were far higher among Jews than Gentiles. Even those from congested tenements surpassed their fellow students. After thousands of years of "unrelenting persecution," modern Jews are "irrepressible and indomitable, holding their place in the very foremost rank of the world's best peoples. It is a spectacle provoking the wonder . . . of the world."

The prevalence of Jewish philanthropy was also an object of admiration. Articles often included detailed descriptions of Hebrew charities and self-help organizations.[41] In the midst of its most virulent campaign against Jewish immigration, the *Times* felt impelled to comment, "The spirit and devotion cannot be too highly praised of those Hebrews of New York who have endeavored to take care of their exiled co-religionists." Various organizations such as the Educational Alliance and the Hebrew Technical Institute received lavish approval. When a new hospital was opened on the East Side, the *World* was careful to note that it was a monument to the thrift of LOCAL people. The opening was an event "in which all east side people felt deep pride."

One of the rare attempts to genuinely analyze the changes and problems of Jewish life in America was included in an article in the *Sun* on the funeral of Rabbi Jacob Joseph.[42] It was far easier for a Jew to live an ideal Orthodox life, the paper remarked, where there were segregated Jewish communities. "It becomes extremely difficult, almost impossible, in this free country . . . with its disintegrating forces." The disadvantages faced by the Orthodox Jew included his beard and appearance and his attempts to adhere to a kosher diet, which made it very uncomfortable for him away from the great cities. Rabbi Joseph had attempted to organize the community, but the separation of church and state left him with only that authority given to him voluntarily. His funeral, a tribute to his personality, was, perhaps also an indication that "a religion for which so much was endured for thousands of years will not be abandoned without a struggle."

The picture an average reader would get of the life and customs of the Russian Jews was, largely, an impression of the exotic and picturesque. However, there was also a strong element of intellectual ambition and upward striving. In one way, these people appeared to be unassimilable in their strangeness. Yet it was clear that they were assimilating through the public schools. On the one hand, there were the quaint markets and the humorous haggling, the "oriental" religious practices; but on the other, there was the City College graduating class and the public library branch with the heaviest use in the city. The combination of sympathy, alien ways, and repulsion must have made it difficult for the readers to determine which was the correct picture of Russian Jews in New York.

There were several well-known authors who made a special effort to understand life in New York's Jewish ghetto. William Dean Howells was a generally sympathetic, if perplexed, observer in his *Impressions and Experiences* (1896).[43] "An East-Side Ramble" described his walk through a Hebrew quarter whose "loathsomeness" blunted a visitor's perceptions. The people did not appear degraded, but were cheerful and courageous enough to keep clean in "an environment where . . . their betters would scarcely have heart to wash their faces." There was none of the "drunkenness or truculence of an Irish or low American neighborhood." Their children all went to school, were "quick and intelligent," and spoke English. He was not amused by the street bazaar, "a sorrowfully amusing satire upon the business ideals of our plutocratic civilization" where the desperately poor preyed upon each other.

Still, while not as optimistic as some about the future in such unrivaled "squalor," he was loath to leave the neighborly intimacy and patient good spirits. Above all, the place left him with a feeling of "men's heroic superiority to their fate."

Mary McKenna wrote of her experiences in working among the Jewish immigrants in *Our Brethren of the Tenements and the Ghetto.*[44] She described Jewish youngsters as so bright that they did not have to enter the lower grades and "they finish the course in less time than the native-born children." The religious Jews were particularly delightful people. "If they give any offense, it is because . . . their separateness had made them ignorant of conventional forms." Despite terrible conditions, Jews preserved their morals, religion, and "a beautiful spirit of helpfulness." They were hospitable, and the "amount of small charity given directly from poor to poorer" was astonishing.

After eight years of social work in the slums, James Bronson Reynolds declared that Jews should be welcomed as immigrants. "I feel that society is much better for their being here. Their eagerness, brightness and fine susceptibility to Americanizing influences are very valuable assets in our social life."[45] Some of the reformers tended to romanticize Jewish immigrants, particularly in view of their apparent eagerness to be Americanized. Other Progressives expressed distaste toward Jews and other aliens as part of an anti—"new" immigrant mentality.

The most prolific writer on the immigrant Jew was Jacob Riis, the well-known reformer, whose views underwent a startling metamorphosis over the years.[46] In his famed 1890 work, *How the Other Half Lives,* his attitude was decidedly ambivalent about "Jewtown." Dirt and disease were endemic and thrift was the watchword. Jews refused to see the light of Christianity since "Money is their God." Immigrant school children jumped ahead of their classmates in mental arithmetic due to the strength of their "instincts of dollars and cents." Conditions in a typical sweatshop were harrowing, yet the worker who complained turned sweater himself at the first opportunity, "and takes his revenge by driving an even closer bargain than his rival tyrant." Charities had the problem of aiding the poorest without attracting "greater swarms." One of the difficulties lay in the gregarious and commercial nature of the Jews, which prevented their dispersal to rural areas. In this earliest and best known of Riis's work, he repeated many of the stereotyped images of the Jew.

By 1892, in his *Children of the Poor,* Riis had become more optimistic about the prospect of Jews as citizens. He still felt burning indignation at the "inhuman packing of human swarms, of bitter poverty . . . sweater slavery . . . darkness and squalor and misery. . . ;." Little children, peddling pitiful wares or staggering under heavy bundles of clothes, rarely laughed. Riis was struck by the number of little workers who claimed to be "just fourteen."

Clearly, it was "not the child which the tenement had dwarfed . . . but the memory of moral sense of the parents." (Notice again this image of "dwarfing.") Despite horrible living conditions, however, the area was the healthiest spot in the city, due to the "temperate habits of the Jew and his freedom from enfeebling vices . . . along with his marvelous vitality." Like most middle-class commentators, Riis feared that the absence of privacy could lead to corruption of morals. "But for the patriarchal family life of the Jew that is his strongest virtue," children would have been ruined in an atmosphere that would have destroyed most gentiles. Despite an expansion of "greed and contentiousness," now that they were free of oppression, they could become good citizens—"They understood the power of knowledge." The ease and speed with which the children learned was equaled only by their excellent behavior and attention. There was no test of strength with their teachers like there was in Italian districts. "Figuring is their strong point. They would not be Jews if it was not." The only real problem was teaching them cleanliness. Although Riis still accepted some negative clichés about Jewish immigrants, the positive aspect were becoming predominant in his views.

Because he had greater contact with the Jewish immigrants, Riis eventually became an energetic propagandist for their prospects. An 1896 article about a garment strike emphasized their "boundless energy and industry." Living in black and bitter poverty, the suffering multitude was "struggling undismayed to cast off its fetters . . . and winning the fight against tremendous odds by the exercise of the same stern qualities that won for their brothers prosperity and praise." Obviously, "nothing stagnates where Jews are. . . . The second generation is the last found in those tenements." Although he still believed that the Jewish religion was sadly in error, Riis concluded, "New York City has no better and more loyal citizens."

By 1898 in *Out of Mulberry Street,* Riis demonstrated how deeply his sympathy and understanding had become engaged with these strange immigrants in a collection of moving tales and bittersweet vignettes. Liberty was a passion in the tenements that led people to strike even, as one cloak-maker, when they did not have enough to feed hungry families. Riis listened as a striker recited the prayer of his fathers, "Blessed art thou, O Lord our God . . . that . . . hast delivered us from bondage to liberty." Riis had even abandoned his disapproval of the "blind" Jewish religion. "Lost Children" was the affecting story of the disappearance of the three-year-old daughter of a peddler who, with his wife, maintained an anxious vigil at police headquarters. Riis visited their grim third-floor tenement flat on a Sabbath eve. The father sat at the head of the table, "every trace of the timid shrinking peddler" laid aside. The little girl's high chair was empty, but "in the strength of domestic affection that burned with unquenched faith in the dark tenement after months of weary failure, I read the history of this strange people that in every land and in every day has conquered even the slum with the hope of home." After two years the little girl was finally found at a children's home and returned. In "The Slippermaker's Fast," Isaac Josephs worked his body into total exhaustion in order to have enough to be able to fast on Yom Kippur "when all the rest of the days he fasted" through necessity. Other stories were in a similar, deeply compassionate vein.

In 1899 Riis produced a series for the *Atlantic Monthly* that passionately defended Jewish immigrants. He described a park where police routinely clubbed Jewish cloak-makers "for the offense of gathering to assert their rights to being men. . . ." The Educational Alliance and the Hebrew Institute taught thousands of children of refugee Jews and passed them on to the public schools, "the best material they receive from anywhere." The Jew, who longed for a home to call his own, was the best material for citizenship.

> I, for one, am a firm believer in this Jew and his boy. Ignorant they are, but with a thirst for knowledge that surmounts any barrier. The boy takes all the prizes in school. His comrades sneer that he will not fight. . . . But I believe that should the time come when the country needs fighting men, the son of the despised immigrant Jew will resurrect on American soil . . . the old Maccabee type . . . .

He even excused Jewish sweatshop owners whom he had bitterly denounced earlier. The Jew only took to clothes making because it was easily learned and he could make his way rapidly. The real sweater was the manufacturer: "the Jew is the victim of the mischief. . . ." Jacob Riis had come a long way in the nine years since he had written "Money is their God."

Perhaps the most humane and intelligent observer of the Lower East Side was Hutchins Hapgood. Introduced to the nuances of its life by Abraham Cahan, he achieved a degree of personal identification with its customs and aspirations unequaled by anyone of his social class and background. His articles appeared in the *Atlantic Monthly, The Critic, The Bookman, The World's Work, Outlook, Boston Transcript, Evening Post,* and the *Commercial Advertiser.* These ultimately led to a classic book, *The Spirit of the Ghetto,* which was illustrated by the nineteen-year-old Jacob Epstein.[47] The book detailed the effective struggle against poverty by a richly varied community of workers, peddlers, intellectuals, and socialists. Reformers supposed the ghetto to be a "place of poverty, dirt, ignorance, immorality . . . where people are queer and repulsive," Hapgood wrote in his introduction. But he was taken by the "charm" of the place. Life was more intense and varied than in any part of New York. Older Jews retained Orthodox customs, eloquently described by Hapgood. He was one of the first observers to comment on the generation gap. There was a struggle within the boy of the second generation. He was ashamed of his parents' limitations, but they remained his conscience, "the visible representatives of a moral and religious tradition by which the boy may regulate his inner life." It was easy to predict that his growing Americanism would triumph "at once over the old traditions and the new socialism," Hapgood perceptively remarked. Moses Rischin has noted that readers were unprepared for such "transparent realism." The Jews he presented were not "exotic wanderers," financial giants, "neither a mystical people nor a tenement proletariat," but rather individuals who might be a source for reform in America.[48]

Hapgood continued to stress the Americanization of the Russian Jew in such articles as "The Rise of the Russian Jew" and "The Earnestness that Wins Wealth." Russian Jews were graduating from high schools and colleges in increasing numbers. Their excitement in ideas and energy in acquiring knowledge had "an interesting analogy to the hopefulness and acquisitive desire of the early Renaissance." Jews came to this country with "stored vitality and ambition" which had been suppressed in Eastern Europe. Even the sting of old caricatures was eased by the attraction Hapgood felt for an eager young "Jew haggler" who persuaded him to sell his old clothes "practically for nothing" by impassioned arguments "at once poetical and logical." The business instinct that shined in their faces was "not cold and calculating. It is the expression of a naive, intense interest in life."

These favorable observers presented a picture of the Jew as excellent potential citizens. They were invariably described as laudably ambitious (for learning as well as wealth), temperate, moral, family loving, intellectual, and rising rapidly above their poverty through the approved work ethic. At a time of mounting sentiment for immigration restriction, the picture of these sympathetic authors provided an interesting countervailing force. No other immigrant group had such passionate defenders who gave them larger-than-life virtues.

Even the most sympathetic journals, however, made it clear that Jews were admired only when they remained within the limits of proper conduct. As the new immigrants crowded into the East Side, a relatively small but visible group became anarchists, frequent riots occurred in the crowded streets, and strikes were commonplace. These were the subjects of most of the coverage of Jewish New Yorkers in the newspapers, causing futher dilemmas. The poverty of the immigrants seemed to call for compassion. Their obvious devotion to the work ethic was frequently praised. Yet it often seemed that they were incapable of comprehending society's need for law and order. Generally docile and law-abiding, they occasionally exploded and over-stepped the legitimate bounds of protest, as defined by the newspapers. In terms of earlier Jewish stereotypes, these activities were even more difficult to understand. The language used was, in itself, significant in its preoccupation with "savagery," "dwarfing" of personality, and "Oriental" qualities. Strikes of poverty-stricken clothing workers elicited sympathy until they erupted into violence. A harmless anarchist demonstration caused alarmed reactions out of proportion to its significance. Misgivings were expressed at the mobbing of a missionary or at kosher-food riots. Upper-class papers, particularly, feared the possible formation of a "dangerous class." These reactions appeared to have been based more upon class fears than upon anti-Semitism. When the Jews themselves were victims of lawlessness during Rabbi Joseph's funeral, the papers unanimously condemned their persecutors.

Strikes on the part of poor "cloakmakers" and "tailors" were generally reported sympathetically until they transgressed conduct accepted by the newspapers. Minor violence erupted in the first major cloak-makers' strikes of 1890 with assaults upon scabs.[49] The strikers, exhibiting a keen sense of public relations, organized a "parade of misery." The papers tended to sympathize. "Starving but Undaunted," ran the headline in the *Tribune*. Even the violence was understandable—"their misery has grown harder to bear and yesterday their despair culminated in riots." The mass-circulation *World* commented that their faces "bore unmistakable signs of privation and want . . . swept by billowings of suffering and sorrow." No paper was more favorable to the cause of the workers, although the *World* never mentioned that they were Jews.

Even the ultraconservative *Sun* was moved to pity the "depths of destitution" of these people. Their parade had revealed a group "physically stunted and deformed by the hardships of an early life spent generally under one form or another of oppression . . . and worn down by the days and nights of unceasing toil . . . since they came to free America." Despite its wretchedness, the *Sun* remarked approvingly "the procession was one of the most orderly ever held in the city." The *Herald* was compassionate enough to start a fund for destitute cloak-makers. However, when the workers rejected a settlement that the paper felt was fair, the *Herald*, a middle-class organ, characterized them as "ignorant and misguided."

The *Times*, probably the New York paper least friendly to Jews, at first favored amelioration of working conditions and donations by "public spirited citizens." However, the paper turned against the workers due to "their riotous behavior" in attacking strikebreakers. Sympathy for the strikers, the paper warned, was diminished by the fact that they were Russian Jews who "originally came here to get work by accepting less than the current rate of wages," and were "of a low grade . . . ignorant of the English language and of the institutions of this country."

In 1891 the *Times* reported a more vivid "outrage" by striking "Polish cloakmakers." A child was disfigured by vitriol thrown by "a lot of unkempt Polish Jews." This story proved that these "are not the most desirable immigrants . . . and strongly emphasizes the propriety of restricting immigration of them." The *Herald* agreed that, though the workers had a right to seek to live above the edge of starvation, "if these strikers seek to revenge their wrongs by riotous proceedings . . . they must be checked by the strong arm of the law." The *Herald* could understand their exasperation, "but there is a right way and a wrong way to achieve reform and smashing machinery and throwing vitriol are the wrong way." The *Sun* complained that while most of the Hebrew cloak-makers were "meek and long-suffering," of late their strikes had been accompanied by unacceptable violence.[50]

The papers were largely sympathetic to the plight of the clothing workers, however. A *Times* feature on the poverty of the cloak-makers in 1894 reported "venerable old patriarchs whose tangled white beards . . . and sunken famished eyes, told with a sorrowful eloquence how heavily that hand of need bore them down in a land of exiles." Here one could not find the fictional Shylocks and Rebeccas, but only "humanity pinched by hunger . . . petrified by despair." The reporter poked fun at those (including his own paper) whose imagination had turned a "simple and innocent" group into "a parcel of frantic, maddened bloodthirsty anarchists." This image of helpless despondency was the reverse of the old stereotype of the Jew as aggressive Shylock or the newer picture of radical troublemaker. When the strikers appeared to be winning, the *World* (again without mentioning their religion) exulted, "The sufferers themselves . . . have accomplished this great thing. They have exemplified the truth that the poor and oppressed laborer must work out his own salvation."[51]

The justice of the workers demands was so widely conceded by 1896 that even occasional outbursts of violence did not call forth storms of denunciation. While opposing "riotous disturbance," the *Tribune* urged that working conditions "be ameliorated for the sake of the whole community." Even the *Times* deplored the fact that a major industry had been established in the city "largely on the labor of poor Jews who have sought refuge here from oppression in other countries." The tailors normally behaved well, the papers agreed, and their misery should be relieved.[52]

By 1900 clothing strikes had become so commonplace that they were treated with a distinct lack of concern. "Cheerful Pantsmakers Strike," the *Tribune* reported. "These strikes are annual affairs on the East Side and little harm . . . results from them." Loud Yiddish discussions and energetic gesturing might have led a stranger to fear a riot was imminent, but there was no danger of that "as the East Side Hebrews are probably the least aggressive people in the world."[53]

The reaction was markedly different when Jewish radicals overstepped the line of acceptable conduct. The depression of 1893 heightened American fears and uncertainties. When unemployed Jewish workers organized protest demonstrations featuring anarchist speakers like Emma Goldman, conservative journals dreaded the impending revolution of Jewish sansculottes.[54] Idle workers stormed a meeting hall, urged on by the fiery words of Emma Goldman. ("You are worse than black slaves . . . if you do not get bread and freedom peaceably, take it by force.") The disturbances quickly dwindled to a series of noisy, harmless meetings, but not before respectable citizens had become thoroughly alarmed. "The murmurs of the hungry multitude . . . have increased," the *Herald* reported dramatically. "the city hears it now as Paris a century ago heard the cry out of St. Antoine . . . foretelling the deluge. . . . Weapons are brandished in hands that have never known any more dangerous weapons than a tailor's needle." Anarchy strode the East Side preaching defiance of law and order to "bewildered foreigners with empty stomachs." Later, the *Herald* reporter went as far as to assert that, despite the wild anarchist claims, one could not find a single really hungry man on the East Side.

The reaction of the normally friendly *Tribune* was an excellent example of how this overstepping of boundaries could produce a great anxiety. The paper feared that social revolution would strike "like a typhoon . . . into the East Side." The Jews had betrayed the image the paper had painted of them as repositories of middle-class virtues. For twenty years "there have arrived in this country a vast number of ignorant and lawless persons," leading to the issue of how practicable it was "for the welfare of society or for the welfare of the ignorant immigrants themselves to suffer the same measure of license in speech which has been permitted among people of Anglo-Saxon blood." The *Tribune* argued that the people who instigated anarchist riots should be locked up, or, even better, shipped out of the country—"they are seldom Americans." The significance of this extreme reaction becomes more apparent when it is recalled that the *Tribune* was the most sympathetic to Jewish immigration of the upper- and middle-class newspapers.

As might be expected, the *Times* agreed completely. However, since it did not expect anything better, its attitude was one of annoyance rather than terror. "It is pretty trying to the American citizen to have a lot of aliens of the lowest grade . . . parading under the lead of agitators." Although the anarchists were later more realistically portrayed as "mild as babes," the image persisted or "unwashed, ignorant, unkempt, childish semi-savages." With no comprehension of our form of government, they were prey to "desperate-talking, firebrand-flinging poltroons of the Goldman kind." The boys, who had been "weaned on the pestiferous milk of nihilism and dynamite throwing," were the real menace. Although few in number, they longed to demolish law and order and devour pamphlets on assassinations. The dangerous nonsense of "creatures like Goldman" found a responsive audience in the "hatchet-faced, sallow, rat-eyed young men of the Russian Jewish colony."

The *Illustrated American,* in an 1893 article, "A Plague of Men," was as troubled about the Russian Jew as the most conservative newspaper.[55] To the surprise of many, "he has evinced an almost frantic desire for disorder and riot." In recent disturbances this product of "ignorance and cruelty" was the first to come tumbling out of tenements to join anarchistic riots. Released from the despotism of the Tsar to the most marvelous freedom in the world, Jews displayed "crazy ingratitude." It was likely that they were "but little removed from insanity," and easy prey to the "half-idiotic frothings" of the anarchists and other advocates of "violent opposition to law and order."

The *World,* appealing to working-class readers, was, as usual, more sympathetic. It concluded that the whole anarchist incident proved "how very small and insignificant the lawless element in New York is . . . how deep-seated is the law-abiding sentiment of our people." Expression of extreme ideas was nothing more than a safety valve that rendered even a "virago" like Emma Goldman harmless.[56]

This incident may well have contributed to the widely held view of later years that Jews were disproportionately anarchist revolutionaries. Once the immediate furor died down, however the papers dropped the issue. The *Tribune,* for example, reverted to its previous genial view of the immigrant Jews as a group of budding American bourgeoisie. Within a few years the paper was able to report a meeting on the East Side that cheered "unkind references to the clergy and the capitalist," and to cheerfully remark that "the audience was a fairly intelligent body . . . exceedingly full of spirit. But it kept in good order."[57]

Riots and disorders were fairly commonplace on the East Side. Most, however, were relatively minor. When they did not appear threatening to the class and ideological interests of the newspapers, they were treated with relative tolerance.[58] A panic in a reading room, for example, might bring forth good natured remarks about "excitable Hebrews." The advertised Yom Kippur dinner at the Herrick, a restaurant on the East Side, led to a small riot. The *World* reported that the socialist customers were quite bold—"as they emerged, each would light a cigarette and puff it leisurely. This was done especially to enrage the religionists." It most certainly had the desired effect. Wild scenes ensued in which the "luckless patrons" were lucky to escape with their skins intact. Although the crowds had "turned sacred Yom Kippur into a season of wild commotion," most of the papers were unconcerned. Only the *Times* voiced mild disapproval, particularly when the crowd jeered four Spanish-American War soldiers in full uniform, putting "religion above patriotism." The incident did confirm a widely held view that Jews were narrow-minded and intolerant.

The newspapers were generally unsympathetic to the many efforts to convert the East Side Jews, regarding these missionary attempts as "appalling impudence." In 1899 "wealthy paralytic" Wilson Dunlop and a small band of followers, including a converted Jew, attempted to preach to an increasingly hostile mob. The resentment culminated in a full-scale riot in which decayed fruit, rotten eggs, and even firecrackers were thrown at the missionary wagon.[59] Some papers sharply condemned the flagrant lawlessness displayed. "Rioting Hebrews Mob Missionary—Firecrackers Thrown Into the Face of the Helpless Paralytic as He Sits in His Wagon," was the *Herald's* headline. The paper reported that the scene would "remind one of Paris and the

Dreyfus agitation. Bitter religious feeling moved the throng . . . one felt the violence of a crazed multitude." Although Jewish resentment was understandable, the *Sun* remarked, "this is turning the tables with a vengeance." As usual, the *Times* was most condemnatory, observing that the authorities should have sustained Dunlop's right to espouse an unpopular cause against a "savage mob." It was dangerous for East Siders to be led to believe that order would not be maintained by the police. "It may be remarked that these particular subjects are in evident need of being 'converted' to common decency before they will be a credit to any religion." The *Times* advocated its usual solution, "an immediate course of instruction in elementary civilization which can be administered through the medium of a policeman's club."

Other newspapers were more understanding. The *Evening Post* accused the missionary of incensing Orthodox Jews by "flaunting . . . the familiar sacred text." The *World* believed that Dunlop's "anti-Hebrew crusade" had succeeded only in inflaming the feelings of the population. The *Journal* disapproved of the missionary activities most strongly. An enterprising *Journal* reporter discovered that Dunlop was a usurer ("Man who Seeks to Convert East Side Jews Makes Money in Quite a Different Business") who had been convicted earlier in Philadelphia. "The crown of martyrdom he has assumed as the object of persecution of the Jews of the Ghetto bids fair to be mingled with the laurels of a Shylock," the *World* remarked wryly at the end of the two-day sensation.

The Kosher Meat riots of 1902, which lasted, in rising and subsiding waves, from May 15 to May 24, spreading from the East Side to Brooklyn, the Bronx, Newark, and even Boston, were more frightening in their evocation of European-like food riots.[60] The high price of meat had led the women to organize a boycott of kosher butchers. As the crowds grew more infuriated, they smashed shop windows, threw meat into gutters, stamped on it, poured kerosene, and even made bonfires out of meat. They did not loot or take meat for themselves. One of the many signs carried in this "revolution of the women" proclaimed, "Boycott, Boycott, Don't Eat Meat. They are Eating the Flesh of our Women." The Yiddish newspapers compared this outbreak "with revolutions of this kind which have occurred in Paris in time past." "There was a wild scene of turmoil," the *Herald* reported, "when all the pent up passions of the Hebrews—usually the meekest of mortals were let loose . . . the spirit of riotry seemed to pervade the east side."

At first, the *Times* was rather mild in its comments since it opposed the Beef Trust. This was the first riot against the trust and the first food riot the *Times* could recall in America. (Actually, there had been several in New York in the 1830s.) "Americans are used to link food riots with persecution . . . and that is what is in the minds of the people who are . . . to gut butcher shops." As the riots continued, however, the *Times* perceived the full implications of the lawlessness. This class of people, especially the women, the paper editorialized, "have many elements of a dangerous class. They are very ignorant. . . . They do not understand the rights and duties of Americans. They have no inbred or acquired respect for law and order." They had known all authority as despotic, so it was important to make them understand "the proper consequences of their lawlessness." They needed far more severe treatment. The *Sun* echoed these sentiments, somewhat more mildly. Kosher butchers, who earned only a scanty living, had their stocks destroyed in a disagreement over the way they conducted business. "These rioters should be taught as impressively as possible that one of the first rules of law is that people mustn't interfere with other people's business."

The two mass-circulation papers were far more sympathetic to the grievances of the Jewish women. Although the *Journal* conceded that the rioters had "thrown law and order to the winds," it described them in favorable terms. They constituted a unique parade of old and young women, "the raven-haired dark-eyed women of the Ghetto, the women of poverty from the slums." They marched together singing "a ringing protest against the oppression of the meat trust in the homes of the poor, aggravated by the oppression of the harpies of the little shops." The *World* felt the demonstrations had gone too far, even though public sympathy was with the poor who had been victimized by "the Beef Trust's extortion." However, public peace required the maintenance of order. In spite of this, the *World* opposed any harsh punishment for the rioters—"Fining and imprisonment of the misguided mothers of families will, however, work great hardships and needlessly aggravate east side suffering." Thus, despite the threat to public order, only the *Times* seemed seriously alarmed about the revolutionary implications of the food riots.

The period's most sensational riot, the culmination of the funeral of Chief Rabbi Jacob Joseph, was an exception in that Jews were the victims, not the perpetrators.[61] The rabbi's funeral drew thousands into the streets in an outpouring of veneration and grief. The police decided to clear a path and, as the *Evening Post* commented, "dashed into the crowd apparently utterly regardless of what they did. . . . One might have thought they were putting down a riot." Later, the procession passed in front of the Hoe Printing Press factory, where the chief sport of the Irish workers had been attacking passing Jews. The workers threw missiles and water on the heads of the mourners. For once, the *Sun* reported, "the meek and futile protest of the Jew was not forthcoming. In its place came a charge into the factory." In response, the police, with the Hoe troublemakers at their side, began to systematically club the mourners. The East Side was aroused to a fever pitch of indignation. Protest meetings were held, and Mayor Low formed a citizen's commission to investigate. The commission ultimately exonerated the Jews and condemned the Hoe employees, the police, and even the local magistrates.

In this clearly anti-Semitic outburst by some Irish New Yorkers, the newspapers and periodicals were unanimous in condemning police actions. The *Journal* ran screaming headlines declaring the events "A DISGRACE," and offering "Proof of OUTRAGES!" The *World* declared, "It is a fact that fills the whole community with a sense of shame that a body of peaceable people, paying the last honors to a beloved pastor, should have been so molested and maltreated." Even *Life* felt that the riot was "highly discreditable to the police." Irish policemen "habitually treat the East Side Jews with contempt and frequently with brutality." Although *Life* had earlier expressed the feeling that the Jew "had contaminated everything in American life he has touched," it did believe that he was entitled to the protection of law enforcement. This was another example of the distinction between private and public anti-Semitism in America. Two of the city's most conservative journals, the *Evening Post* and the *Times,* were most dismayed. The *Post* charged that the police had indulged in "wholesale brutality." They thought they could do as they pleased since they had gotten away with scandalous treatment of Negroes on the West Side two years earlier. "Here is a splendid opportunity," the *Post* admonished sternly, "to teach some police brutes that there is a limit to the freedom with which they vent their racial dislikes upon an unoffending people." This race prejudice was all the more discreditable since "our Jewish fellow citizens are notably orderly and law-abiding. The police resorted to unchecked violence of a kind generally characteristic of Russian Cossacks."

The *Times* was even more indignant, showing great consistency in its opposition to lawlessness, even when the culprits were policemen. "These poor Hebrews have certain rights in their own quarter which even a McSweeny should respect," the paper commented caustically. The contrast between police behavior at the funeral of Archbishop Corrigan and that of Rabbi Joseph had made the whole episode clear. "These unhappy Jews are not only not protected by the police; they are in need of protection against the police." The paper also condemned magistrates who had belittled accounts brought to them of "the ill-treatment of these unhappy exiles." These conditions of injustice, the *Times* concluded, "demand to be remedied in the interests of our pretensions to civilization."

One widely held view of the Jewish immigrants had been expressed earlier by a New York magistrate, "The Jews come to this country laboring under the delusion that they can do as they please." Although they had been persecuted in Europe, their troubles here were "in themselves." They complained about others, but "the Hebrew is the first man in this city to commit an assault and he does it in such a way that the sympathy is for him." Christians too had some rights, the justice remonstrated, and were tired of being "insulted . . . maltreated by these filthy and intolerant immigrants . . . these half-civilized and arrogant foreigners."[62] The newspapers of this era dealt with strikes, riots, disorders, and anarchism that did not fit the old image of the German Jews, but that seemed endemic to the new immigrants. Surprisingly, despite this, the most common adjective used to describe the Jews was "meek." Some of the papers, particularly the *Times*, feared the presence of a large number of "excitable," unassimilated lower-class foreigners who might form a "dangerous class." With the exception of the anarchist scare of 1893, most of the other journals did not regard immigrant Jews as dangerous or lawless unless they overstepped prescribed boundaries. It is particularly significant that violence directed against Jews was deplored as vigorously as violence by Jews. One unfortunate legacy of this period, however, may well have been the later picture of the "Jew troublemaker."

A reader of newspapers and magazine in the later part of the century would have emerged with an extremely complex and ambiguous perception of immigrant Jews. One reason for this was the presence of two distinct groups. One image had been established by the relatively small group of prosperous, assimilated German Jews. The arrival of "hordes" of Eastern Europeans, so much more exotic and lower class, profoundly altered the picture. Interestingly, as more poured in, their virtues, as well as their limitations, became more apparent. The older view of the Jew did not disappear. It existed side by side with the new, almost opposite, image.

Shylock, already firmly established, continued to make his appearance in the pages of newspapers and magazines. His later counterpart, the fabulously successful and all-powerful international banker, could also be found on occasion. But numerous poor relations were pushing aside these older figures. The downtrodden Russian cousin, bowed by years of persecution, was strange-looking, persisted in speaking an odd jargon, and followed a peculiar "Oriental" religious service. He worked at the lowest paying jobs, yet he struggled to educate his children. He himself seemed indigestible by American society, but his children were clearly assimilating. He was the "meekest of mortals," but he frequently erupted and seemed incapable of understanding society's need for order. At times he was feared as a "savage," yet his intellectual strivings and charitable inclinations were widely admired. He could be a dangerous anarchist, but, unlike other immigrants, he was a frequent ally of upper-class reformers. He was definitely working class, but he was portrayed as middle class and, therefore, praiseworthy in his striving for a better life. Writers worried that the Eastern Jew was a stranger, not only to the American way of life and to Christianity, but to Western culture itself. Could our civilization absorb him?

One must also remember that the newspapers and magazines were far from monolithic in their viewpoints. In the 1890s the *Times* and the *Tribune* presented opposing images even though they appealed to a similar class. No newspaper was more hostile and anxious to exclude Jews as undesirables than the *Times*. While the *Tribune's* features on life in the lower East Side often had the character of modern descriptions of tribal life among the Maori, they were almost invariably friendly. The *Tribune* tended to ascribe American bourgeois virtues to the Jewish immigrants and was, therefore, particularly dismayed by any violence. The other upper-class papers (*Commercial Advertiser, Evening Post,* and *Sun*) were at times humanitarian, at times patronizing, and on rare occasions (particularly in the case of the *Sun*) genteelly anti-Semitic. The *Herald,* mildly sensational and middle class in appeal, tended to favor Russian Jewish immigration, reserving its condemnation for Italian immigrants. The *World* and the *Journal,* the two mass newspapers, were sympathetic on such issues as strikes and food prices but devoted little space to the life of New York's Jews. Even the *Times* approved of wealthy Americanized German Jews. Its disapproval was more anti-immigrant than anti-Semitic. This was, after all, a period of rising restrictionist sentiment. No acts comparable to the New Orleans lynching of Italians victimized Jewish immigrants. All of the papers, except the *Journal,* expressed concern about society's need for order. All were hostile to transgressions against the predefined limits set up by society. They opposed violations of law and order, whether committed by Jews or directed against Jews.

The magazines also exhibited varying viewpoints. Despite an occasional exception, all opposed Russian persecution. *Harper's Weekly* was the most steadfast in its friendly attitudes through the 1880s and 1890s. In the later part of this period *Atlantic Monthly, Outlook, The World's Work, The Bookman,* and *Munsey's Magazine* all featured basically positive images. Other periodicals expressed a decided dichotomy. The *Century Magazine* and *Illustrated American,* for example, might include a blatantly anti-Semitic article in one issue and a vigorous defense of Russian Jews in another. Even *Life* and *Frank Leslie's,* most often hostile, were occasionally moved to defend the Jewish immigrant.

The frequent reader of the press would find it difficult to arrive at any one consistent image of the Eastern European Jew. Journals of the same class appeal and quality often contradicted each other and themselves. Novels, plays, and humor magazines barely even acknowledged the presence of Russian Jews in America. In the New York newspapers and national magazines, however, the Eastern Jew was far more than a "complication." He had become, in fact, the central and contradictory Jewish figure. Some of the paradoxes inherent in the perceptions of the immigrant continued to plague the assimilated American Jew long after his children had achieved the integration into American society so ardently desired.

Conclusion

THE COMPLEX AND CONTRADICTORY IMAGE OF THE JEW WAS AN ELABO-
rate and highly inconsistent stereotype. The Jew was successful and lower
class, clannish and social climbing, capitalist and anarchist-communist, dangerous and docile. It included the high-minded German philanthropist and
the wild-eyed Russian anarchist, the shrewd driving businessman and the
meek tailor bowed by centuries of oppression, the chosen people and the
Christ-killers.

There were many other ethnic clichés in this era: the drunken, slow-witted
Irishman, the plodding German, the lazy, dirty Mexican, and the excitable
Italian were but a few examples. The nineteenth century was not sensitive to
ethnic slights and hostility. As Irving Howe has cogently observed, the image
of the "melting pot" was very popular "with clear presuppositions as to who
would melt whom." With so many arriving so rapidly, members of the
community "demanded a rapid, complete assimilation," as Robert Wiebe has
noted. In one sense, the miserly and often comically dishonest clothes dealer
or pawnbroker of the humor magazines or burlesque houses was simply
another manifestation of suspicion of all new immigrants. It is difficult to
assert that the presentation of the Jew was more cutting than the crafty, cruel
Chinese, for example. The reiteration of the negative Jewish image, however,
had the potential of unleashing forces of historic anti-Semitism. It is important to remember that the Jews were not simply another ethnic group. Jews
also constituted a religion that, by its mere presence, challenged the basic
assumptions of Christianity by stubbornly rejecting the true Messiah. This
was the substantial difference between the Jew and even a nationality that was
the object of much suspicion and contempt, such as the Italian. The Italians,
portrayed as credulous, superstitious "Papists," were, nonetheless, Christians. They had not blindly rejected Christ, leading to centuries of accumulated hostility. The Jews appeared as a more permanent minority which,
perhaps because of this religious difference, would never be totally assimilated. Religious fanaticism, dislike of aliens, and social and economic competition could join together in reaction to the Jew.

Even in the first half of the century, as this book has shown, there was a

179

widespread and often expressed system of ideas unfavorable to Jews. Nevertheless, group hostility found a much more popular target at this time in Catholics, who seemed to be a far greater danger to American ideals. Mormons presented a basic challenge to individualism and a capitalist society. Much effort was also expended, then and later, in keeping blacks in the place American society had assigned to them. The Jew had no such clearly delineated place. Despite the presence of myriad fictional Shylocks, conditions for the Jews in America were more than tolerable. The vigor with which the Jewish press objected to the relatively minor slight involved in the use of the word "jew" is testament to the comparative weakness of American anti-Semitism. The presence of a variety of ethnic, religious, and racial groups that absorbed much of the animosity, undoubtedly helped to mute anti-Jewish expressions.

In many ways there were basic compatibilities between American values and Jewish traditions. These militated against the spread of any significant anti-Semitic movement. The congruences included Old Testament teachings (of greater significance in the United States than in Europe), ideals of religious freedom, and distrust of any centralized religious authority. Constitutional and legal safeguards of rights for everyone preserved the same guarantes for Jews. Just about everyone agreed that Jews were entitled to legal equality. In addition, the American self-image of a new society, which cast off European prejudices and promised refuge for the oppressed, operated in opposition to European-style anti-Semitism. Certainly there was rejection and contempt in America, as there had been in Europe. The difference was that "the dominant credo of the society was in constant contradiction with this behavior . . . its dominant religion preached brotherhood. Weak as the spirit was compared to the flesh, it still made life in America different from life in Europe."[1]

One must remember, however, that an element of irrational anti-Jewish feelings always existed. This view condemned the Jews as unassimilable and basically disloyal to the institutions of any country in which they lived. Whatever the Jew actually did or did not do could not alter these basic preconceptions. In this sense, the real issue was the perceiver, rather than the Jew. Anna Dawes's comment was typical: the Jews always insisted, she claimed, on "remaining a foreign element in every community and an indigestible substance."[2] The later influx of Russian Jews only served to reinforce this preexisting image. Not only was the Jew alien to America and to the Protestant experience, but possibly to Western tradition and civilization as well—an unwanted remnant of an "Oriental" past.

The dichotomy, so obvious in the images of the Jew, was central in the historic religious aspect. On the one hand, Jews were the people who once had been chosen by God, but who were now condemned for rejecting Him. Religious textbooks and religious fiction, popular in the nineteenth century, both routinely reflected this attitude. Yet equally ardent Christians believed that the Jews would eventually return on the road to salvation and, in the process, help to bring universal salvation in accordance with divine plan. The second view led to a generally kindly, if patronizing, attitude.

Literary stereotypes remained remarkably constant throughout the century, generally more reflective of European conventions than changing American realities. Shylock was frequently central, almost invariably with a beautiful daughter who was deeply ashamed of her usurious dad. The Jew in these stories could hide his true feelings, making it impossible for others to know what he was thinking or plotting. He was rarely what he appeared to be. This reinforced a deeper fear of the Jew pursuing a horrible revenge upon the Christian world. More well-meaning authors generally confined themselves to impossibly noble Sheva types whose lives also revolved around the money function. In some ways the Jew was larger than life, the subconscious father figure flowing from religious sources. Popular sources, such as the theater and dime novels, tended to further simplify these archetypes. However, the obvious willingness to accept a Jew as hero (as in *The Jew Detective*) is indicative of less-heated emotions behind the stereotypes. This is also true of the tendency to place the vilest villains in foreign settings.

Comic magazines also perpetuated the picture of the Jew as a man for whom greed was the central motivation. "The lust for gain is so strongly rooted in his organism, that it extinguishes every other feeling, every other passion."[3] This image had an obvious relationship to the American stress on productivity as a prime value in contradistinction to the parasitic unproductive middleman. (Consider, for example, the early mistrust of banks and bankers.) Shylock and his comic counterparts, from this angle, were the prototypical nonproducers.

The economic image of the Jew, however, was not necessarily unfavorable. Jews were often praised as exemplars of the competitive values of American capitalism. The Jews achieved success by the very diligence, hard work, and thrift that were central values in the business-oriented society. An attack on their success might be interpreted as a repudiation of the American success ethos. If the indolent could destroy the industrious, the bottom of society tear down the top, America would become no better than such reprehensible nations as Russia and Romania. The conscientious Jewish businessman was also held up as a model of charitableness and lawfulness. Despite its obvious anti-Semitic potential, the treatment of wealthy Jews, like the Rothschilds, was generally favorable. Famous Jews were more often regarded as examples of success gained in the face of overwhelming obstacles than as Shylocks. Much of the ambivalence about the economic image of the Jew appeared to reflect the divisions in the American mind about the values of capitalism itself.

In the 1870s the success of the German Jewish immigrants led to a newer image of status seekers, although the older, contradictory view of the Jew as clannish and aloof continued to have some potency. A noticeable segment of German Jews achieved wealth and some prominence. They displayed their fortunes ostentatiously and were socially aggressive, adding another burden to the existing picture of the Jew as a Shylock and a foreigner. It was true that Jews did not display the most grotesque eccentricities of the Gilded Age. Men like Jim Fisk or Diamond Jim Brady were certainly not Jews. The rapid rise of the German Jew, however, shook a status-conscious society. The Jew was expected to become an American, but not at too rapid a pace. This was the beginning of a basic contradiction that persisted to the twentieth century. The Jew was enjoined to cease being so clannish, but found many obstacles placed in his path when he attempted to assimilate into the mainstream of American society. The Saratoga and Coney Island incidents were manifestations of the growing acceptance of the picture of the Jew as parvenu. Restrictions, however, had existed well before these publicized cases. Yet the almost universal indignation of the press shows that this image was far from universally accepted as late as 1879. By the 1880s and 1890s, however social exclusion had become commonplace. By this point, Herbert Gold sardonically suggests, the Jewish role was "chiefly to be outrageous . . . money, sex, power, occult rites. . . . And loud talking in summer resorts."[4]

Newspapers and magazines were far more responsive to changes in the Jewish position in America than literary, theatrical, and religious sources. Foreign and domestic issues concerning Jews were widely and often sympathetically covered. American ideals of freedom and equality often vied with a "counter-tradition" of racism and suspicion of foreigners. Contradictions multiplied as a periodical might defend Jewish rights in ringing tones on one page, then attack the Jew's obnoxious qualities on the next. The major journals exhibited profound internal ambivalence. *Niles Weekly Register, North American Review, Century,* and *Puck* all exhibited basically ambiguous attitudes. Even generally favorable publications such as the *New York Tribune, Atlantic Monthly, The Bookman,* and *Harper's Weekly* included occasional unflattering pieces. Such periodicals as *Life, Leslie's* and the *New York Times,* which were basically hostile, would, at times, break into an impassioned defense of the ill-treated Jew. All opposed organized anti-Semitism and persecution. Neither class attitudes nor the type of publication could reliably predict the attitude a given publication would take toward Jews. The images were surprisingly unhistorical. That is, contrary to commonly expressed views of many historians, changes were rarely direct reflections of economic events like depressions or political incidents such as elections. The underlying assumptions were surprisingly constant throughout the century. The advent of the Russian Jew was the cause of the first real major change.

Prior to the 1890s, despite some social ostracism among the upper classes, the condition of the Jew in America remained quite acceptable. Anti-Semitism simply did not have the same significance that it had in Europe, a fact often noted with satisfaction by the press. At this time, social mobility had enabled a sizable number of Jews to become wealthy. The children and grandchildren of the German Jewish immigrants of the middle of the century were increasingly educated and genteel. This was obscured in the press by the mass exodus of Eastern European Jews, who concentrated in a handful of ghettos, most spectacularly in New York's Lower East Side. These Jews were far more alien, mysterious and out of synchronization with American standards. By this point, many journals had accepted the German "Hebrew" and concentrated their ire on the "low class Jew." These strange Jews generated real anxiety as to their ability ever to assimilate into American society. Their alleged proclivity for disorder and radical causes led to a permanent image of the Jew as a dangerous revolutionary. Robert Wiebe has perceptively described the terrifying vision of a shattered society, beset by class cleavages like those in Europe, which obsessed many of the elite in the late nineteenth century. They dreaded the social disorder and class crisis that would result from "the horror of a European working class arriving with industrialization."[5] The Russian Jew certainly was a part of these fears.

Yet these same Jews also exhibited praiseworthy ambition. As Jacob Riis had observed, nothing stagnated in the presence of Jews. They were obviously hard working, perhaps too much so. They were devoted to family virtue. Their children were remarkable successes in school. Unlike Italians and other "new" immigrants, it seemed clear that the Jews would not long remain in the lower classes. There was a tremendous increase in articles about the Jews in the 1890s. Interestingly, these pieces were favorable more often than not. In an era when hostility to the Jews seemed to be increasing, the images presented continued to be contradictory.

Their massive concentrations in the hated cities also helped to foster the idea of the "international Jew." This image had existed to some extent earlier in the century, but it now achieved greater prominence in such books as *Caesar's Column*. Prophets of anti-Semitism, whether Populist writers or alienated aristocrats like Henry Adams, tended to be "despairing critics of the power of money in American society."[6] Distrust of the immigrant Jew as a part of an international conspiracy was typical of the nineteenth-century conspiracy mentality. It was intertwined with fears about the dangerous influence of Eastern cities and of industrial and finance capitalism. Those cities, "swollen with foreigners" were seen as the centers of a "vast conspiracy against mankind" by "international parasites" who would "sacrifice our homes and our children upon the altar of mammon."[7] Ideological anti-Semitism, which was endemic in Europe, had its primary appeal in areas where there were few Jews and the supposed Jewish conspirator was a figure of mystery and distance, rather than a continual menace. The Jew was perceived as an international financier by those least likely to have ever met a financier or to have studied finance. The Jew, as an individual, was frequently accepted in these same rural communities. The Populists, the subjects of an almost unending debate as to their role in furthering anti-Semitism, were as divided in their attitudes as most Americans.

A multitude of antithetical images of the Jew were in evidence by the end of the century. Deep seated psychological reactions coexisted with American ideology. The Jew as God's own peculiar people who produced Christ and rejected him, chosen and condemned, continued with somewhat diminished force. In fact, these underlying assumptions, still enduring today, might well have lain behind the uneasiness about Jewish ability to become part of society. (A similar ambivalence can be seen in the attitudes of many fundamentalists today who, while very positive in their public statements, still doubt that Jews can reach heaven.) Shylock and Sheva, irredeemably wicked and unbelievably noble, the harsh rejecting father and the permissive giving father, dominated popular and serious literature, along with the beautiful Rebecca, both mother and lover. They were relatively untouched by the newer immigrants. The usurious miser to whom wealth was life existed along with the kindly philanthropist and the conspicuous consumer. The perpetual alien who adamantly refused to become a part of American society, was a partner of the patriotic Jewish American, grateful to his new land of liberty and eager for assimilation. The group in which criminality was so commendably rare showed an alarming tendency to be disorderly. The powerful international financier was a cousin of the helpless, poverty-stricken tenement cloak-maker. The boorish social climber stood beside the intellectual or artistic genius.

Other groups were also subject to American ambivalence. Harold Isaacs found the Chinese to be objects of both hostility and affection, admiration and contempt. They were stereotyped as honest, industrious, and thrifty, yet devious and inscrutable.[8] Similarly, Italians were hard working, but dangerously excitable. As Stuart Miller has remarked, the human mind is not a tidy filing system. New precepts do not replace older contradictory ones. Instead, they are "filed away side by side."[9] Such "biformities," as Michael Kammen has described them, were particularly characteristic of American society. Erik Erikson, in *Childhood and Society,* noted "whatever one may consider a truly American trait can be shown to have its equally characteristic opposite." In *Leaves of Grass,* Walt Whitman wrote: "Do I contradict myself?/ Very well then. I contradict myself,/(I am large, I contain multitudes.)"[10] These contradictions particularly affected the impossible-to-comprehend Jew, beside whom the dimwitted, drunken Irishman, the hotheaded Italian, and other accepted ethnic images were straightforward and easy to grasp. (The Italian, for instance, was attacked less frequently, but he was not defended as vigorously either.)

The underlying religious and psychological assumptions about Jews were much the same in America as in Europe, although the ambivalence was far more pronounced in this country. One could debate the relative importance of the two equally valid but paradoxical conclusions: negative images of Jews were less virulent and positive ones more widespread in America than elsewhere, yet hostile stereotypes did persist in the face of professed American ideals and the real role of Jews in America. Both are significant. Practices of social discrimination were commonplace, but it is essential to distinguish such actions from anti-Semitism instituted or encouraged by the government. The basic thrust of American society for legal rights for all whites became a weapon that could eventually be used by Jews struggling against anti-Semitism. It is difficult to disagree with Harold Isaacs's view that Jews who came to America from Europe "found the barriers against them located much further out than any that had hemmed them in before."[11]

By the end of the nineteenth century endless expansive opportunities came to be seen as far more limited. The nation, as Robert Weibe has commented, "seemed filled." What had once been welcomed as signs of progress had become "omens of disaster." The cities were crowded with immigrants who, once viewed as needed labor in a land of opportunity, now "swarmed and smothered native Americans." In the more nervous early twentieth century "ideological deviants" had to be either converted or eliminated. In this transition the elite found that traditional ethnic distinctions could be utilized to bring order to society. This could be accomplished by means of segregation, immigration restriction, and job discrimination based upon ethnicity. In the first quarter of the twentieth century restrictions in such areas as business, finance, medicine, and law were particularly aimed at Jews "classically stereotyped as the adaptable infiltrators, whose existing positions of strength and commitments to educational achievement made many of them immediate candidates for the new elite." However, as Wiebe has pointed out, skills ultimately prevailed over cultural stereotypes. Jews moved into newer areas of opportunity in the framework of a new pluralism.[12]

In the twentieth century color clearly became a more vital difference than ethnicity or religion. Americans, however, continued their tendency to dread conspiracies like those earlier ones of "international finance" or the Mormon Church. Misgivings were often expressed about aliens who might be obeying foreign masters. These did not center on Jews, however. Anti-communism replaced anti-Catholicism as the most widespread fear. When these twentieth-century anxieties did provide a breeding ground for group antipathy, an inheritance of deeply held negative images of the Jew was available from the nineteenth century. Less obvious, perhaps, is that there was another, opposite set of images, a counterinheritance of admiration for the Jew, also usable in the later period. It may well be that these latter perceptions ultimately triumphed.

Notes

Introduction

1. Harold Isaacs, *Scratches on Our Mind* (New York, 1958), 381, 390.
2. Harold Isaacs, *Idols of the Tribe* (New York, 1975), 26, 42.
3. Walter Lippmann, *Public Opinion* (New York, 1922), 81.
4. Robert Wiebe, *The Segmented Society* (New York, 1975), 21, 53.
5. Charles H. Stember, "The Changing Image of the Jew and the Contemporary Religious Situation," in *Jews in the Mind of America* (New York, 1966), 319.
6. Nathan W. Ackerman and Marie Jahoda, *Anti-Semitism and Emotional Disorder: A Psychoanalytic Interpretation* (New York, 1950), 56.
7. Nicholas Berdayev, *Christianity and Anti-Semitism* (New York, 1954), 6.
8. Herbert Gold, in *"Kike,"* ed. Michael Selzer (New York, 1972), xv.
9. Henry Loeblowitz-Lennard, "The Jew as Symbol," *Psychoanalytic Quarterly* 16 (January 1947): 36; Leon Poliakov, *The History of Anti-Semitism* (New York, 1965), 1 : 159–60.
10. Joshua Trachtenberg, *The Devil and the Jews* (New York, 1943), 4.
11. Isaacs, *Idols,* 190.
12. Ben Halpern, "Anti-Semitism in the Perspective of Jewish History," in *Jews in the Mind of America,* ed. Charles H. Stember (New York, 1966), 283.
13. Hannah Arendt, *The Origins of Totalitarianism* (New York, 1951), 28.
14. Charles E. Silberman, *A Certain People* (New York, 1985), 24.
15. Edward H. Flannery, *The Anguish of the Jews* (New York, 1964), 248.
16. Carey McWilliams, *Mask for Privilege* (Boston, 1948); Oscar Handlin, "American Views of the Jew at the Opening of the Twentieth Century," *Publications of the American Jewish Historical Society* 40 (June 1951): 325, 327.
17. John Higham, "Anti Semitism in the Gilded Age," *Mississippi Valley Historical Review* 43 (March 1957); "Social Discrimination against Jews in America: 1830–1930," *Publications of the AJHS,* September 1957.
18. Michael Dobkowski, *The Tarnished Dream: The Basis of American Anti-Semitism* (Westport, Conn., 1979), 235, 239.
19. Isaacs, *Idols,* 193–94.
20. Wiebe, *Segmented Society,* 21, 52, 68.
21. Michael Kammen, *People of Paradox* (New York, 1972), 100, 110, 113–16, 251, 265.
22. Harold Fisch, *The Dual Image* (London, 1971), Introduction.
23. Abram Isaacs, "Has Judaism a Future?" *North American Review,* July 1897, 149–50.

Chapter 1. The Religious Image

1. Nicholas Berdyaev, *Christianity and Anti-Semitism* (New York, 1954), 6.

2. Fred Gladstone Bratton, *The Crime of Christendom* (New York, 1969), 168.

3. The continued potency of this religious image of the Jew in the twentieth century can be seen in a study by Charles Y. Glock and Rodney Stark, *Christian Beliefs and Anti-Semitism* (New York, 1969), 62–65.

4. *Harper's Magazine* 17 (July 1858): 267.

5. Hannah Adams, *The History of the Jews* (Boston, 1817), 7, 43, 53, 287, 290, 543. See also Rev. Michael Russell, *Palestine of the Holy Land* (New York, 1833), 19, 301.

6. Elizabeth Peabody, *Sabbath Lessons* (Salem, Mass., 1813), 32, 49–50, 60; A. A. *Annals of the Jewish Nation* (New York, 1832), iii–iv, 311, 354. See also H. P. Peet, *Scripture Lessons for the Young* (New York, 1846).

7. M. Johnstone, *Stories from the History of the Jews* (New York, 1853), 194, 199–200, 206, 215, 231, 238–39. For similar views see E. C. Forbes, *Easy Lessons on Scripture History* (New York, 1859), 98–99.

8. It should be noted that only in the second half of the twentieth century Protestant religious groups began to reexamine Sunday school texts in the light of studies revealing the extent of anti-Semitism found in these books. A good description of the kind of material in modern Sunday school books can be found in: James Brown, "Christian Teaching and Anti-Semitism: Scrutinizing Religious Texts," *Commentary*, December 1957, 494–501.

9. *The Churchman*, 24 March 1855, quoted in *American Israelite*, 29 April 1855. Similar views were expressed by the *Christian Intelligencer* and the *Catholic Telegraph*, quoted in *American Israelite*, 7 August 1858 and 29 January 1869.

10. Rev. Charles A. Goodrich, *A Pictorial Descriptive View and History of All Religions* (New York, 1860), 42–44, 52. Hannah W. Richardson, *Judea in Her Desolations* (Philadelphia, 1861), iii, 269–70.

11. W. D. Morrison, *The Jews Under Roman Rule* (New York, 1891), 360–61. John W. Mears, *From Exile to Overthrow* (Philadelphia, 1881), 238–45. See also F. W. Farmer, *The Herods* (New York, 1898).

12. Nathaniel Hawthorne, "The Star of Calvary," in *An American Anthology, 1781–1900* ed. Edmund Stedman (New York, 1900), 191.

13. Quoted in Adams, *History*, 2:214–15.

14. *Reports of the Society for Meliorating the Condition of the Jews*, 1823, 6, 10, 15, 20, 30, 38–39; 1825, 16–17, 32. David M. Eichhorn, "A History of Christian Attempts to Convert the Jews of the United States and Canada," (Ph.D. diss., Hebrew Union College, 1938) contains much interesting material on conversionist efforts.

15. John Hoyland, *Epitome of History* (Philadelphia, 1816), 2:43, 45, 51, 303, 342. Also, Jonathan Goodwin, *The Return and Conversion of the Jews* (Middletown, Conn., 1843), 5, 8, 16, 18, 58.

16. Isaac Mayer Wise, *Reminiscences* (Cincinnati, Ohio, 1901), 63, 70.

17. Moses Stuart, *Sermon at the Ordination of the Reverend G. Schouffler as Missionary to the Jews* (Andover, Mass., 1831), 5–8, 19, 20. Also, Alexander Keith, *The Land of Israel* (New York, 1844), 381. This reflected views similar to those popularized by the English author, Rev. H. H. Milman, *The History of the Jews* (New York, 1832). Milman was widely read in the United States. For a typically ambiguous mixture of admiration, condemnation, and conversionist fervor, see also, American Sunday School Union, *The Jew At Home and Abroad* (Philadelphia, 1845).

18. *Harper's Weekly* 32 (3 March 1888): 155–56; and *New England and Yale Review* 16 (March 1890): 245–50. Support for conversion attempts exists in modern America. In the Glock and Stark study 48% of all Protestants supported efforts to convert the Jews (p. 66).

19. *Niles Weekly Register* 11 (14 December 1816): 260. Also, 26 (17 July 1824): 326; 30 (3 June 1826): 234.

20. *Philadelphia Sunday Dispatch*, 28 May 1871.

21. *New York Times,* 11 June 1872; *Detroit Post,* 28 July 1876. Similar views could be found in the *New York Sun,* 1 December 1879.

22. For examples: *New York Tribune,* 28 May 1898; *Evening Journal,* 19 July 1899.

23. Religious literature is covered more extensively in Louis Harap, *The Image of the Jew in American Literature* (Philadelphia, 1974), 135–88.

24. All the songs quoted in this chapter come from the collection of the Newberry Library, Chicago.

25. Some good examples are: Rev. Jarvis Gregg, *Selumiel* (Philadelphia, 1833); *Hadassah, the Jewish Orphan* (Philadelphia, 1834); Sarah Pogson Smith, *Zerah, the Believing Jew* (Philadelphia, 1837).

26. William Ware, *Zenobia* (New York, 1843).

27. Lee M. Friedman, "Jews in Early American Literature," *More Books: The Bulletin of the Boston Public Library* 17, no. 10, 463; Don B. Seitz, "A Prince of Best Sellers," *Publisher's Weekly,* 21 February 1931, 940.

28. Joseph Holt Ingraham, *Prince of the House of David* (Philadelphia, 1855), vii, 400. Also J. H. Ingraham, *Pillar of Fire* (Boston, 1888), i.

29. Lew Wallace, *Ben Hur, A Tale of Christ* (New York, 1880), 545.

30. Some Examples are F. Marion Crawford, *Zoroaster;* Elizabeth Stuart Phelps, *The Master of Magicians* and *The Story of Jesus Christ;* Rose Porter, *A Daughter of Israel;* Eldbridge Brooks, *Son of Issacher;* E. F. Burr, *Aleph, the Chaldean;* J. Breckinridge Ellis, *Shem;* Mary Elizabeth Jennings, *Asa of Bethlehem;* Caroline Atwater Mason, *The Quiet King;* William A. Hammond, *The Son of Perdition;* all published from 1885 to 1900.

31. Florence M. Kingsley, *Titus* (New York, 1894), *Stephen* (New York, 1896), *Paul* (New York, 1897), and *The Cross Triumphant* (New York, 1898). The quote is from *Paul,* 348, vi.

32. William D. Mahan, *The Archko Volume* (Philadelphia, 1887), 16–17.

33. Mrs. T. F. Black, *Hadassah* (Chicago, 1895), 196.

34. Sarah Schoonmaker Baker, *The Jewish Twins* (New York, 1860), 134; Mrs. C. A. Ogden, *Into the Light* (Boston, 1899), 322; Henriette N. W. Baker, *Lost But Found* (Boston, 1871), 322, and *Rebecca the Jewess* (Boston, 1879), i; H. H. Boyeson, *A Daughter of the Philistines* (Boston, 1883), 176; Annie F. Johnston, *In League with Israel* (New York, 1896), 303.

35. *Scribner's Monthly* 13 (November 1876): 130; *Harper's Magazine,* October 1879.

36. *Ironclad Age,* 26 April 1887, quoted in *Israelite,* 6 May 1887.

37. Cited in Rudolf Glanz, *The Jew in Old American Folklore* (New York, 1961), 13.

38. *North American Review* 33 (July 1826): 102–4; *Nation* 5 (14 November 1867): 388. For a similar point of view, see also Thomas Jefferson's letter to Joseph Marx, cited in Abraham Karp, ed., *The Jewish Experience in America* (New York, 1969), 26.

39. *Niles Weekly Register* 69 (3 January 1846): 283–48.

40. *Frank Leslie's Illustrated Newspaper,* 4 November 1882.

41. Philip Cowen, ed., *Prejudice against the Jews* (New York, 1928), 62, 18–19. This was a republication of a symposium in the *American Hebrew*, 4 April 1890.

42. *New York Tribune*, 27 September 1891.

43. *Constitutional Whig*, 9 January 1829.

44. *North American Review* 32 (January 1831): 254, 263; 60 (April 1845): 330; *Boston Journal*, quoted in Philip S. Foner, *Jews in American History* (New York, 1945), 50.

45. Zebulon Vance, "The Scattered Nation," in Clement Dowd, *The Life of Zebulon Vance* (Charlotte, N.C., 1897), 371–74, 385. Similar ideas were expressed by Daniel Webster, quoted in Bertram Korn, *Eventful Years and Experiences* (Cincinnati, 1954), 49; and by Theodore Parker, in John Weiss, ed., *The Life and Correspondence of Theodore Parker* (New York, 1969), 2: 497.

46. Sidney Lanier, quoted in Joseph L. Baron, ed., *Stars and Sand* (Philadelphia, 1943), 431–32; Crawford Howell Toy, *Judaism and Christianity* (Boston, 1890), 237; Charles Loring Brace, *The Unknown God* (New York, 1890), 72.

47. *Harper's New Monthly Magazine* 88 (January 1894): 262–64.

48. Lydia Maria Child, *The Progress of Religious Ideas Through Successive Ages* (New York, 1855), 2: 152–53; 3: 439–42.

49. *North American Review*, July 1824, 113.

50. *Niles Weekly Register* 25 (1 November 1823); 26 (13 March 1824).

51. *United States Gazette*, 14, 15, 16 April 1843.

52. *Chicago Democrat*, 11 June 1851; *Chicago Daily Journal*, 14 June 1851; *Daily Democratic Press*, 3 April 1855.

53. James Parton, "Our Israelitish Brethren," *Atlantic Monthly*, 26 (October 1870): 392, 394–95.

54. *Jew At Home*, 111, 114, 120, 123.

55. *New York Times*, 3 April, 1870; 5 September 1870; 16 October 1870; 8 January 1871; 18 December 1870; 10 March 1872; 22 April 1872; 12 May 1878.

56. Quoted in Leon L. Watters, *The Pioneer Jews of Utah* (New York, 1952), 73–75, 85–86.

57. Quoted in *American Israelite*, 13 August 1875.

58. *New York Tribune*, 26 September 1889; 9 August 1890.

59. *New York Tribune*, 10 October 1894; 6 Sepetember 1896; 24 September 1899; 6 April 6 1898; 16 February 1896; *Evening Post*, 25 September 1897; 12 December 1895; *New York Times*, 7 October 1897.

60. Quoted in Morris Schappes, ed., *Documentary History of the Jews of the United States* (New York, 1871), 240–42.

Chapter 2. Literary Images

1. Edgar Rosenberg, *From Shylock to Svengali* (Stanford, Calif., 1960), 35, 160, 34, 84, 69, 164, 297.

2. Livia Bitton-Jackson, *Madonna or Courtesan? The Jewish Woman in Christian Literature* (New York, 1982), 30.

3. Stephen Bloore, "The Jew In American Dramatic Literature: 1794–1930," *Publications of the AJHS* 40 (June 1951): 347.

4. See, for example, Joshua Kunitz, *Russian Literature and the Jew* (New York, 1929); George L. Mosse, *Jews and Germans* (New York, 1970); Charles C. Lehrmann, *The Jewish Element in French Literature* (Rutherford, N.J., 1961); Stephen Wilson, *Ideology and Experience: Anti-Semitism in France* (Rutherford, N.J., 1982); Alfred Low, *Jews in the Eyes of Germans* (Philadelphia, 1979)

5. Philip S. Foner, *Mark Twain: Social Critic* (New York, 1958), 222.

6. Leslie Fiedler, "What Can We Do about Fagin?" *Commentary* 7 (May 1949): 413.

7. Louis Harap, "The Image of the Jew in American Drama, 1794–1823," *American Jewish Historical Quarterly*, 60 (March 1971): 243. For a contemporary comment, see Mordecai M. Noah, *Travels in England, France, Spain and the Barbary States in the Years 1813–14 and 15* (New York, 1819, 309–10).

8. Susanna H. Rowson, *Slaves in Algiers* (Philadelphia, 1794), 17, 51, 71.

9. James Ellison, *The American Captive* (Boston, 1812); Royall Tyler, *The Algerine Captive* (1797; reprint, Gainsville, Fla., 1967), 2: 167, 215; James Fenimore Cooper, *The Bravo* (New York, 1852).

10. Leslie Fiedler, *The Jew in the American Novel* (New York, 1959), 8; George Lippard, *The Quaker City* (Philadelphia, 1876), 149–50. A similar character can be found in Charles F. Briggs, *Bankrupt Stories* (New York, 1843) 310.

11. Peter Hamilton Meyers, *The Miser's Heir* (Philadelphia, 1854), 92–94. See also Julia Ward Howe, *The World's Own* (Boston, 1857), 107.

12. Joseph H. Ingraham, *The Clipper Yacht* (Boston, 1845), 10, 14.

13. John Beauchamp Jones, *Border War: A Tale of Disunion* (New York, 1859), 74; and *The Western Merchant* (Philadelphia, 1877), 133.

14. Henry James, "Impressions of a Cousin," *Tales of Three Cities* (Boston, 1887), 28, 58.

15. F. Marion Crawford, *Witch of Prague* (New York, 1891), 46, 193, 219.

16. Edgar Fawcett, *New York, A Novel* (New York, 1898), 61–26, 78; Richard Henry Savage, *An Exile from London* (New York, 1896), 51, and *The White Lady of Khaminavatka* (New York, 1898), 13.

17. Frank Norris, *McTeague* (1899; reprint, New York, 1968), 31–33, 157, 234–35.

18. Nathaniel Hawthorne, "A Virtuoso's Collection," *Mosses from an Old Manse* (Boston, 1894), 2: 276–77.

19. Nathaniel Hawthorne, "Ethan Brand," *Complete Novals and Selected Short Stories of Nathaniel Hawthorne* (New York, 1937), 1191–92.

20. See George W. Anderson, *The Legend of the Wandering Jew* (Providence, 1970), 153–160. F. Marion Crawford, *A Roman Singer* (New York, 1894). The Wandering Jew was also the central character in Lew Wallace's *Prince of India*, cited in the previous chapter.

21. Fiedler, *Novel*, 7.

22. J. Ingraham, *Clipper*, 51.

23. Louis Harap, "Fracture of a Stereotype: Charles Brockden Brown's Achsa Fielding," *American Jewish Archives* 24 (November 1972): 192. Charles Brockden Brown, *Arthur Mervyn* (New York, 1800, 1962), 2: 379, 389, 297, 298, 400, 402, 407.

24. Henry Harland, *As It Was Written* (New York, 1885), 12, 24.

25. E. S. March, *A Stumbler in Wide Shoes* (New York, 1896), 54. See also Theodore Sedgewick Fay, *Sidney Clifton* (New York, 1839), 1.

26. Jean-Paul Sartre, *Anti-Semite and Jew* (New York, 1948), 48–49.

27. J. Ingraham, *Clipper*, 9, 20.

28. George Lippard, *The Nazarene* (Philadelphia, 1854), 210, 226–27, 231.

29. Bitton-Jackson, *Madonna or Courtesan?*, 56.

30. J. Ingraham, *Clipper*, 20; Kathleen O'Meara, *Narka the Nihilist* (New York, 1887), 296.

31. Nathaniel Hawthorne, *The Marble Faun*, in *Complete Novels*, 601–19.

32. Henry James, *The Tragic Muse* (New York, 1890, 1936), 1: 61, 204–5, 220.

33. Herman Melville, *Clarel* (New York, 1876, 1960), 56, 497.

34. Ellen Schiff did find examples of "la belle juive" in American dramas in the 1930s. See Ellen Schiff, "What Kind of Way is That for Nice Jewish Girls to Act? Images of Jewish Women in Modern American Drama," *American Jewish History* 70 (September 1980): 106–18.

35. Harap, "Drama," 245; Edward Coleman, "Plays of Jewish Interest on the American Stage, 1752–1821," *Publications of the AJHS,* no. 33 (1934): 183; Lee M. Friedman, "Jews in Early American Literature," *More Books: The Bulletin of the Boston Public Library* 17, no. 10, 462.

36. George Walker, *Theodore Cyphon or the Benevolent Jew* (Alexandria, Va., 1803), 2:157. See also Joseph Butler, *Fortune's Footfall* (Harrisburg, Pa., 1798); Harap, "Drama," 256.

37. William Gilmore Simms, *Pelayo* (New York, 1838), 1: 84, 99; 2: 270.

38. Otto Ruppius, *The Peddler* (Cincinnati, 1871), 8, 12.

39. J. Richter Jones, *The Quaker Soldier* (Philadelphia, 1866), 98–109, 549.

40. Edwin Whipple, *North American Review* 124 (January 1877): 50–51.

41. See, for examples, Amelia Barr, *Bow of Orange Ribbon* (New York, 1886); Stuart Cumberland, *The Rabbi's Spell* (New York, 1888); Cecily Sidgewick, *Lesser's Daughter* (New York, 1894). Hezekiah Butterworth, "Wych Hazel, The Jew," *In Old New England* (New York, 1895), contains a far more interesting example of the Sheva-like character.

42. Caroline Willard, *A Son of Israel* (Philadelphia, 1898), 6, 11, 87, 94.

43. Robert W. Chambers, *Cardigan* (New York, 1901), 150, 219, 458, 496, 507. For similar examples see: Richard Henry Savage, *Lost Countess Falka, A Story of the Orient* (New York, 1896); Caroline Atwater Mason, *Woman of Yesterday* (New York, 1900). Greater ambivalence is shown in Henry Gillman, *Hassan: A Fellah* (Boston, 1898).

44. Harold Frederick, *Gloria Mundi,* in *Major Works of Harold Frederick,* vol. 5 (New York, 1969), 35, 36, 158, 179, 182, 403. See also Harap, *Image,* 396.

45. Ellen Schiff, *From Stereotype to Metaphor: The Jew in Contemporary Drama* (Albany, 1982), 17.

46. Quoted in Arnold Rogow, ed., *The Jew in a Gentile World* (New York, 1961), 244–45.

47. Edmund Wilson, "The Jews," in *A Piece of My Mind: Reflections at Sixty* (New York, 1956), 93–94.

48. Quoted in Joseph L. Baron, ed., *Stars and Sand* (Philadelphia, 1943), 133.

49. Friedman, "Jews in Early American Literature," 463; Rogow, *Jew in a Gentile World,* 255–57.

50. Sol Liptzin, *The Jew in American Literature* (New York, 1966), 43.

51. See Cowen, *American Hebrew,* 18; Oliver Wendell Holmes, *Over the Teacups,* in *The Writings of Oliver Wendell Holmes* (Cambridge, 1871), 4: 194–97; *The Professor at the Breakfast Table* (Grosse Point, Mich., 1968), 163.

52. James Russell Lowell in *North American Review* 65 (July 1847): 212–14; *Letters of James Russell Lowell* (New York, 1894), 208, 234, 415–16; *New Letters of James Russell Lowell* (New York, 1932), 328; "Democracy," in *Complete Writings of James Russell Lowell* (New York, 1904), 7: 15–16; *Atlantic Monthly* 179 (January 1897): 128–29.

53. Quoted in Ernest Saveth, *American Historians and European Immigrants: 1875–1925* (New York, 1948), 62.

54 Cowen, *American Hebrew,* 106.

55. Henry Adams, *The Education of Henry Adams* (New York, 1931), 238. See also Worthington C. Ford, ed., *Letters of Henry Adams* (Boston, 1938), 2:33; 3:111, 120,

144, 150–51, 233, 238, 241, 256, 338; and Harold Dean Cater,*Henry Adams and His Friends* (Cambridge, 1947), 362, 375, 377, 422, 438, 466, 473, 482, 599, 501–2.

56. Kenton J. Clymer, "Anti-Semitism in the Late Nineteenth Century: The Case of John Hay," *AJHS Quarterly* 60 (June 1971):347.

57. Wilson, *A Piece of My Mind* 98, 101.

58. Quoted in Harap, *Image,* 368, and Barbara Solomon, *Ancestors and Immigrants* (Cambridge, 1956), 181.

59. Henry James, "Glasses," *Embarrassments* (New York, 1896), 93; *The American Scene* (New York, 1907), 127–29.

60. For a more complete discussion, see Louise Abbie Mayo, "Herman Melville, the Jew and Judaism," *American Jewish Archives* 38, no. 2 (November 1976): 172–97.

61. Herman Melville, *Clarel: A Poem and Pilgimage in the Holy Land* (1876; reprint, New York, 1960), 56–66, 87–89, 530, 8–10, 55, 498, 505, 203, 205, 267, 78, 88, 213, 543, 54, 110, 134, 513.

62. Fiedler, *Novel,*9.

63. John James Clarke, "Henry Harland: A Critical Biography," (Ph.D. diss., Brown University, 1957), 34.

64. Harland, *Written,* 104–6.

65. *New York Times,*5 October 1885.

66. Henry Harland, *Mrs. Peixada* (New York, 1886), 78, 101–3, 252–53.

67. Henry Harland, *The Yoke of the Thorah* (New York, 1887), 63–64, 68, 171, 219–20.

68. *American Hebrew,*February 1888.

69. *New York Times,*26 June 1887; *New York Tribune,* 22 May 1887.

70. Henry Harland, *Uncle Florimond* (New York, 1888), 63, 94.

71. *American Hebrew,* 5 October 1888.

72. *Lippincott's Monthly Magazine,* May 1888, 657–66.

73. Henry Harland, *Grandison Mather* (New York, 1889), 167, 125, 136, 144.

74. Edward King, *Joseph Zalmonah* (Boston, 1894), 4, 9, 18, 20. See also Maurice Hindus, "Edward Smith King and the Old East Side," *American Jewish Historical Quarterly* 64 (June 1975): 321–30.

75. Abraham Cahan, *Yekl* (New York, 1896), 23–24, 28–9, 37, 71, 75, 176; David M. Fine, *The City, the Immigrant and American Fiction, 1880–1920* (Metuchen, N.J., 1977), 54.

76. Nancy H. Banks, "The New York Ghetto," *The Bookman* 4 (October 1896): 157–58; Howells quoted in Rudolf and Clara M. Kirk, "Abraham Cahan and William Dean Howells, the Story of a Friendship," *AJHS Quarterly* 52 (September 1962):51–52.

77. Abraham Cahan, "A Ghetto Wedding," *Atlantic Monthly* 81 (February 1898):270, 273.

78. Abraham Cahan, *The Imported Bridegroom and Other Stories of the New York Ghetto* (New York, 1898), passim.

79. Abraham Cahan, "The Apostate of Chego-Chegg," *Century* 37 (November 1899):94, 103.

80. Abraham Cahan, "Rabbi Eliezer's Christmas," *Scribner's* 26 (December 1899): 664.

81. Jules Chametzky, *From the Ghetto: The Fiction of Abraham Cahan* (Amherst, Mass. 1977), 77.

82. Fine, *The City. . . ,* 73. See, for example, Herman Bernstein, *In the Gates of Israel* (New York, 1902).

83. Jonathan Sarna, "The 'Mythical Jew' and the 'Jew Next Door' in Nineteenth

Century America," in *Anti-Semitism in American History*, ed. David Garber (Urbana, Ill., 1986), 57–78. However, he is not able to explain the reason for this dissonance.

Chapter 3. Popular Images

1. Michael Joseph Denning, "Dime Novels: Popular Fiction and Working Class Culture in Nineteenth Century America" Ph.D. diss., Yale University, 1984).

2. Cecil Robinson, *With the Ears of Strangers* (Tucson, 1963), 25.

3. Sylvanus Cobb, *The Marmeluke* (Boston, 1852), 27; Edward Judson, *Ned Buntline's Life Line* (New York, 1849), 14, 19, 125; *Morgan or The Knight of the Black Flag* (New York, 1860), 15, 16, 19, 20, 24, 87, 115–16, 187; *Rose Seymour: or the Ballet Girl's Revenge* (New York, 1865), 44, 46.

4. Albert Aiken, *White Witch* (New York, 1871), 11, 29; *The Genteel Spotter* (New York, 1884), 6, 11, 12, 22; *Lone Hand in Texas* (New York, 1888), 10–13; *Dick Talbot the Ranch King* (New York, 1892), 16.

5. Albert Aiken, *California Detective* (New York, 1878), 8, 30, 31; *The Phantom Hand* (New York, 1877), 5; *Lone Hand on the Caddo* (New York, 1888), 3; *Lone Hand the Shadow* (New York, 1889), 2–4, 8, 13; *The Fresh of Frisco* (New York, 1891), 24.

6. Gilbert Jerome, *Dominick Squeek, the Bow Street Runner* (New York, 1884), 24–26, 43–44; *Old Subtle: Or The Willing Victim* (New York, 1885), 18, 32.

7. Jesse Cowdrick, *The Detective's Apprentice* (New York, 1885), 6.

8. Edward Wheeler, *Apollo Bill, the Trail Tornado* (New York, 1882), 9; *Boss Bob, King of the Bootblacks* (New York, 1886), 5, 7, 12–15; *Jim Bludsoe, the Boy Phenix* (New York, 1878), 4, 8, 11, 14; *The Ventriloquist Detective* (New York, 1887), 2, 5.

9. Prentiss Ingraham, *Gold Plume, the Boy Bandit* (New York, 1881), 7, 9; *The New Monte Cristo* (New York, 1886), 6, 7; *The Jew Detective* (New York, 1891), 2–4, 14, 27; "Jule the Jewess," in *Banner Weekly* 15, nos. 734–45 (December 1896–February 1897). Joseph Ingraham also wrote a dime novel with a Jewish character, *Ramero* (New York, 1869), 89.

10. Ellen Schiff, "Anti-Semitism on the American Stage," in Gerber, ed. *Anti-Semitism*, 82.

11. T. Allston Brown, *A History of the New York Stage* (New York, 1903).

12. Quoted in Toby Lelyveld, *Shylock on the Stage* (Cleveland, 1960), 54, 56.

13. *Ibid.*, 65.

14. William Winter, *Life and Art of Edwin Booth* (London, 1893), 198–200.

15. *New York Times,* 4 February 1867.

16. *Cincinnati Christian Herald,* quoted in *American Israelite,* 14 April 1865; William Cullen Bryant, "Shylock Not a Jew," in Joseph Baron, *Stars and Sand* (Philadelphia, 1943), 59–60; also quoted in Lelyveld, *Shylock on the Stage,* 75.

17. Lelyveld, *Shylock on the Stage,* 129.

18. *Pineywoods Tavern or Sam Slick in Texas* (Philadelphia, 1858), 37.

19. Herbert W. Kline, "The Jew that Shakespeare Drew?" *American Jewish Archives* 23 (April 1971): 72; *New York Herald,* 7 November 1883; *Evening Bulletin,* 24 December 1895; *Chicago Tribune,* 10 January 1884; Lelyveld, *Shylock on the Stage,* 83; Henry James, *Scenic Art, Notes in Acting and the Drama* (New Brunswick, N.J., 1948).

20. Lelyveld, *Shylock on the Stage,* 92; *New York Mirror,* 7 January 1888; William Archer, *The Dramatic Year* (Boston, 1889), 182; Norman Hapgood, *The Stage in America* (New York, 1901), 166–67; Henry A. Clapp, *Reminiscences of a Dramatic Critic* (Boston, 1902), 135.

21. John Brougham, *Much Ado about a Merchant of Venice* (New York, 1858), 2, 9,

24; George M. Baker, *The Peddler of Very Nice* (Boston, 1866), 208–9, 212–14; *"Shylock", a Burlesque*, As Performed by Griffin and Christy Minstrels, Arranged by George W. H. Griffin (New York, 1876?), 3, 4, 6, 8.

22. John Brougham, *The Lottery of Life* (New York, 1867?); Dion Boucicault, *Flying Scud*, in *Favorite Plays of the Nineteenth Century*, ed. Barrett Clark (Princeton, 1943), 139; Charles Townsend, *Jail Bird* (New York, 1893?), 7, 10; Steele Mackaye, *Money-Mad*, cited in Louis Harap, *Image*, 216.

23. Hornblow, *History of Theatre in America*, 1 : 204.

24. Thomas Dibdin, *The Jew and the Doctor* (New York, 1807), 13, 16, 33, 35.

25. Sidney Grundy, *An Old Jew* (New York, 1894), 23, 118.

26. Hapgood, *Stage in America*, 246–27.

27. George H. Jessop, *Sam'l of Posen or The Commercial Drummer*, in *America's Lost Plays*, vol. 4 (Bloomington, 1964), 159, 183.

28. *New York Daily Graphic*, 17 May 1881; *American Hebrew*, 5 April 1889; *New York Times*, 20 May 1894; Harap, *Image*, 232.

29. Stephen Bloore, "The Jew in American Dramatic Literature, 1794–1930," *Publications of the A.J.H.S.* 40 (June 1951):351–52.

30. Henry C. DeMille and David Belasco, *Men and Women*, in *America's Lost Plays*, vol. 17, ed. Robert H. Hall (Princeton, 1941), 304.

31. *American Israelite*, 4 April 1901.

32. Edward W. Tullidge, *Ben Israel* (Salt Lake City, 1875), 16, 32.

33. Hornblow, *History of Theatre in America*, 2 : 152; T. Allston Brown, *A History of the New York Stage* (New York, 1903), 2 : 220.

34. Augustin Daly, *Leah the Forsaken* (New York, 1862?): A. H. Quinn, *A History of American Drama* (New York, 1927), 10; George William Curtis, *Harper's Weekly*, 7 March 1863.

35. *Eltone Out and Outer Comic Songbook* (New York, 1839); Rudolph Glanz, *The Jews of California* (New York, 1960), 126; Bernard Sobel, *Burleycue* (New York, 1931), 120.

36. Schiff, "Anti-Semitism," 84; Douglas Gilbert, *American Vaudeville, Its Life and Times* (New York, 1940), 73, 288; Sobel, *Burleycue*, 142, 143.

37. Brown, *History . . . New York Stage*, 1 : 89; F. E. Chase, *A Ready Made Suit, A Mock Trial* (Boston, 1885?), 21–23; Felix Isman, *Weber and Fields* (New York, 1924), 258; Harry E. Shelland, *Great Libel Case* (New York, 1900), 3, 12.

38. M. J. Landa, *The Jew in Drama* (New York, 1969), 201.

39. *A Collection of Songs Collected from the Works of Mr. Dibdin* (Philadelphia, 1799), 260. For many good examples see Rudolph Glanz, *The Jew in Old American Folklore* (New York, 1961), 130–31; *The Jew in Early American Wit and Graphic Humor* (New York, 1973), 62.

40. Thomas Haliburton, *Letterbag of the Great Western* (New York, 1840), 89–90.

41. *Spirit of the Times* 14 (1844–45): 544; 19 (1850): 604.

42. *The Spectator* (New York, 1845), 58; *The Bulls and the Bears on Wall Street* (New York, 1854), 166; *The Knickerbocker* 50 (1857): 477.

43. John J. Appel, "Jews in American Caricature: 1820–1914," *American Jewish History* 71 (September 1981): 103–33; William F. Lichter, "Political Reflections of an Age" (Ph.D. diss. New York University, 1970); Dobkowski, *Tarnished Dream*, 60.

44. *Life*, 14 June 1883, 281.

45. *Puck*, 16 April 1895, 98; 6 January 1892, 342; 16 May 1894, 197; 31 August 1898; 7 December 1898; 4 October 1899.

46. *Life*, 20 February 1896, 133; 8 April 1897, 278; 21 December 1899, 536; 12 May 1898, 406; 5 April 1883, 161; 15 January 1891, 38; 16 January 1898, 45; *Judge*

1 (1881):5; *Puck* 21 (1887):371; 23 April 1895, 154; 5 October 1897; 1 February 1899.

47. *Life,* 24 November 1887, 294; 24 March 1898, 226; *Puck,* 16 December 1896; 23 February 1898; *Tid-Bits* 1 (1884): 8.

48. *Life,* 20 September 1883, 142; 5 November 1885; 204; *Judge,* 17 March 1894, 162; 22 October 1898.

49. *Judge,* 3 February 1894, 68; 13 January 1894, 24; *Puck,* 15 May 1895, 196; 19 June 1895; 29 January 1895; 22 April 1896; 18 November 1896; 20 October 1897; 11 May 1898; 12 June 1899; *Life* 25 (1895): 125; 17 May 1900, 424. The endurance of this basic joke can be seen in modern "Borscht Belt" routines. For example, Cohen: "You here in Miami? How's business?" Schwartz: "I was flooded out." Cohen: "How do you make a flood?"

50. *Puck,* 23 September 1891, 70; 19 September 1894; 14 December 1898; *Judge,* 10 July 1882, 8–9; *Life,* 10 October 1901, 290–91.

51. *Puck,* 21 April 1897; 27 July 1898; 3 January 1900; *Puck Library* (1887), 6–7; *Judge,* 22 July 1882, 8–9; 20 January 1883, 2; *Life,* (1897), 215; 19 December 1901, 535.

52. James Harvey Young, *The Toadstool Millionaires* (Princeton, 1961), 141; *Hostetter's Illustrated,* 1891, 15; 1898, 15; 1901, 31; *Harper's Magazine* 32 (1865–66):134, 409; *Harper's Monthly* 92 (December 1895): 159–60; James S. Buck, *Pioneer History of Milwaukee* (Milwaukee, 1886), 4:115; *Texas Sifting,* quoted in *Puck* 12 (1882–83): 320.

53. *John Donkey,* vol. 1 (1848), 335, 323.

54. *California Mailbag,* vol. 2, 60.

55. *Puck,* 8 December 1880, 228–29; 27 June 1877, 2; 4 July 1887, 16; 30 July 1879, 323; 8 December 1880, 220; 11 May 1881; 6 August 1879, 346.

56. *Life,* 10 April 1902.

57. *Puck,* 29 July 1891, 362.

58. Appel, 105.

59. *Harper's Magazine* 50 (1874): 698.

60. Glanz, *Humor,* 237.

61. Cecil Robinson, *With the Ears of Strangers: The Mexican in American Literature* (Tuscon, 1963), 20, 33, 54; Appel, 107, 115; Fine, *The City,* 59; Harold Isaacs, *Scratches on Our Minds: American Images of China and India* (New York, 1958), 112; Stuart Creighton Miller, *The Unwelcome Immigrant: The American Image of the Chinese* (Berkeley, 1969), 147, 149, 185.

Chapter 4. The Press and Periodicals

1. *Banking and Insurance Chronicle,* 28 March 1867, 97–98; 12 April 1867, 114, 115; *Insurance Monitor,* March 1867, 143; April 1867, 225, 227, 229, 230, 231.

2. *New York Herald,* 9 April 1867, 16 April 1867; *Evening Post,* 7 April 1867; *Sunday Dispatch,* 21 April 1867.

3. *American Israelite,* 24 January 1873, 11 September 1890; *Police Gazette,* quoted in Rudolf Glanz, *Studies in Judaica Americana* (New York, 1970), 148. David Gerber documents similar fears of Jewish business untrustworthiness as early as the 1850s in "Cutting Out Shylock: Elite Anti-Semitism and the Quest for Moral Order in the Mid-Nineteenth Century American Marketplace," in Gerber, *Anti-Semitism,* 201–25.

4. *New York Herald,* 20, 21 June 1877; *New York Times,* 19 June 1877.

5. Matthew Hale Smith, *Sunshine and Shadow in New York* (Hartford, 1868), 453.

6. *New York Tribune,* 1 June 1876; *American Israelite,* 29 June 1877.

7. *New York Herald,* 20, 21, 22, 23, 24 June 1877; *Evening Post,* 20 June 1877; *Commercial Advertiser,* 19 June 1877; *New York Sun,* 20, 25 June 1877; *Daily Graphic,* 21, 26 June 1877; *New York Tribune,* 20, 23, 25, 27 June 1877; *Harper's Weekly* 21 (July 7, 1877): 518–19; *New York Times,* 21, 23 June 1877; *American Israelite,* 29 June 1877. Non–New York newspapers were surveyed and extensively quoted in *Herald,* 22, 23 June 1877.

8. *New York Herald,* 22, 23, 24, 25, 26, 28 July 1879; *New York Sun,* 23 July 1879; *Commercial Advertiser,* 23 July 1879; *Evening Post,* 23 July 1879; German papers quoted in the *Herald,* 25 July 1879.

9. *New York Evening Mail,* 23 July 1879; *New York Times,* 27 July, 20 October 1879; *Brooklyn Daily Eagle,* 23, 24 July 1879.

10. *Puck,* 30 July 1879, 322; *Nation,* 31 July 1879, 68; *Harper's Magazine,* October 1879.

11. *American Israelite,* 6 August 1880; *Nation,* 12 May 1881, 327; *Puck,* 11 May 1881, 178.

12. *North American Review,* September 1881, 263–77.

13. *The Forum,* July 1887, 523–31.

14. *New York Herald,* 23 April 1893; *New York Times,* 22 April 1893; *Evening Post,* 17 April 1893, 22 April 1893; *New York Sun,* 24 April 1893.

15. *New York Sun,* 15 June 1899; *New York Tribune,* 13 October 1902.

16. *Niles Weekly Register,* 27 December 1823, 4 October 1845; Abraham Karp, *The Jewish Experience in America* (New York, 1969), 165; Bertram Korn, *The Early Jews of New Orleans* (Waltham, Mass., 1969), 257–58.

17. *Evening Post,* 10 October 1822; William L. MacKenzie, *The Lives and Opinions of Ben'n Franklin Butler and Jesse Hoyt* (Boston, 1845), 37; *Niles Weekly Register,* 24 September 1825, 1 October 1825, 21 January 1826; Isaac Goldberg, *Major Noah: An American Jewish Pioneer* (Philadelphia, 1936), 252.

18. *New York Herald,* 16 March 1840.

19. Philip Hone, *The Diary of Philip Hone* (New York, 1927), 1:543; *Niles Weekly Register* 67 (21 September 1844), (16 November 1844): 164; *Commercial Advertiser,* 24 March 1851; *Evening Post,* 24 March 1851.

20. George G. Foster, *New York Naked* (New York, m.d.), 80–82; *Lippincott* 1 (28 June 1868): 666–70.

21. Joseph Holt Ingraham, *The Sunny South* (Philadelphia, 1860), 307–8.

22. *American Israelite,* 22 March 1861, 16 September 1864; *Harper's Magazine* 26 (1863): 675.

23. Reprinted in the *New York Tribune,* 9 April 1885.

24. *The Asmonean* 11 (1854): 140; Rudolf Glanz, "The Rothschild Legend in America," *Jewish Social Studies* 19 (January–April 1957):15, 19; *New York Times,* 19 October 1874.

25. *Frank Leslie's Illustrated Weekly,* 23 January, 16 March, 13 April, 27 April, 6 July 1893.

26. *Atlantic Monthly* 32 (December 1873):651; *The Century* 1 (April 1882): 939–42.

27. For a complete discussion see Glanz, "Rothschild"; *Niles Weekly Register* 30 (22 April 1826): 144; 37 (28 November 1829):214; 49 (1835):40.

28. *Philadelphia Times,* 21 November 1856; *Harper's Weekly,* 8 April 1882, 219; 13 May 1882; *Illustrated American* 5 (24 January 1891): 422; *Nation* 71 (1900): 103.

29. Glanz, "Rothschild," 9–10, *New York Times*, 4 January 1878; *New York Tribune*, 26 September 1886, 1 May 1887.

30. *Spirit of the Times* 5 (1835): 12; Glanz, "Rothschild," 11; *Harper's Weekly* 1 (1857): 253; *Overland Monthly* 2 (1869): 288; *Munsey's Magazine* 7 (April 1892): 37, 40. For the opposite point of view see Brooks Adams, *Law of Civilization and Decay* (New York, 1943), 306.

31. *Niles Weekly Register* 63 (5 October 1842): 977; *Harper's New Monthly Magazine* 73 (November 1883): 890–97; *New York Times*, 16, 21 October 1883, 19, 22, 26, 27 October 1884; *New York Tribune*, 24 October 1884; *Pioneer Press*, quoted in W. Gunther Plaut, *Jews in Minnesota* (New York, 1969), 85; Ambrose Bierce, in Edmund Clarence Stedman, *An American Anthology* (Boston, 1900), 444.

32. *Life* 27 (17 May 1896): 364.

33. *Atlantic Monthly* 75 (April 1895): 571.

34. *New York Times*, 18 June 1878; *Atlantic Monthly* 46 (October 1880): 566.

35. Charles Stember, *Jews in the Mind of America* (New York, 1966), 248; *National Anti-Slavery Standard* 1 (17 February 1842). See also *Feast of Wit* (Philadelphia, 1821), 61; *Table Talk*, 14 August 1833.

36. *Spirit of the Times* 14 (1844–45): 506; *American Israelite*, 11 May 1855, 1 May 1858; Rudolf Glanz, *The Jews of California* (New York, 1966), 52.

37. *Harper's Weekly* 3 (1859): 739; *Atlantic Monthly* 20 (1867): 603; *Banking and Insurance Chronicle*, 2 May 1867, 138; *New York Tribune*, 5 August 1883; *American Hebrew* 18, no. 6 (1883); *A Day on Coney Island* (New York, 1880), 11; *Cincinnati Gazette*, 20 July 1871; *New York Times*, 29 May 1877.

38. Harap, *Image*, 81; B. G. Rudolph, *From a Minyon to a Community* (Syracuse, 1970), 38; *American Israelite*, 18 May 1855; *Harper's Weekly*, 19 November 1859. See also *New York Ledger*, 3 September 1858.

39. Glanz, *Folklore*, 118; *Jewish Messenger*, 12 July 1861; Joseph A. Scoville, *The Old Merchants of New York City* (New York, 1877), 2:121; Charles F. Daly, *The Settlement of the Jews in North America* (New York, 1893), 73, 87, 89, 97.

40. *Niles Weekly Register*, 6 October 1832, 69 (4 October 1845): 139; *New York Evening Mirror*, 2 March 1855; *American Israelite*, 11 May 1855; *Los Angeles Star*, 11 October 1862; *New York Tribune*, 25 February 1880; *New York Times*, 6 November 1863, 4 February 1877, 3 August 1883; Philip Cowen, ed., *Prejudice against the Jews* (New York, 1928), a symposium in *The American Hebrew*, 4 April 1890, 80–81.

41. *American Israelite*, 22 June 1860, 27 May 1881.

42. *The Independent* 41 (12 September 1889): 17; *Life* 13 (24 January 1889): 46; *The Methodist Review* 75 (March 1893): 29; *American Hebrew*, symposium, 50–131.

43. Robert Wiebe, *The Segmented Society* (New York, 1975), 146.

44. *De Bow's Review* 5 (August 1868): 695, 697, 700.

45. *New York Times*, 24 November 1871; *Harper's Weekly* 17 (26 July 1873): 642; 19 February 1881; *Harper's New Monthly Magazine* 55 (July 1877): 300; 88 (January 1894): 262–66; Henry George, "Moses: A Lecture," in *The Writings of Henry George* (New York, 1898), 8:21; *American Hebrew*, 2 July 1880.

46. *Brooklyn Daily Eagle*, 2 April 1874; *American Israelite*, 26 March 1875; Jacob Riis, *Children of the Poor* (New York, 1923), 190; *Atlantic Monthly*, July 1898, 131.

47. *Washington Sentinel*, 21 May 1854; *Sunday Dispatch*, 28 May 1854.

48. *Jewish Messenger*, 21 May 1861; Glanz, *California*, 372; *Chicago Tribune*, 16 August 1862.

49. *Philadelphia Evening Telegraph*, 19 October 1872; *North American Review* 126 (March–April 1878): 302; *New York Herald*, 8 October 1886; *New York Sun*, 25 March 1887; *American Hebrew*, symposium, 37, 43, 58, 134.

50. *Monthly Chronicle of Interesting and Useful Knowledge*, 1839, 552; *Harper's*

Magazine 17 (July 1858): 267–86; 22 (1866): 404.

51. *New York Times,* 7 August 1865, 29 November 1874, 15 July 1877; *Nation* 14 (29 February 1872): 137; *New York Tribune,* 7 August 1875.

52. *New York Sun,* 16, 19 September 1870. For a discussion of "The Jew as Racial Alien," by Robert Singerman, see Gerber, *Anti-Semitism,* 103–28. Singerman does concede that the term "race" was used in the nineteenth century to "designate virtually any physical, linguistic or ethnic group."

53. Glanz, *Folklore,* 64; *Life* 18 (6 August 1891): 60.

54. Jonathan Sarna, "Anti-Semitism and American History," *Commentary* 71 (March 1981): 45.

55. *California Mail Bag* 2 (1872): 67; John Higham, "Anti-Semitism in the Gilded Age," *Mississippi Valley Historical Review* 43 (March 1957): 566.

Chapter 5. Political and Ideological Images

1. Richard Morris, "The Jews, Minorities and Dissent in the American Revolution," *Migration and Settlement: Proceedings of the Anglo-American Historical Conference* (London, 1971), 158–60.

2. *The Democrat* (New York, 1795), Introduction.

3. *Niles Weekly Register,* 16 January and 29 May 1819, 21 October 1820, 14 January 1826; Joseph Blau and Salo Baron, *The Jews of the United States: 1790–1840* (Philadelphia, 1963), 1:42–43; *National Intelligencer,* 14 October 1820; George Houston, *Israel Vindicated* (New York, 1823), 95, 99.

4. Leon Huhner, "The Struggle for Religious Liberty in North Carolina with Special Reference to the Jews," *Publications of the AJHS* (1907), 60–62, 64.

5. See Bertram Korn, *American Jewry and the Civil War* (Philadelphia, 1960).

6. *The Thirteenth Annual Report of the American and Foreign Anti-Slavery Society,* 11 May 1853 (New York, 1853); *New York Tribune,* 7 January 1861.

7. E. Merton Coulter, *The Confederate States of America* (Baton Rouge, 1950), 237; *Southern Illustrated News* 2 (1863): 100; *American Israelite,* 22 March 1861, 28 February 1862, 25 July 1862, 6 March 1863; *New York Times,* 15 March 1862; *Jewish Messenger,* 4 April 1862, 12 February 1864; *Harper's Weekly,* 1 August 1863.

8. Korn, *American Jewry,* 128–9; 148–9; *American Israelite,* 9 January 1863; *Philadelphia Public Ledger,* 13 January 1863; *New York Times,* 18 January 1863.

9. *New York Herald,* 31 July 1865; *Harper's Magazine* 33 (1866): 560.

10. John Higham, in Charles Stember, *Jews in the Mind of America* (New York, 1966), 248–49. See also Richard Hofstader, *The Age of Reform* (New York, 1955), 77.

11. Irwin Unger, *The Greenback Era* (Princeton, 1964), 201–12; Brick Pomeroy, *The Great Campaign,* 22 August 1876.

12. Elizabeth Bryant, "Types of Mankind as Affecting the Financial History of the World: Delivered before the Greenback Labor Club of the District of Columbia, October 7, 1878," 1–8.

13. *Irish World,* 30 June 1877.

14. *American Israelite,* 6 July and 10 August 1893, 22 July and 15 October 1896; Walter Nugent, *The Tolerant Populists: Kansas Populism and Nativism* (Chicago, 1963), 108, 192.

15. Thomas May Thorpe, *What is Money?* (New York, 1894), 66; Ebenezer Wakely, *The Gentile Ass and the Judean Establishment* (Chicago, 1895), frontispiece, 5; James B. Goode, *The Modern Banker* (Chicago, 1896), 125; Tom Watson, *The People's Party Campaign Book* (Washington D.C., 1892), 12.

16. William H. Harvey, *A Tale of Two Nations* (Chicago, 1894), 96; *Coin's Finan-*

cial School (Chicago, 1894), 123, 144; *Coin's Financial School Up-to-Date* (Chicago, 1895), 68.

17. Ignatius Donnelly, *Caesar's Column* (Cambridge, 1960), 32, 150–52, 283.

18. Martin Ridge, *Ignatius Donnelly: The Portrait of a Politician* (Chicago, 1962), 264, 395–96; Norman Pollack, "The Myth of Populist Anti-Semitism," *American Historical Review* 68 (October 1962): 77–78; Ignatius Donnelly, *The Golden Bottle* (New York, 1968), 280–81.

19. Nugent, *The Tolerant Populists*, 111; *American Israelite*, 8 June 1893; William Jennings Bryan, *The First Battle: A Story of the Campaign of 1896* (Chicago, 1897), 580–81.

20. H. P. C. Worthington, *Hell for the Jews* (New York, 1879), 4–16.

21. Sarna, *Commentary*, 45; Telemachus Timayonis, *The Original Mr. Jacobs* (New York, 1888), 5–307, and *Judas Iscariot* (New York, 1888), 3–273.

22. Goldwin Smith, "New Light on the Jewish Question," *North American Review* 153 (August 1891): 129–42; responses: September 1891, 257, 271; November 1891, 521–22.

23. *Catholic World*, December 1891, 360–71; August 1892, 649–58; September 1892, 857–58; October 1893, 50, 54.

24. *New York Sun*, 17 March 1849. See also *American Insraelite*, 23 May 1856.

25. *Atlantic Monthly* 46 (October 1880): 566–67; *Puck* 8 (8 December 1880): 220; *New York Times*, 20 October 1881; *Century* 2 (May 1882); 3 (February 1883): 608–9.

26. *Chicago Evening Journal*, 15 November 1890; *Detroit News*, 23, 25 March, 3, 5, 7, 20 April 1893; *New York Herald*, 6 December 1895; *New York Sun*, 10 December 1895; *New York Tribune*, 14 December 1895; *Life*, 26 December 1895, 410; *Review of Reviews*, January 1896; *American Israelite*, 19 December 1895—this issue cited papers around the country, including *Detroit Tribune, Park City Times, Philadelphia Ledger*, as well as those in paragraph. *New York Tribune*, 16 January 1898; *New York Times*, 13 December 1900.

27. *North American Review*, October 1856, 352; January 1894, 94–95; July 1897, 149–50.

28. James Parton, "Our Israelitish Brethren," *Atlantic Monthly* 26 (October 1870): 386–403; "The Scattered Nation," reproduced in Clement Dowd, *The Life of Zebulon B. Vance* (Charlotte, 1897), 370–94; Johanna von Bohne, *Jew and Gentile* (New York, 1889), 8, 11–13; M. Bourchier Sanford, "In Favor of the Jew," *North American Review* 152 (January 1891): 126–28; Madison C. Peters, *The Jews in America* (Philadelphia, 1905), 76–133; *Review of Reviews*, March 1893, 222, April 1893, 336; Mark Twain, "Concerning the Jews," *Harper's Monthly Magazine* 99 (June 1899): 528–35; M. S. Levy, "A Rabbi's Reply to Mark Twain," *Overland Monthly*, October 1899, 364, 366; Mark Twain, "The American Jew as Soldier," *Mark Twain on the Damned Human Race* (New York, 1962), 177–78. See also Selig Adler, "Zebulon Vance and the 'Scattered Nation,'" *Journal of Southern History* 7 (August 1941): 369.

29. *Niles Weekly Register*, 24 July 1815, 293; 24 August 1816, 429; 9 November 1816; 9 October 1819, 94; 16 October 1819, 111; 6 November 1819, 157; 22 October 1822, 99; 18 November 1826, 182; 5 October, 23 November, 1833; 23 June 1842, 258; 7 January 1843, 304; 18 February 1843, 400; 2 September 1843, 2; 30 September 1843, 67; 9 March 1844, 27.

30. *North American Review* 12 (January 1821): 225–27; 22 (April 1826): 427–28; 83 (October 1856): 352–62; 86 (January 1858): 203–6.

31. *New York Courier*, 20 September 1840; *American Literary Magazine* 1 (November 1847): 318–19.

32. *New York Times,* 25 May 1852; *New York Evening Post,* 5 August 1857.

33. *American Israelite,* 7 August 1857; *New York Herald,* 8 August 1857.

34. Bertram Korn, *American Reaction to the Mortara Case* (Cincinnati, 1957), 118–121, 146–147; *Philadelphia Public Ledger,* 25 November 1858; *Jewish Messenger,* 14 January 1859; *Irish American* 4 December 1859.

35. *Nation* 15 (10 October 1872): 227; *New York Times,* 23 March 1872, 13 January 1873, 19 October 1874, 6 June 1879, 14 September 1879, 25 January 1880; *Frank Leslie's Illustrated Newspaper,* 2 August 1879; *Harper's Weekly* 23 (5 April 1879): 226; *New York Herald,* 7 January 1877; *Chicago Daily Times,* 3 April 1885.

36. *American Israelite,* 12 December 1879, 21 January 1881; *New York Times,* 24, 25 November 1880, 9, 20, 29 December 1880, 6 January 1881; *Nation* 29 (2 October 1879): 217; (7 January 1880, 24 June 1880): 469; 9, 31 December 1880): 403.

37. *Nation* 56 (12 January 1893): 24; *The Forum,* December 1893, 412–16, 445–49. See chapter 6 for a detailed discussion of public perceptions of Russian persecutions.

38. Rose Halpern, "American Reaction to the Dreyfus Case" (Master's thesis, Columbia University, 1941), 32, 35–37, 41, 47, 49, 52, 57, 59, 61; Ronald A. Urquart, "American Reaction to the Dreyfus Affair" (Ph.D. diss., Columbia University, 1972), 97–101, 146, 165, 174; *New York Sun, Herald, World, Times,* all 6 January 1895; *Harper's Weekly,* 19 August 1899, 828; 16 September 1899, 927; 23 September 1899, 930; *New York Tribune,* 24 February 1898, *Puck* 45 (28 June 1899); *Review of Reviews,* March 1898, 311; *Atlantic Monthly,* May 1898, 589–91.

39. *Century,* May 1883, December 1889; *New York Times,* 6 May 1891; *Harper's Weekly* 41 (13 November 1897); *North American Review* 167 (August 1898): 200; November 1898; 169 (July 1899): 299–301.

40. *Niles Weekly Register* 10 (3 August 1816): 373; Hannah Adams, *History of the Jews* (Boston, 1817), 467.

41. *Albany Gazette,* 29 January 1820; *Commercial Advertiser,* 16 October 1822.

42. *Charleston Courier,* 20 March 1841; Israel T. Naamuni, "Gold Rush Days" *Commentary* 6 (September 1948): 265; Pomroy Jones, *Annals and Recollections of Oneida County* (Rome, N.Y., 1851), 541.

43. *American Literary Magazine* 1 (November 1847): 319; *New York Times,* 25 May 1852.

44. Eliza Woodson Farnham, *California Indoors and Out* (New York, 1856), 264; *Jewish Messenger,* 23 October 1857, 69.

45. *New York Herald,* 27 September 1869; *Times,* 3 April 1870; *Tribune,* 22 November 1876.

46. *Frank Leslie's Illustrated Weekly,* 4 March 1882; Irving A. Model, "Attitude of the American Jewish Community Toward East European Immigration," *American Jewish Archives,* June 1950, 34; *American Hebrew* 20, No. 9 (1884): *The Poetical Works of Joaquin Miller* (New York, 1923), 309–10.

47. Lewis MacBrayne, "The Promised Land," *McClure's,* November 1902, 71.

48. *Jewish Messenger,* 6 May 1898.

Chapter 6. Eastern European Jews

1. Robert H. Wiebe, *The Segmented Society* (New York, 1975), 67–68.

2. *North American Review,* April 1845, 353, 356–57, 359.

3. Quoted in *American Israelite,* 3 May 1861. Also see 6 September 1872 for a similar view expressed by the *Chicago Post.*

4. *New York Times,* 21 January 1872.

5. *Brooklyn Daily Eagle,* 15, 16, 17 December 1875, 13 February and 10 May

1876; *New York Herald,* 16, 17, 18, 19, 21 December 1875, 11, 13, 14, February, 11 March, 10 May 1876; *New York Tribune,* 16 December 1875, 14 February and 10 May, 1876; *New York World,* 13, 15 February 1876.

6. *New York Times,* 19 August 1877; 11 July, 1880.

7. *New York Tribune,* 6 July, 4 September, 9 November, 1881; 24, 29, January, 2 February 1882.

8. *New York Times,* 28, 29, 30, 31 January, 3 February, 15 March 1882.

9. *Evening Post,* 1 February 1882; *Commercial Advertiser,* 15 March 1882. See also *Harper's Weekly* 26 (11 February 1882). Also *Cincinnati Commercial,* quoted in *American Israelite,* 9 June 1882.

10. *Weekly Witness,* quoted in *American Israelite,* 16 June 1882; *Century Magazine* 1 (April 1882): 908–9, 919, 949. See also letters to the editor in the *New York Tribune,* 10 July, 5 February, 1882.

11. *New York Tribune,* 19 January, 2, 24, 27 May, 13, 28 June, 3 September 1882.

12. *New York Tribune,* 5 August 1883.

13. *New York Times,* 15, 28 September 1881; 16 February, 7 March, 16, 19 June, 8 August, 5, 15 October 1882; 12 July, 1883; 24 July 1884.

14. *Harper's Weekly* 26 (11 February, 1882): 93, 96; 18 February, 1882, 109; 4 March 1882, 131; *Cincinnati Commercial,* 9 June 1882; *St. Paul Globe,* 17 July 1882; *Minneapolis Tribune,* 18 July 1882. See also *New York Sun,* 8 May 1883; *Baltimore American,* 12 July 1883.

15. *Frank Leslie's Illustrated Newspaper,* 4 March, 6, 19 August 1882. See also *Commercial and Financial Chronicle* 35 (19 August 1882); *Judge* 2, No. 40 (1882): 6; *Household Book of Wit and Humor* (Philadelphia, 1883).

16. *New York Sun,* 22 February 1885; *Harper's Weekly* 33 (30 November 1889): 955; *American Israelite,* 30 September 1889.

17. *New York Times,* 3, 19, May, 12 June 1885.

18. *Illustrated American* 4 (21 March 1891): 238; 10 (19 March 1892): *Harper's New Monthly Magazine,* March 1894, 603–14; *Littell's Living Age,* 19 September 1891, 748–52; *Century Magazine* 33 (February, 1893, July 1893).

19. *New York Tribune,* 12 August, 10 November, 21 December 1890; 19 June 1898.

20. *New York Sun,* 16 August 1890.

21. *New York Times,* 13 September 1894; *Evening Post,* 24 September 1898; *Tribune,* 6 May 1895, 30 December 1900; *Sun,* 6 December 1895.

22. *New York Times,* 3 November 1902.

23. *Arena,* December 1890, 119–20; *The Forum,* March 1891, 104–11; December 1893, 412, 414, 445. See also *New York Tribune,* 12 August, 21 December 1890.

24. Quoted in Baron, ed., *Stars and Sand* 233–34.

25. *Cincinnati Times-Star,* 29 January 1891; *Journal and Messenger,* quoted in *American Israelite,* 11 June 1891; *Detroit News,* 1 September 1892; *Detroit Free Press,* 3 October 1892; *North American Review* 152 (May 1891): 607; *Illustrated American,* 19 March 1892, 213; *Frank Leslie's Illustrated Newspaper,* 2 February 1893; *Life* 23 (1894): 100. See also *Chicago Record Herald,* 16 October 1901.

26. *Reports of the Industrial Commission on Immigration,* vol. 15 (Washington D.C., 1901), xxvi, 11, 22, 29, 94, 192–94, 197, 327, 346.

27. *Puck* 29 (1891): 246, See also *McClure's Magazine* 20 (November 1902): 67, 69, 74.

28. *New York Times,* 26 August, 19 October, 9 November, 14 December 1890; 6 February, 3 April, 7 August, 17 July, 22 January, 13 February, 24 May, 17 August 1891.

29. *New York Times,* 7, 14, 28, September, 5, 12, 19, 26 October, 2, 9, 16, 23, 30

November, 7, 14, 21 December 1891; Harold Frederic, *The New Exodus,* in *The Major Works of Harold Frederic* (New York, 1969), 3, 16, 26, and passim.

30. *New York Times,* 21 December 1891.

31. *New York Times* 7 May, 25 August, 12 September, 11 December 1893. See also 17 August 1902.

32. *New York Tribune,* 12 August 1890; 31 May, 5 June, 21 December 1891; 3 May 1892; 9 September 1899, 1 October 1902.

33. *New York World,* 18 May 1891.

34. Barbara M. Solomon, *Ancestors and Immigrants* (Cambridge, Mass., 1956), 119, 121.

35. *New York Times,* 27 August 1895, 6 September 1895, 14 November 1897, 30 July, 6 March 1893.

36. *New York Tribune,* 2 August 1896; 11 August 1895; 9 January and 15 September 1898; 20 August 1899; 30 September, 22 April, 25 February 1900; 28 July 1901.

37. *Evening Post,* 4 March 1895, 11 April 1896, 9 May 1896.

38. *Commercial Advertiser,* 12, 26 February, 26 March, 9 April, 14, 21 May, 6 August, 29 October, 19 November, 17, 24, 31 December 1898; 1, 22 April, 3 June 1899; 14, 28 April, 9 June 1900; 26 January, 2, 22 March 1901.

39. *Harper's Weekly* 34 (19 April 1890): 306; 39 (6 July 1895): 636–73; 3 August 1895, 725; 40 (29 August 1896): 10 November 1899, 1125; *Century Magazine* 21 (January 1892): 324–82; February 1892, 513–32; November 1899; *The Bookman* 7 (May 1898): August 1898; *Frank Leslie's Illustrated Newspapers,* 23 March 1893, *Puck* 42 (1897): 8–9; *Atlantic Monthly* (82 September 1898): 130–23; 68 (October 1900): 538; *Munsey's Magazine* 23 (August 1900): 609–19; *Outlook* 72 (1 November 1902): 530–93; 8 July 1905, 631–73; *The World's Work* 7 (March 1904): 4555–67.

40. *New York Times,* 23 March 1901; *Evening Post,* 11 April 1896, 3 October and 10 January 1903; *Herald,* 27 December 1891; *Atlantic Monthly* 82 (1898): 132; *New York Tribune,* 24 March and 31 July 1895; 20 February and 18 September, 1898; 12 November 1899; 6 January and 23 June 1902.

41. *New York Tribune,* 28 June 1891, 5 October 1902; *New York Times,* 11 July 1891; 19 May and 2 June 1895; *World,* 26 May 1902.

42. *Sun,* 3 August 1902.

43. William Dean Howells, *Impressions and Experiences* (New York, 1896), 138–39, 141, 143, 146–47, 148.

44. Mary J. McKenna, *Our Brethren of the Tenements and the Ghetto* (New York, 1899), 7, 10–11, and passim. See also Myra Kelly, *Little Citizens* (New York, 1904) for a charming if patronizing view.

45. Quoted in Melvin Dubofsky, *When Workers Organize* (Amherst, Mass., 1968), 36.

46. Jacob Riis, *How the Other Half Lives* (New York, 1890, 1957), 76–100; *The Children of the Poor* (New York, 1892, 1923), 35–53; *Review of Reviews,* January 1896, 58–62; *Out of Mulberry Street* (New York, 1898), 33–43, 67–70, 153–55; "The Tenants" *Atlantic Monthly* 84 (August 1899): 157; September 1899, "The Genesis of the Gang," 304; October 1899, "Letting in the Light," 497–99; "Justice for the Boy," November 1899, 647. See also Jeffrey S. Gurock, "Jacob Riis: Christian Friend or Missionary Foe? Two Jewish Views," *American Jewish History* 71, no. 1 (September 1981): 29–41. Gurock feels that privately Riis remained conversionist or, at least, insensitive in his attitudes toward Jews. This does not, however, alter the impact of his writings.

47. Hutchins Hapgood, *The Spirit of the Ghetto* (New York, 1901, 1966), Preface, 22–25, 47, and passim. See also *The World's Work* 6 (1903): 3459–65. A different

view of Hapgood is expressed in Fine, *The City*. Fine sees Hapgood as "still the outsider with his nose pressed to the windows of the ghetto," similar to later anthropologists who were drawn to simpler, unspoiled cultures out of feelings of discontent with their own "civilization."

48. Moses Rischin, Introduction, Hutchins Hapgood, *Spirit of the Ghetto* (Cambridge, Mass., 1983).

49. *New York Tribune,* 4, 11 July 1890; *Sun,* 4, 9 July 1890, *World,* 9 July 1890; *Herald,* 3, 17 July 1890; *Times,* 2, 4, 16, 20 July, 1890.

50. *New York Times,* 10 March 1891; *Herald,* 10 March 1891; *Sun,* 10 March, 1891. See also *Tribune,* 29 March 1893.

51. *New York Times,* 13, 26 September 1894; *World,* 4, 7 September 1894; *Tribune,* 16 November 1894.

52. *Herald,* 3 August 1896; *Tribune,* 2, 9 August 1896; *Times,* 3 August 1896.

53. *New York Tribune,* 25 July 1900, 13 January 1901.

54. *Herald,* 18, 19, 22 August 1893; *World,* 22 August 1893; *Tribune,* 18, 20, 22, 23 August 1893; *Times,* 18, 20, 21, 23 August 1893. See also *Brooklyn Daily Eagle,* 26 July 1892; 17, 25 May 1895.

55. *Illustrated American,* 13 September 1893, 365.

56. *World,* 23 August 1893.

57. *New York Tribune,* 6 February 1897.

58. *World,* 26 September 1898; *Tribune,* 26 September 1898; *Herald,* 26 September 1898; *Times,* 26, 27 September 1898.

59. *Herald,* 18, 19 June 1899; *Sun,* 20 June 1899; *Times,* 18–21 June 1899; *Evening Post,* 17 June 1899; *World,* 19, 21 June 1899; *New York Evening Journal,* 19, 20 June 1899.

60. *Tribune,* 16, 17, 19, 23, 25, 27 May 1902; *Herald,* 16–26 May 1902; *Times,* 16–19, 22–24 May 1902; *Sun,* 16, 17, 23, 24 May 1902; *Journal,* 15–19 May, 1902; *World,* 16, 17, 19, 20 May 1902. See Also Paula E. Hyman, "Immigrant Women and Consumer protest: The New York City Kosher Meat Boycott of 1902," *American Jewish History* 70 (September 1980): 91–105.

61. *Sun,* 31 July 1902; *Herald,* 31 July, 17 September 1902; *Times,* 31 July, 1, 5, 7, 13, 14, 20 August, 16 September 1902; *Tribune,* 3 August 1902; *Journal,* 31 July, 1, 4 August 1902; *World,* 1 August 1902; *Evening Post,* 30, 31 July, 16 September 1902; *Life* 40 (1902): 266.

62. *Sun,* 17, 18 July 1893; *Times,* 17, 18 July 1893.

Conclusion

1. Isaacs, *Idols,* 194.

2. Anna L. Dawes, *The Modern Jew* (Boston, 1886), 41.

3. *The Quarterly Sentinel* 6 (May 1899): 6.

4. Herbert Gold in *"Kike,"* Michael Selzer, (New York, 1972), xii.

4. Wiebe, *The Segmented Society,* 119–22.

6. Higham, in Stember, *Jews in the Mind of America* 249.

7. Lazar Ziff, *The American 1890s: Life and Times of a Lost Generation* (New York, 1966), 74, 81.

8. Issacs, *Scratches,* 72, 109.

9. Stuart Creighton Miller, *The Unwelcome Immigrant: The American Image of the Chinese* (Berkeley, 1969), 8.

10. Kammen, *People of Paradox,* 97, 113.

11. Isaacs, *Idols,* 194.

12. Wiebe, *The Segmented Society,* 70–78, 105–8.

Bibliography

Primary Sources—Books

A. A. *Annals of the Jewish Nation*. New York, 1932.

Adams, Brooks. *Law of Civilization and Decay*. New York, 1943.

Adams, Charles Follen. *Leedle Yawcob Strauss and Other Poems*. Boston, 1878.

Adams, Hannah. *A Dictionary of All Religions and Religious Denominations*. New York, 1817.

———. *The History of the Jews*. Boston, 1817.

Adams, Henry, *The Education of Henry Adams*. New York, 1931.

———. *Henry Adams and His Friends*. Compiled by Harold Dean Cater. Cambridge, Mass.: 1947.

———. *Letters of Henry Adams*. Vols. 1–3. Edited by Worthington C. Ford. Boston: 1938.

Aguilar, Grace. *Home Scenes and Heart Studies*. New York, 1852.

———. *Vale of Cedars*. New York, 1850.

Aiken, Albert. *The California Detective*. New York, 1878.

———. *Dick Talbot the Ranch King*. New York, 1892.

———. *The Fresh of Frisco at Santa Fe*. New York, 1891.

———. *The Genteel Spotter*. New York, 1884.

———. *The Lone Hand in Texas*. New York, 1888.

———. *The Lone Hand on the Caddo*. New York, 1888.

———. *Lone Hand the Shadow*. New York, 1889.

———. *The Phantom Hand*. New York, 1897.

———. *The White Witch*. New York, 1871.

American Cycolpedia. Vol. 8. New York, 1874.

Archer, William. *The Dramatic Year*. Boston, 1889.

American Society for Meliorating the Condition of the Jews. *First Report*. New York, 1823.

American Sunday School Union. *The Jew at Home and Abroad*. Philadelphia, 1845.

Baker, George M. *The Peddler of Very Nice*. Boston, 1866.

Baker, Henriette N. W. *Lost But Found*. Boston, 1871.

———. *Rebecca the Jewess*. Boston, 1879.

Baker, Sarah Schoonmaker. *The Jewish Twins*. New York, 1860.

Barnes, Alfred. *Questions on the Historical Roots of the New Testament*. New York, 1832.

Barr, Amelia. *Bow of Orange Ribbon*. New York, 1886.

Bates, Arlo. *Mr. Jacobs*. Boston, 1883.

Beauvallet, Leon. *Rachel and the New World*. New York, 1867.

Berean Tract and Bible Mission 1876–8.

Bible Study Union Graded Lessons for Sunday Schools and Bible Classes. Intermediate Grade. 1894–99. Protestant Episcopal Church.

Bigland, J. *A Compendius History of the Jews*. London, 1820.

Black, Mrs. T. F. *Hadassah*. Chicago, 1895.

Boucicault, Dion. *Flying Scud*. In *Favorite American Plays of the Nineteenth Century*, edited by Barrett H. Clark. Princeton, 1943.

Boyeson, H. H. *A Daughter of the Philistines*. Boston, 1883.

Brace, Charles Loring. *The Unknown God*. New York, 1890.

Brooks, Eldbridge S. *Son of Issacher*. London, 1890.

Brooks, Rev. J. W. *The History of the Hebrew Nations*. London, 1841.

Brougham, John. *Much Ado About a Merchant of Venice*. New York, 1858.

Brown, Charles Brockden. *Arthur Mervyn*. New York, 1800, 1962.

Brown, T. Allston. *A History of the New York Stage*. 3 vols. New York, 1903.

Browne, J. Ross. *Crusoe's Island*. New York, 1864.

Bryan, William Jennings. *The First Battle: A Story of the Campaign of 1896*. Chicago, 1897.

Bryant, Elizabeth. "Types of Mankind as Affecting the Financial History of the World: Delivered Before the Greenback Labor Club of the District of Columbia, October 7, 1879." Washington D.C., 1879.

Buck, James S. *Pioneer History of Milwaukee*. Milwaukee, 1886. Vol. 4.

The Bulls and the Bears on Wall Street. New York, 1854.

Butler, Joseph. *Fortune's Football*. Harrisburg, Pa., 1798.

Butterworth, Hezekiah. *In Old New England*. New York, 1895.

Cahan, Abraham. *The Imported Bridegroom and Other Stories of the New York Ghetto*. New York, 1898.

———. *Yekl*. New York, 1899.

Caine, Hall. *The Scapegoat*. New York, 1891.

Caleb Asher. Philadelphia, 1845.

Carter, C. Soule. *Questions Adapted to the Text of the New Testament*. Boston, 1865.

Chambers, Robert W. *Cardigan*. New York, 1901.

Chase, F. E. *A Ready Made Suit, A Mock Trial*. Boston, 1885?.

Child, Lydia Maria. *The Progress of Religious Ideas through Successive Ages*. 3 vols. New York, 1885.

Church, Alfred J., and Seely, Raymond. *The Hammer*. New York, 1892.

Clark, Gordon. *Shylock: As Banker, Bondholder, Corruptionist, Conspirator*. Washington, D.C., 1894.

Clarke, James Freeman. *Legend of Thomas Didymus, the Jewish Sceptic*. New York, 1881.

Claxton, Rev. R. Bethell. *Questions on the Gospels*. Philadelphia, 1860.

Cowdrick, Jesse C. *The Detective's Apprentice*. New York, 1885.

Cowen, Philip, ed., *Prejudice against the Jews*. New York, 1928. A Symposium in the *American Hebrew*, 4 April 1890.

Crawford, F. Marion. *A Roman Singer*. New York, 1894.

———. *Mr. Issacs*. New York, 1883.

———. *The Witch of Prague*. New York, 1891.

Crofts, Mrs. Wilbur F. *The Lesson Handbook for Primary and Intermediate Teachers*. Boston, 1883.

Cumberland, Stuart. *The Rabbi's Spell*. New York, 1888.

Daly, Augustin. *Leah, the Forsaken*. New York, 1862?.

Daly, Charles P. *The Settlement of the Jews in North America*. New York, 1893.

Dawes, Anna L. *The Modern Jew*. Boston, 1886.

A Day on Coney Island. New York, 1880.

DeMille, Henry C. and Belasco David, "Men and Women" in *America's Lost Plays* (Princeton, 1941), Vol. XVII.

The Democrat. New York, 1795.

Dibdin, Thomas. *A Collection of Songs Collected from the Works of Mr. Dibdin*. Philadelphia, 1799.

———. *The Jew and the Doctor*. New York, 1807.

Donnelly, Ignatius. *Caesar's Column*. Cambridge, Mass., 1960.

———. *The Golden Bottle*. New York, 1968.

Dowd, Clement. *The Life of Zebulon Vance*. Charlotte, N.C., 1897.

Draper, John William. *History of the Intellectual Development of Europe*. New York, 1865.

Dwight, Serena E. *The Hebrew Wife*. New York, 1836.

Ellison, James. *The American Captive*. Boston, 1812.

Eltone Out and Outer Comic Songbook. New York, 1839.

Faber, Rev. George S. *A General and Connected View of the Prophecies*. Boston, 1809.

Farmer, F. W. *The Herods*. New York, 1898.

Farnham, Eliza Woodson. *California Indoors and Out*. New York, 1856.

Fawcett, Edgar. *New York, A Novel*. New York, 1898.

Fay, Theodore Sedgewick. *Sidney Clifton*. New York, 1839.

Feast of Wit. Philadelphia, 1821.

Forbes, E. C. *Easy Lessons on Scripture History*. New York, 1859.

Foster, George G. *New York by Gaslight*. New York, 1850.

———. *New York in Slices*. New York, 1849.

———. *New York Naked*. New York?.

Francis' Guide to New York and Brooklyn. New York?.

Frederic, Harold. *The Market Place*. New York, 1899.

———. *Gloria Mundi* and *The New Exodus*. In *The Major Works of Harold Frederic*. 5 vols. New York, 1969.

Garland, Hamlin. *The Rose of Dutcher's Coolly*. Cambridge, Mass., 1969.

Geissinger, Rev. D. H. *Lessons in the Life of Our Lord Jesus Christ*. New York, 1881.

George, Henry. *The Writings of Henry George*. Vol. 8. New York, 1898.

Gillman, Henry. *Hassan: A Fellah*. Boston, 1898.

Goode, James B. *The Modern Banker*. Chicago, 1896.

Goodrich, Rev. Charles A. *A Pictorial Descriptive View and History of All Religions*. New York, 1860.

Goodwin, Jonathan. *The Return and Conversion of the Jews*. Middletown, Conn., 1843.

Gregg, Rev. Jarvis. *Selumiel*. Philadelphia, 1833.

Grellet, Stephen. *Lessons for Schools from the Holy Scriptures*. Philadelphia, 1865.

Griffin, George W. H. *"Shylock," A Burlesque as Performed by Griffin and Christy's Minstrels*. New York, 1876?.

Griswold, Rufus. *Poems and Poetry of America*. New York, 1873.

Grundy, Sidney. *An Old Jew*. New York, 1894.

Hadassah,—the Jewish Orphan. Philadelphia, 1834.

Haliburton, Thomas. *Letter-Bag of the Great Western*. New York, 1840.

Halsey, Harlan Page. *Mephisto*. New York, 1899.

Hapgood, Hutchins. *The Spirit of the Ghetto*. New York, 1902, 1983.

Hapgood, Norman. *The Stage in America*. New York, 1901.

Harland, Henry. *As It Was Written*. New York, 1885.

———. *Grandison Mather*. New York, 1889.

———. *Mrs. Peixada*. New York, 1886.

———. *The Yoke of the Thorah*. New York, 1887.

———. *Uncle Florimond*. New York, 1888.

Harvey, William H. *A Tale of Two Nations*. Chicago, 1894.

———. *Coin's Financial School*. Chicago, 1894.

———. *Coin's Financial School Up-To-Date*. Chicago, 1895.

Hatton, Joseph. *By Order of the Czar*. London, 1891.

Hawthorne, Julian. *Sebastian Strome*. New York, 1880.

Hawthorne, Nathaniel. *"Ethan Brand"* and *The Marble Faun*. In *Modern Library Complete Novels and Selected Short Stories of Nathaniel Hawthorne*. New York, 1937.

———. *Mosses from an Old Manse*. Boston, 1894.

Hobson, J. A. *Problems of Poverty*. London, 1891.

Holmes, Oliver Wendell. *Over the Teacups*. In *The Writings of Oliver Wendell Holmes*. Cambridge, Mass., 1871.

———. *The Professor at the Breakfast Table*. Grosse Point, Mich., 1968.

Homer, A. N. *Hernani the Jew*. Chicago, 1897.

Hone, Philip. *The Diary of Philip Hone*. 2 vols. New York, 1927.

Horton, Edward A. *Scenes in the Life of Jesus*. Boston, 1895.

Hosmer, J. *History of the Jews*. Boston, 1847.

Household Book of Wit and Humor. Philadelphia, 1883.

Houston, George. *Israel Vindicated*. New York, 1823.

Howe, Julia Ward. *The World's Own*. Boston, 1857.

Howells, William Dean. *Impressions and Experiences*. New York, 1896.

———. *Their Wedding Journey*. New York, 1872.

Hoyland, John. *Epitome of History*. Vol. 2. Philadelphia, 1816.

Iddo, An Historical Sketch Illustrating Jewish History During the Time of the Maccabees. Philadelphia, 1841.

Ingersoll, Ernest. *A Week in New York* New York, 1891.

Ingraham, Joseph H. *Ramero*. New York, 1869.

―――. *The Clipper Yacht or Moloch the Money-Lender*. Boston, 1845.

―――. *The Pillar of Fire*. New York, 1857, 1888.

―――. *The Prince of the House of David*. New York, 1855.

―――. *The Sunny South*. Philadelphia, 1860.

―――. *The Throne of David*. Boston, 1871.

Ingraham, Prentiss. *Gold Plume, the Boy Bandit*. New York, 1881.

―――. *The Jew Detective*. New York, 1891.

―――. *The New Monte Cristo*. New York, 1886.

―――. *Jule the Jewess*. In *Banner Weekly* 15 (December–February 1897).

Jackson, Melvin. *Travels of Paul*. New York, 1903.

James, Henry. *Embarrassments*. New York, 1890.

―――. *Tales of Three Cities*. Boston, 1887.

―――. *The American Scene*. New York, 1907.

―――. *The Tragic Muse*. 2 vols. New York, 1936.

―――. *Scenic Art, Notes on Acting and the Drama*. New Brunswick, N.J., 1948.

Jerome, Gilbert. *Dominick Squeek, the Bow Street Runner*. New York, 1884.

―――. *Old Subtle or the Willing Victims*. New York, 1885.

Jessop, George H. *Sam'l of Posen or the Commercial Drummer*. In *America's Lost Plays*. Bloomington, 1964. Vol. 4.

Johnston, Annie F. *In League With Israel*. New York, 1896.

Johnstone. *Stories from the History of the Jews*. New York, 1853.

Jones, J. Richter. *The Quaker Soldier*. Philadelphia, 1866.

Jones, John Beauchamp. *Border War: A Tale of Disunion*. New York, 1859.

―――. *The Western Merchant*. Philadelphia, 1877.

Judson, Edward Z. C. *Morgan or the Knight of the Black Flag*. New York, 1860.

―――. *Ned Buntline's Life Line*. New York, 1849.

―――. *Rose Seymour; or the Ballet Girl's Revenge*. New York, 1865.

Keith, Alexander. *The Land of Israel*. New York, 1844.

Kelly, Myra. *Little Citizens*. New York, 1904.

King, Edward. *Joseph Zalmonah*. Boston, 1894.

King, Moses. *King's Handbook of New York City*. Boston, 1892.

Kingsley, Florence M. *Paul*. New York, 1897.

―――. *Stephen*. New York, 1896.

―――. *The Cross Triumphant*. New York, 1898.

―――. *Titus*. New York, 1894.

Kitto, Johan. *An Illustrated History of the Holy Bible*. Norwich, N.Y., 1868.

Lazarus, Emma. *The Poems of Emma Lazarus*. Cambridge, 1889.

Lippard, George. *The Empire City*. Philadelphia, 1864.

―――. *The Nazarene*. Philadelphia, 1854.

———. *The Quaker City*. Philadelphia, 1876.

Lowell, James Russell. *Complete Writings of James Russell Lowell*. Boston, 1904.

———. *Letters of James Russell Lowell*. New York, 1894.

———. *New Letters of James Russell Lowell*. Boston, 1932.

MacKenzie, William L. *The Lives and Opinions of Benj'n Franklin Butler and Jesse Hoyt*. Boston, 1845.

Mahan, William D. *The Archko Volume*. Philadelphia, 1887.

March, E. S. *A Stumbler in Wide Shoes*. New York, 1896.

Mason, Caroline Atwater. *Woman of Yesterday*. New York, 1900.

Matthews, Brander, and Jessop, George H. *A Tale of Twenty-Five Hours*. New York, 1892.

Matthews, Cornelius. *A Pen and Ink Panorama of New York City*. New York, 1853.

Mayer, Nathan. *Differences*. Cincinnati, 1867.

McCabe, James D., Jr. *Lights and Shadows of New York Life*. Philadelphia, 1872.

McKenna, Mary T. *Our Brethen of the Tenements and Ghetto*. New York, 1899.

Mears, John W. *From Exile to Overthrow*. Philadelphia, 1881.

Melville, Herman. *Clarel: A Poem and Pilgrimmage in the Holy Land*. New York, 1960.

———. *Journey of a Visit to Europe and the Levant*. Edited by Howard C. Horsford. Princeton, 1955.

The Metropolis Explained and Illustrated. New York, 1871.

Miller, Joaquin. *The Building of the City Beautiful*. Chicago, 1893.

———. *The Poetical Works of Joaquin Miller*. New York, 1923.

Miller's New York as It Is. 1859, 1862, 1866, 1877.

Milman, Rev. H. H. *The History of the Jews*. New York, 1832.

Mitchell, S. Weir. *Hugh Wynne: Free Quaker*. New York, 1897.

Montresor, F. F. *Into the Highways and Hedges*. New York, 1896.

Morford, Henry. *The Practical Guide to New York City and Brooklyn*. New York, 1877.

Morrison, W. D. *The Jews under Roman Rule*. New York, 1891.

Myers, Peter H. *The Miser's Heir, or the Young Millionaire*. Philadelphia, 1854.

Norris, Frank. *McTeague*. New York, 1968.

O'Meara, Kathleen. *Narka, the Nihilist*. New York, 1887.

Ogden, Mrs. C. A. *Into the Light*. Boston, 1899.

Palmer, E. H. *A History of the Jewish Nation*. Boston, 1875.

Parsons, Edward. *History of the Jews in All Ages*. London, 1832.

Peabody, Elizabeth. *Sabbath Lessons*. Salem, Mass., 1813.

Peet, H. P. *Scripture Lessons for the Young*. New York, 1846.

Pennell, Joseph. *The Jew At Home*. New York, 1892.

Pentecost, George. *Bible Studies*. New York, 1891 and 1893.

Peters, Madison C. *The Jews in America*. Philadelphia, 1905.

Phelps, Elizabeth Stuart. *The Story of Jesus Christ*. New York, 1898.

Pick, Rev. Bernhard. *Historical Sketch of the Jews since Their Return from Babylon*. Chicago, 1897.

Pineywoods Tavern or Sam Slick in Texas. Philadelphia, 1858.

Pomeroy, Brick. *The Great Campaign*. 22 August 1876.

Reports of the Industrial Commission on Immigration. Vol. 15. Washington, D.C. 1901.

Richards, Maria T. *Life in Israel*. New York, 1852.

———. *Life in Judea*. Philadelphia, 1854.

Richardson, Hannah W. *Judea in Her Desolations*. Philadelphia, 1861.

Riggs, James Stevenson. *A History of the Jewish People*. New York, 1900.

Riis, Jacob. *How the Other Half Lives*. New York 1957.

———. *Out of Mulberry Street*. New York, 1898.

———. *The Children of the Poor*. New York, 1923.

Rowson, Susanna. *Slaves in Algeria*. Philadelphia, 1794.

Ruggles, Edward. *A Picture of New York in 1846*. New York, 1846.

Ruppius, Otto. *The Peddler*. Cincinnati, 1877.

Russell, Rev. Michael. *Palestine of the Holy Land*. New York, 1833.

Saltus, Edgar. *Enthralled, A Story of International Life.* . . . London, 1894.

Saunders, F. *New York in a Nutshell*. New York, 1853.

Savage, Richard Henry. *An Exile from London*. New York, 1896.

———. *Lost Countess Falka*. New York, 1896.

———. *White Lady of Khaminavatka*. New York, 1898.

Scoville, Joseph A. *The Old Merchants of New York City*. Vol. 2. New York, 1877.

———. *Vigor*. New York, 1864.

Shelland, Harry E. *Great Libel Case*. New York, 1900.

Shiel, M. P. *The Lord of the Sea*. New York, 1924.

Sidgwick, Cecily. *Lesser's Daughter*. New York, 1894.

Simms, William Gilmore. *Pelayo*. 2 vols. New York, 1938.

Siviter, Anna Pierpont. *Nehe*. Boston, 1901.

Smith, Matthew Hale. *Sunshine and Shadow in New York*. Hartford, 1868.

———. *Wonders of a Great City*. Chicago, 1877.

Smith, Sarah Payson. *Zerah, the Believing Jew*. Philadelphia, 1837.

Southworth, Mrs. E. D. E. N. *Ishmael; or In the Depths*. Philadelphia, 1884.

———. *Miriam, the Avenger*. Philadelphia, 1855?.

———. *Self-Raised; or From the Depths*. New York, 1865.

The Spectator. New York, 1845.

Spindler, Karl. *The Jew*. New York, 1894.

Stedman, Edmund S., ed. *An American Anthology 1791–1900*. New York, 1900.

Stevenson, Robert Louis. *Across the Plains*. London, 1892.

Stokes, George. *The Manners and Customs of the Jews and Other Nations Mentioned in the Bible*. Hartford, 1833.

Stranger's Guide to the City of New York. New York, 1852.

Strong, George Templeton. *The Diary of George Templeton Strong*. (4 vols. New York, 1952.

Stuart, Moses. *Sermon at the Ordination of the Rev. Wm. G. Schouffler as Missionary to the Jews*. Andover, Mass., 1831.

The Sun's Guide to New York. New York, 1892.

Sweetser and Ford. *How to Know New York City*. New York, 1888.

Thorpe, Thomas May. *What is Money?* New York, 1894.

Timayonis, Telemachus. *Judas Iscariot. New York, 1888.*

————. *The Original Mr. Jacobs*. New York, 1888.

Towndrow, T. *Dinsmore's Twenty Miles Around New York*. New York, 1858.

Townsend, Charles. *Jail Bird*. New York, 1893?

Toy, Crawford Howell. *Judaism and Christianity*. Boston, 1890.

Tullidge, Edward W. *Ben Israel*. Salt Lake City, 1875.

Twain, Mark. *Mark Twain on the Damned Human Race*. New York, 1962.

Tyler, Royall. *The Algerine Captive*. Gainsville, Fla. 1967.

Vidaver, Dr. H. *Ancient and Modern Anti-Semitism*. Baltimore, 1882.

Vincent, J. H. *First Year With Jesus*. New York, 1867.

von Bohne, Johanna. *Jew and Gentile*. New York, 1889.

Wakely, Ebenezer. *The Gentile Ass and the Judean Establishment*. Chicago, 1895.

Walker, George. *Theodore Cyphon or the Benevolent Jew*. Alexandria, Va., 1803.

Wallace, Lew. *Ben Hur, A Tale of the Christ*. New York, 1933.

————. *The Prince of India*. 2 vols. New York, 1893.

Ware, William. *Julian*. 2 vols. New York, 1841.

————. *Zenobia*. New York, 1843.

Watson, Tom. *The People's Party Campaign Book*. Washington, D.C., 1892.

Weiss, John. *The Life and Correspondence of Theodore Parker*. New York, 1864. Vol. 2.

Wheeler, Edward L. *Apollo Bill: The Trail Tornado*. New York, 1882.

————. *Boss Bob, the King of the Bootblacks*. New York, 1886.

————. *Jim Bludsoe Jr.; The Boy Phenix*. (New York, 1878.

————. *The Ventriloquist Detective*. New York, 1887.

Whittaker Series of Lessons for Bible Classes and Sunday Schools 1895–6.

Willard, Caroline. *A Son of Israel*. Philadelphia, 1898.

Winder, William. *Life and Art of Edwin Booth*. London, 1893.

Wise, Isaac Mayer. *Reminiscences*. Cincinnati, 1901.

Wister, Owen. *Philosophy 4*. New York, 1903.

Wolf, Simon. *The American Jew as Patriot, Soldier and Citizen*. Philadelphia, 1895.

World Almanac. 1868.

Worthington, H. P. C. *Hell for the Jews*. New York, 1879.

Primary Sources—Periodicals and Newspapers

Albany Gazette. 1820.

American Hebrew. 1884–1900.

American Israelite. 1854–1900.

American Literary Magazine. Vol. 1. 1847.

Arena. 1890–92.

The Asmonean. 1854.

Atlantic Monthly. 1857–1901.

Banking and Insurance Chronicle 2 (1867).

The Bookman. 1895–1901.
The Brooklyn Daily Eagle. 1875–1902.
California Mail Bag 2 (1872).
The Catholic World. 1891–93.
Century Magazine. 1881–1901.
Charleston Courier. 1841.
Chicago Daily Journal. 1851.
Chicago Daily Democratic Press. 1855.
Chicago Democrat. 1851.
Chicago Daily Times. 1885–90.
Chicago Evening Journal. 1890.
Chicago Tribune. 1884–1900.
Cincinnati Commercial. 1882.
Cincinnati Times-Star. 1891.
Commercial and Financial Chronicle 35 (1882).
Continental Monthly 1–3 (1863).
De Bow's Review 5 (1868).
Detroit Free Press. 1892–96.
Detroit News. 1892–93.
Detroit Post. 1876.
The Forum. 1887–93.
Frank Leslie's Illustrated Weekly (Newspaper). 1857–1900.
Harper's New Monthly Magazine. 1850–1901.
Harper's Weekly. 1857–1901.
Hostetter's Illustrated. 1876–1900.
Illustrated American. 1890–98.
The Independent. 1889.
The Insurance Monitor and Wall Street Review. 1867.
The Irish American. 1858–1902.
The Irish World and American Industrial Liberator. 1876–1902.
Jewish Messenger. 1857–1900.
John Donkey 1 (1848).
Judge. 1882–94.
The Knickerbocker. 1857.
Ladies' Garland 1–3.
Life. 1883–1902.
Lippincott's Magazine. 1867–80.
Littell's Living Age. 1891–98.
M'lle New York 1–2.
Minneapolis Tribune. 1882.
Munsey's Magazine. 1892–1900.
The Nation. 1866–1901.
National Anti-Slavery Standard. 1840–58.

New Englander and Yale Review. 1890.
New York Commercial Advertiser. 1822–1902.
New York Courier. 1840.
New York Daily Graphic. 1876–82.
New York Evening Journal. 1897–1902.
New York Evening Mail. 1879–80.
New York Evening Mirror. 1855.
New York Evening Post. 1820–1902.
New York Evening Telegraph. 1872–75.
New York Herald. 1840–1902.
New York Ledger. 1858.
New York Sun. 1849–1902.
New York Times. 1852–1902.
New York Tribune, 1857–1902.
New York World. 1890–1902.
Niles Weekly Register. 1813–1849.
North American Review. 1815–1900.
The Outlook. 1900–1905.
Overland Monthly. 1899.
Philadelphia Evening Bulletin. 1892–26.
Philadelphia Public Ledger. 1858–63.
Philadelphia Sunday Dispatch. 1854.
Popular Science Monthly. 1899.
Scribner's Monthly. 1876–99.
Spirit of the Times. 1835–50.
Southern Illustrated News 2 (1863).
Tid-Bits. 1884.
The Truth Teller. 1825–28.
Washington Sentinel. 1845.
The World's Work. 1900–1905.
Popular Song Collection of the Newberry Library, Chicago.

Secondary Works—Books

Ackerman, Nathan, and Jahoda, Marie. *Anti-Semitism and Emotional Disorder: A Psychoanalytic Interpretation.* New York: Harper 1950.

Anderson, George K. *The Legend of the Wandering Jew.* Providence: Brown University Press, 1970.

Baron, Joseph L., ed. *Candles in the Night.* New York: Farrar, 1940.

———. *Stars and Sand.* Philadelphia: Jewish Publication Society, 1943.

Baron, Salo W. *Steeled by Adversity.* Philadelphia: American Jewish Historical Society, 1971.

Berdyaev, Nicholas. *Christianity and Anti-Semitism.* New York: Philosophical Library, 1954.

Bitton-Jackson, Livia. *Madonna or Cortesan? The Jewish Woman in Christian Literature.* New York: Seabury Press, 1980.

Blau, Joseph L., and Salo W. Baron, ed. *The Jews of the United 1790–1840.* 2 vols. New York: Columbia University Press, 1963.

Bratton, Fred Gladstone. *The Crime of Christendom.* Boston: Beacon Press, 1969.

Chametzky, Jules. *From the Ghetto: The Fiction of Abraham Cahan.* Amherst, Mass.: University of Massachusetts Press, 1977.

Clarke, John James. "Henry Harland: A Critical Biography." Ph.D. diss., Brown University, 1957.

Coulter, E. Merton. *The Confederate States of America.* Baton Rouge: Louisiana State University Press, 1950.

Denning, Michael Joseph. "Dime Novels: Popular Fiction and Working Class Culture in America." Ph.D. diss., Yale University, 1984.

Dobkowski, Michael. *The Tarnished Dream: The Basis of American Anti-Semitism.* Westport, Conn.: Greenwood Press, 1979.

Dubofsky, Melvin. *When Workers Organize.* Amherst: University of Massachusetts Press, 1968.

Eichhorn, David M. "A History of Christian Attempts to Convert the Jews of the United States and Canada." Ph.D. diss., Hebrew Union College, 1938.

Ezekial, Herbert T., and Lichenstein, Gaston. *The History of the Jews of Richmond.* Richmond: H. T. Ezekial, 1917.

Fiedler, Leslie A. *The Jew in the American Novel.* New York: Herzl Institute, 1959.

Fine, David. *The City, The Immigrant and American Fiction: 1880–1920.* Metuchen, N.J.: Scarecrow Press, 1977.

Fisch, Harold. *The Dual Image.* London: Ktav, 1971.

Flannery, Edward H. *The Anguish of the Jews.* New York: Macmillan, 1964.

Flower, Edward. "Anti-Semitism in the Free Silver and Populist Movements and the Election of 1896." Master's thesis, Columbia University, 1952.

Foner, Philip S. *Jews in American History.* New York: International Pubs. Co., 1945.

———. *Mark Twain: Social Critic.* New York: International Pubs. Co., 1958.

Gerber, David A., ed. *Anti-Semitism in American History.* Urbana: University of Illinois Press, 1986.

Gilbert, Douglas. *American Vaudeville, Its Life and Times.* New York: McGraw, 1940.

Glanz, Rudolf. *The Jew in Early American Wit and Graphic Humor.* New York: Ktav, 1973.

———. *The Jew in Old American Folklore.* New York: Ktav, 1961.

———. *The Jews of California.* New York: Ktav, 1960.

———. *Studies in Judaica Americana.* New York: Ktav, 1970.

Glock, Charles Y., and Stark, Rodney. *Christian Beliefs and Anti-Semitism.* New York: Greenwood Press, 1966.

Goldberg, Isaac. *Major Noah: An American Jewish Pioneer.* Philadelphia: Jewish Publication Society, 1936.

Grau, Robert. *Forty Years Observation of Music and the Drama.* New York: Broadway Publishing Co., 1909.

Gross, Theodore L., ed. *The Literature of American Jews.* New York: Free Press, 1973.

Gutstein, Morris A. *A Priceless Heritage.* New York: Bloch, 1953.

Handlin, Oscar. *Adventure in Freedom*. New York: McGraw Hill, 1954.

———. *Race and Nationality in American Life*. Boston: Little Brown and Co., 1957.

Halpern, Rose. "American Reaction to the Dreyfus Case." Master's thesis, Columbia University, 1941.

Harap, Louis. *The Image of the Jew in American Literature*. Philadelphia: Jewish Publication Society of America, 1974.

Higham, John. *Send These to Me: Jews and Other Immigrants in Urban America*. New York: Atheneum, 1975.

———. *Strangers in the Land*. New York: Atheneum, 1963.

Hornblow, Arthur. *A History of the Theatre in America*. 2 vols. Philadelphia: J. P. Lippincott, 1911.

Howe, Irving. *World of Our Fathers*. New York: Harcourt, Brace, Jovanovich, 1976.

Isaacs, Harold R. *Idols of the Tribe*. New York: Harper, 1975.

———. *Scratches on Our Minds*. New York: Greenwood Press, 1969.

Isman, Felix. *Weber and Fields*. New York: Boni & Liveright, 1924.

Johannsen, Albert. *House of Beadle and Adams*. Vol. 1. Norman: University of Oklahoma Press, 1950.

Kammen, Michael. *People of Paradox*. New York: Oxford University Press, 1972.

Karp, Abraham, ed. *The Jewish Experience in America*. New York: Ktav Press, 1969.

Kohn, S. Joshua. *The Jewish Community of Utica, 1847–1948*. New York: American Jewish Historical Society, 1954.

Korn, Bertram. *American Jewry and the Civil War*. Philadelphia: Atheneum, 1960.

———. *American Reaction to the Mortara Case*. Cincinnati: American Jewish Archives, 1957.

———. *The Early Jews of New Orleans*. Waltham, Mass.: American Jewish Historical Society, 1969.

———. *Eventful Years and Experiences*. Cincinnati: American Jewish Archives, 1954.

Kunitz, Joshua. *Russian Literature and the Jew*. New York: Columbia University Press, 1929.

Landesman, Alter. *Brownsville*. New York: Bloch Publishing Co., 1969.

Leavitt, M. B. *Fifty Years in Theatrical Management*. New York: Broadway Publishers, 1912.

Lehrmann, Charles C. *The Jewish Element in French Literature*. Rutherford, N.J.: Fairleigh Dickinson University Press, 1961.

Lelyveld, Toby. *Shylock on the Stage*. Cleveland: Western Reserve University Press, 1960.

Levinger, Lee J. *Anti-Semitism in the United States*. Westport, Conn.: Greenwood Press, 1972.

Lipset, Seymour Martin, and Raab, Earl. *The Politics of Unreason*. New York: Anti-Defamation League of B'nai Brith, 1970.

Liptzin, Sol. *The Jew in American Literature*. New York: Bloch Publishing Co., 1966.

Low, Alfred. *Jews in the Eyes of the Germans*. Philadelphia: Institute for the Study of Human Issues, 1979.

Loewenstein, Rudolph M. *Christians and Jews: A Psychoanalytic Study*. New York: International University Press, 1951.

McWilliams, Carey. *A Mask for Privilege*. Boston: Little Brown and Co., 1948.

Mersand, Joseph. *Traditions in American Literature*. New York: The Modern Chapbooks, 1939.

Miller, Stuart Creighton. *The Unwelcome Immigrant: The American Image of the Chinese*. Berkeley: University of California Press, 1969.

Moraes, Henry Samuel. *The Jews of Philadelphia*. Philadelphia, 1894.

Mosse, George. *Germans and Jews*. New York: Fertig Howard Inc., 1970.

Nugent, Walter. *The Tolerant Populists: Kansas Populism and Nativism*. Chicago: University of Chicago Press, 1963.

Plaut, W. Gunther. *The Jews in Minnesota*. New York: American Jewish Historical Society, 1959.

Poliakov, Leon. *The History of Anti Semitism*. New York: Vanguard, 1965.

Quinn, A. H. *A History of the American Drama*. Vol. 1. New York: Harper, 1927.

Reznikoff, Charles and Engelmann. *The Jews of Charleston*. Philadelphia: Jewish Publication Society, 1950.

Rischin, Moses. *An Inventory of American Jewish History*. Washington: Oxford University Press, 1954.

———. *The Promised City*. Cambridge, Mass.: Harvard University Press, 1977.

Robb, James A. *Working Class Anti-Semite*. London: Burns and MacEachern, 1954.

Robinson, Cecil. *With the Ears of Strangers: The Mexican in American Literature*. Tuscon: University of Arizona Press, 1963.

Rogow, Arnold A., ed. *The Jew in a Gentile World*. New York: Macmillan, 1961.

Rosenbach, Abraham S. *An American Jewish Bibliography*. New York: A. S. W. Rosenbach, 1926.

Rosenberg, Edgar. *From Shylock to Svengali*. Stanford, Calif.: Stanford University Press, 1960.

Rourke, Constance. *American Humor: A Study of the National Character*. Garden City, N.Y.: Doubleday, 1953.

Rudolph, B. G. *From a Minyon to a Community*. Syracuse: Syracuse University Press, 1970.

Samuels, Ernest. *Henry Adams: The Major Phase*. Cambridge: Harvard University Press, 1964.

Sanders, Ronald. *The Downtown Jews*. New York: Harper, 1969.

Sartre, Jean-Paul. *Anti-Semite and Jews*. New York: Schocken, 1948.

Saveth, Ernest. *American Historians and European Immigrants: 1875–1925*. New York: Columbia University Press, 1948.

Schappes, Morris, ed., *Documentary History of the Jews in the United States*. New York: Schocken, 1971.

Schiff, Ellen. *From Stereotype to Metaphor: The Jew in Contemporary Drama*. Albany: State University of New York Press, 1982.

Selzer, Michael, ed. *"Kike."* New York: World Publishers, 1972.

Sloan, Irving J., ed. *The Jews in America, 1621–1970*. Dobbs Ferry, N.Y.: Oceana, 1971.

Sobel, Bernard. *Burleycue*. New York: Farrar, 1931.

Solomon, Barbara. *Ancestors and Immigrants*. Cambridge: Harvard University Press, 1956.

Stember, Charles H., et al. *Jews in the Mind of America*. New York: Basic Books, 1966.

Stern, Norton B. *California Jewish History*. Glendale, Calif.: A. H. Stein, 1967.

Trachtenberg, Joshua. *The Devil and the Jews*. New York: Yale University Press, 1943.

Tumin, Melvin M. *An Inventory and Appraisal of Research in American Anti-Semitism*. New York: Anti-Defamation League, 1961.

Unger, Irwin. *The Greenback Era*. Princeton: Princeton University Press, 1964.

Urquart, Ronald A. "American Reaction to the Dreyfus Affair." Ph.D. diss., Columbia University, 1972.

Volkman, Ernest. *A Legacy of Hate: Anti-Semitism in America*. New York: Watts, Franlin Inc., 1982.

Wiebe, Robert H. *The Segmented Society: An Introduction to the Meaning of America*. New York: Oxford University Press, 1975.

Watters, Leon L. *The Pioneer Jews of Utah*. New York: American Jewish Historical Society, 1952.

Wilson, Garff B. *A History of American Acting*. Bloomington: Indiana University Press, 1966.

Wilson, Edmund. *A Piece of My Mind: Reflections at Sixty*. Garden City, N.Y.: Doubleday, 1958.

Wilson, Stephen. *Ideology and Experience: Anti-Semitism in France*. Rutherford, N.J.: Fairleigh Dickinson Press, 1982.

Young, James Harvey. *The Toadstool Millionaires*. Princeton: Princeton University Press, 1961.

Zaretz, Charles E. *The Amalgamated Clothing Workers of America*. New York, 1934.

Ziff, Larzer. *The American 1890s: Life and Times of a Lost Generation*. New York: Viking, 1966.

Secondary Works—Articles

Adams, Harold E. "Minority Caricatures on the American Stage." *Studies in the Science of Society* (New Haven) (1937).

Adler, Selig. "Zebulon Vance and the 'Scattered Nation.'" *The Journal of Southern History* 7, no. 3 (August 1941).

Barzelay, Isaac. "The Jew in the Literature of the Enlightenment." *Jewish Social Studies* 18 (October 1956).

Beckwith, Martha. "The Jews' Garden." *Journal of American Folklore* 64, no. 253 (April–June 1951).

Bloore, Stephen. "The Jew in American Dramatic Literature: 1794–1930." *Publications of the American Jewish Historical Society* 40 (June 1951).

Broches, Z. "A Chapter in the History of the Jews of Boston." *YIVO* 9 (1954).

Brown, James. "Christian Teaching and Anti-Semitism: Scrutinizing Religious Texts." *Commentary*, December 1957.

Chyst, Stanley F. "Three Generations: An Account of American Jewish Fiction, 1896–1969." *J.S.S.* 34 (January 1972).

Clymer, Kenton J. "Anti-Semitism in the Late Nineteenth Century: The Case of John Hay." *AJHS Quarterly* 60 (June 1971).

Coleman, Edward. "Jewish Prototypes in American and English Romans a Clef." *Publications of AJHS* 35 (1939).

———. "Plays of Jewish Interest on the American Stage, 1752–1821." *Publications of AJHS* 33 (1934).

Dinnerstein, Leonard. "A Neglected Aspect of Southern Jewish History." *AJHS Quarterly* 71 (September 1971).

———. "A Note on Southern Attitudes Toward Jews." *J.S.S.* 32 (January 1970).

Eckardt, A. Roy. "Theological Approaches to Anti-Semitism." *J.S.S.* 33 (October 1971).

Feldman, Egal. "The Social Gospel and the Jews." *AJHS Quarterly* 58 (March 1969).

Ferkiss, Victor C. "Populism: Myth, Reality, Current Danger." *Western Political Quarterly* 14 (September 1961).

———. "Populist Influence on American Fascism." *Western Political Quarterly* 10 (June 1957).

Fiedler, Leslie. "What Can We Do About Fagin?" *Commentary* 7 (May 1949).

Fried, Lewis. "Jacob Riis and the Jews: The Ambivalent Quest for Community." *American Studies* 20 (Spring 1979).

Friedman, Lee M. "Jews in Early American Literature." *More Books: The Bulletin of the Boston Public Library* 17, no. 10.

———. "Mrs. Child's Visit to a New York Synagogue in 1841." *Publications of AJHS* 38 (March 1949).

Glanz, Rudolf. "Jew and Yankee: A Historic Comparison." *Jewish Social Studies* (January 1944).

———. "Jews in Early German-American Literature." *J.S.S.* 4 (April 1942).

———. "The Rothschild Legend in America." *J.S.S.* 19 (January–April 1957).

———. "Jewish Social Conditions as Seen by the Muckrakers." *YIVO* 9 (1954).

Greenberg, Leonard. "Some American Anti-Semitic Publications of the Late Nineteenth Century." *Publications of AJHS* (1947).

Gurock, Jeffrey. "Jacob Riis: Christian Friend or Missionary Foe? Two Jewish Views." *AJHS* (September 1981).

Handlin, Oscar. "American Views of the Jew at the Opening of the Twentieth Century." *Publications of AJHS* 40 (June 1951).

———, and Handlin, Mary. "The Acquisition of Political and Social Rights by Jews of the United States." *American Jewish Yearbook*, 1955.

Harap, Louis. "Fracture of a Stereotype: Charles Brockden Brown's Achsa Fielding." *American Jewish Archives* 24 (November 1972).

———. "The Image of the Jew in American Drama 1794–1823." *AJHS Quarterly* 60 (March 1971).

Higham, John. "Anti-Semitism in the Gilded Age: A Reinterpretation." *Mississippi Valley Historical Review* (March 1957).

———. "Social Discrimination against Jews in America: 1830–1930." *Publications of AJHS* 49 (September 1957).

Hindus, Maurice. "Edward Smith King and the Old East Side." *AJHS* 64 (June 1975).

Holbo, Paul S. "Wheat or What? Populism and American Fascism." *Western Political Quarterly* 14 (September 1961).

Holmes, William F. "White Capping: Anti-Semitism in the Populist Era." *AJHS Quarterly*, March 1974.

Huhner, Leon. "The Struggle for Religious Liberty in North Carolina with Special Reference to the Jews." *Publications of AJHS*, 1907.

Hurvitz, Nathan. "Jews and Jewishness in the Street Rhymes of American Children." *J.S.S.* 16 (April 1954).

Hyman, Paula E. "Immigrant Women and Consumer Protest: The New York City Kosher Meat Boycott of 1902." *AJHS* 70 (September 1980).

Karp, Abraham J. "America Discovers the Eastern European Jewish Immigrant." *Jewish Book Annual* 38 (1980–81).

Kirk, Rudolf and Clara M. "Abraham Cahan and William Dean Howells: The Story of a Friendship." *AJHS Quarterly* 52 (September 1962).

Kline, Herbert W. "The Jews that Shakespeare Drew?" *American Jewish Archives* 23 (April 1971).

Lifschutz, E. "Jewish Immigrant Life in American Memoir Literature." *YIVO* 5 (1950).

Liptzin, Sol. "Attitude's Toward Heine's Jewishness in England and America." *YIVO* 2–3 (1947–48).

Loeblowitz-Lennard, Henry. "The Jew as Symbol." *Psychoanalytic Quarterly* 16 (January 1947).

Model, Irving Aaron. "Attitude of the American Jewish Community Toward East European Immigration as Reflected in the Anglo-Jewish Press 1880–90." *American Jewish Archives,* June 1950.

Morris, Richard. "The Jews, Minorities and Dissent in the American Revolution." *Migration and Settlement: Proceedings of the Anglo-American Historical Conference* (London, 1971).

Mosse, George L. "The Image of the Jew in German Popular Culture: Felix Dahn and Gustav Freytag." *Leo Baeck Institute Yearbook* 2 (1951).

Naamuni, Israel T. "Gold Rush Days." *Commentary* 6 (September 1948).

Nichols, Jeanette R. "Bryan's Benefactor: Coin Harvey and His World." *The Ohio Historical Quarterly* 67 (October 1958).

Pinsker, Polly. "English Opinion and Jewish Emancipation 1830–60." *J.S.S.* 14 (January 1952).

Pollack, Norman. "Handlin on Anti-Semitism: A Critique of 'American Views of the Jew.'" *Journal of American History* 51 (December 1964).

———. "The Myth of Populist Anti-Semitism." *American Historical Review,* October 1962.

Raphael, Marc Lee. "The Utilization of Public Local and Federal Sources for Reconstructing American Jewish Local History: The Jews of Columbus Ohio." *AJHS Quarterly* 65 (September 1975).

Rockaway, Robert. "Anti-Semitism in an American City, Detroit 1850–1914." *AJHS Quarterly* 64 (September 1974).

———. "The Eastern European Community of Detroit 1881–1924." *YIVO* 152 (1974).

Sarna, Jonathan. "Anti-Semitism and American History." *Commentary* 71 (March 1981).

Schiff, Ellen. "What Kind of Way Is That for Nice Jewish Girls to Act? Images of Jewish Women in Modern American Drama." *American Jewish History* 70 (September 1980).

Schoenberg, Philip Ernest. "American Reaction to the Kishinev Pogrom." *AJHS Quarterly,* March 1974.

Seitz, Don B. "A Prince of Best Sellers." *Publisher's Weekly,* 21 February 1931.

Silver, Louis. "Jews in Albany 1655–1914." *YIVO* 9 (1954).

Steinberg, Abraham H. "Jewish Characters in Fugitive American Novels of the Nineteenth Century." *YIVO* 11 (1956–57).

Tuerk, Richard. "Jacob Riis and the Jews," *New York Historical Society Quarterly* 63 (July 1979).

Tumin, Melvin. "Anti-Semitism and Status Anxiety: A Hypothesis." *J.S.S.,* October 1971.

Woodward, C. Vann. "The Populist Heritage and the Intellectual." *American Scholar* 29 (Winter 1959–60).

Zlotnick, Joan. "Abraham Cahan, a Neglected Realist." *American Jewish Archives* 23 (April 1971).

Index